THE NEW STATE

GROUP ORGANIZATION THE SOLUTION OF POPULAR GOVERNMENT

BY

M. P. FOLLETT

AUTHOR OF
"THE SPEAKER OF THE HOUSE OF REPRESENTATIVES"

WITH INTRODUCTION BY
LORD HALDANE

Martino Publishing
Mansfield Centre, CT
2016

Martino Publishing
P.O. Box 373,
Mansfield Centre, CT 06250 USA

ISBN   978-1-61427-978-5

© *2016 Martino Publishing*

Cover Design Tiziana Matarazzo

Printed in the United States of America On 100% Acid-Free Paper

THE NEW STATE

GROUP ORGANIZATION THE SOLUTION
OF POPULAR GOVERNMENT

BY

M. P. FOLLETT

AUTHOR OF
"THE SPEAKER OF THE HOUSE OF REPRESENTATIVES"

WITH INTRODUCTION BY
LORD HALDANE

LONGMANS, GREEN AND CO.

LONDON & NEW YORK

1923

First Edition, December, 1918
New Impression, January, 1920
Third Impression, with Introduction by Viscount Haldane, September, 1920

INTRODUCTION

BY

VISCOUNT HALDANE

I HAVE ventured to ask the authoress of what Professor Bosanquet has recently called "the most sane and brilliant of recent works on political theory," to let me write a few pages introductory to the next issue of her book. My reason has been, not the thought of being able to improve on anything that she has said in it, but the desire to help to make the book known in my own country by pointing out its bearing on our own political problems. For to me the book is one of real importance. It is the exposition of a principle which is not stated for the first time, but which, in the form and connection in which she states it, seems to place many difficulties in a new light, and to lay to rest controversies, some at least of which have arisen out of misinterpretation of what is fundamental. Vagueness about first principles is at once the source of confusion in conception and of waste of valuable energy. Now Miss Follett's book sets itself firmly to avoid this vagueness.

"The New State" has a double purpose. It seeks to establish a point of view from which self-production and variation in the forms of the State may be rendered intelligible, and it endeavours to show the lines on which these forms may be adapted in the solution of practical questions. The relations of Labour to Capital are becoming progressively difficult as the labouring classes are advancing in education and ability for searching reflection. The questions which are every day arising cannot be wholly separated from their theoretical basis. This basis is being discussed everywhere, sometimes crudely, but more and more with insight and knowledge. The authoress has therefore undertaken to examine and re-state it, and she does so with a learning and grasp which it would be difficult to surpass.   There are few fields of research which she has not explored.

About the theory that underlies the book I propose to write very briefly, its importance notwithstanding.   For what is most to the point to-day is that, as illustrated in their application to politics, a set of practicable ideas, in vital respects not only fresh but full of promise, are set forth for consideration.

I will therefore refer to Miss Follett's philosophical views only in so far as is necessary to make my interpretation of the practical side of the book intelligible.   The great point in her theory is that the controversy between Monism and Pluralism arises out of views that are too contracted on both sides. Monism is often thought to suggest that the state is a self-subsisting entity into which all sovereign power is really gathered up and is exercised outside the central government only by permission or delegation.   Such a conception the pluralists naturally find to be too narrow to contain the facts.   They pronounce it to be not only ethically objectionable, but incapable of explaining our actual experience of legislation and administration alike.   Hobbes' "Leviathan" and the German notion of the state they put on the same level.   The most acute among the critics of the monistic state are careful not to fall into the journalistic habit of representing the late German Government as the outcome of idealist metaphysics. They know too much not to be aware that the great theorists of a hundred years ago in Germany did not wish for anything of the kind.   It was not Hegelianism, as Miss Follett and the best-informed thinkers have come to understand it, but the violent reaction against idealism which set in throughout Germany soon after Hegel's death, that gave rise to the dominance of militarism.

Hegel does not appear to have been a particularly pleasant person in controversy.   He indulged at times in diatribes against his opponents, and he has paid the usual penalty of being miscalled and misrepresented.   But had he lived in Boston in 1920, instead of in Germany a century earlier, he would probably, as far as I can judge from his writings, have said something not very different from what Miss Follett says.

His concern was to explain the existing state of things in his own country and in Great Britain, the constitution of which was for him a subject of keen interest. For Hegel, as for others, it was only after the day's work had been done that philosophy could come on the scene to survey it. The American Constitution would for him have been an actual fact, embodying what he pronounced, in his Philosophy of Right, to be "freedom of individual thought, the principle of the modern world that all essential aspects of the spiritual whole should attain to their rights by self-development." "From this standpoint," he says, "one can hardly raise the idle question as to which form is the better, monarchy or democracy." We venture to reply simply that the forms of all constitutions of the state are one-sided, if they are not able to contain the principle of free individuality, and do not know how to correspond to completed reason. He denounces "the confusion of the force of right with the right of force." It was he who said of Napoleon that he had brought "the highest genius to victory, only to show how little victory could achieve." He was a conservative, but in the first place he was a thinker. He knew that the forms of government might display infinite variety, according to the moods of those who were behind them. And therefore, when he had been carrying the proof sheets of a book to the printers in Jena, and had been passed by Napoleon who was entering the town at the head of his troops, he made the dry observation in a letter, that he had met the World Spirit and that it was on horseback.

I have referred to Hegel's teaching only because Miss Follett refers to it in much the same sense. His task was simply to take the facts as he found them and to discover what was their meaning. As the result he held that human institutions belonged to the region, not of inert externality, but of mind and purpose, and were, therefore, dynamic and self-developing. Miss Follett's principle is not different. She would fain avoid the approach to metaphysical discussion. Like Mr. Bosanquet she finds in the obvious facts of social experience the ground on which she seeks to build up her structure. The cardinal doctrine of her book is that the state is what its members make it to be. Sovereignty is a relative notion. The individual is sovereign over himself in so far as he can develop, control and unify his manifold nature. The group is sovereign in so far as its members in unity direct themselves in the expression of the common purposes they are evolving. A state is sovereign only in so far as it does the same thing, and it gives rise to the power of a great group unified by common ends. It is the expression of elements of identity in purpose. We are not isolated atoms. We live and we think only in communion with others of our kind, and it is so that we evolve the collective will which, in its fullest and most imperative form, gives rise as its outcome to sovereignty. This will is not a mere aggregate of isolated wills. It evolves itself only through living with others in group life, out of actual identity of ideas and purposes amid their differences. The form of the state and the meaning of the resulting sovereignty may vary, following general opinion at different periods and under different conditions, and so may the mode of expressing the imperative. But all ultimately comes back to the will of the people of the state. It was this will, as he interpreted it, that Cromwell expressed when he beheaded Charles the First. It was this will that was embodied when the British people first succeeded in laying down definite constitutional limitations on the power of their kings. It was this will that Lincoln proved to have expressed when he placed beyond doubt the unity of the nation as a nation in the American Civil War.

It is not true that each group within the state has an isolated sovereignty. Each group may control itself, but only within the limits of its existence and influence as a group. It is like the individual, with a general will which is distinctive, but a will the purposes of which fall within the larger purposes of the state group. Wills are not atomic. They may and do act under the guidance of various ends, some of which are less individual than others. The general will so evolved is no entity separate from these individual wills. It is their common expression. But it may, as in war time, present these individual wills as unified at a tremendous level. Reality does not always exist at the same level, and human purposes may embody reality at varying degrees. The will is no static thing but is a form of the dynamic activity characteristic of mind. At some of these degrees each may stand for the whole, and when this is so the private mind coincides with the group mind. Thus there is no isolated sovereignty, nor does the unified state begin from any pre-existing unity in its control of its groups. It may be evolved only gradually, or it may be that on occasions the individual wills effect their unification *per saltum*. History contains examples of both methods. There are many forms in which sovereignty is given shape, just as there are many forms of the state. In Great Britain the instrument of the unified state is, in principle at all events, Parliament. In America it is the Federal and State Governments and their Executives, with that Supreme Court, the delegation to which of some degree of sovereign power under the original Constitution the genius of John Marshall brought to clear light when he rendered judgment in Marbury v. Madison. Such a judgment as his would not have been rendered in England. But then the written constitution of the United States is an instrument differing radically from that of Great Britain. There sovereign power is differently distributed. Yet in both countries the *ultima ratio* is the collective will of the people.

Sovereignty is thus a fact with many forms, and not an abstract or uniform principle. It is a consequence of the existence of the state rather than the state itself. Whoever can gain the approval of the people gets this power. Sovereignty in the subordinate group is not different in nature from state sovereignty, but it is only relative sovereignty, and it is subordinate to that of a larger entirety. As I have said, the individual man is no static or isolated atom. Relations to his fellow men are of the essence of his life, and they are ever in active process of development. He is always to some extent engaged in developing these relations. And so it is with the subordinate groups. They are always seeking to bring themselves into relation with each other, it may be in a trade-union congress or it may be in a different kind of association for the promotion of some common cause. All these groups may be of great value. Ideally all are essential, for the functions which mankind has to fulfil are not activities in isolation from each other. It would be to the good if the teacher could always have the practical training of a parent. Man must identify himself, so far as he can, with the experience of humanity generally. But we are finite and must limit our purposes if we would accomplish anything actual. What pluralism really has to impress is that a rich experience cannot be adequately gained excepting through many actual relations in group life. What it is apt to overlook is that none of these group relationships is more than a stage towards a more complete whole within which they all take their places, and that consequently, even as a citizen, man has to identify himself with group life in many forms before he has fully developed his humanity. In some of such groups I may be an employer; in others an employee. I may be a workman and also a shareholder; a clerk, and the representative of my fellow citizens on a local authority; a lawyer and a fellow of a college or a professor. I may thus not only get education in opposing points of view, but I may contribute to apparently opposing points of view. Only apparently opposing, however, because there is a larger outlook which is open to me, from which they fall into their places. It is through this larger outlook that what is called a true general will develops itself.

Individuals and groups stand in no antithesis. The group will is just the individual will at a different level of purpose. The sovereign state itself is nothing apart from the citizens who compose it, and whose assent to its objects and its organisation it embodies. The hesitation in accepting this view has arisen from the idea that individual human beings exist only as segregated atoms, with purposes which are entities apart and merely resembling each other. But our experience tells us that such is not the true character of mind, and the state, like the subordinate group, is the embodiment of mind. We cannot obtain our full stature or even be what we are apart from active relationships, to our parents, or to our churches, or to our social and political surroundings. When I pay my rates and taxes I accept this as a fact. No one group can completely enfold me, and that is because of the multiplicity of my nature. Nor can any number of groups exhaust the capacity of the modern citizen. Group organisation is a method or instrument in politics, but the ultimate unit is always the individual, because his activities and range are more extensive than those of any group organised only for special purposes and in this sense subordinate to his full life by reason of the limitation of its purposes. Beyond the ends by which the group is thus confined lie the wide purposes of the nation state. This state is no Absolute. For it too may participate in movements which go beyond itself, and concern no one people but mankind generally. That is the principle of a League of Nations or a Concert of Powers, or whatever else the form of union may be. But here too there is no contradiction between the will of the member and that of the community. The will of the latter is just that of the former at a higher level or degree and in a different aspect, a result depending not on mechanical addition, but on identity in modes of thought and the action which embodies it. These are not separable. Majority rule must if it is to be of value, possess an intellectual foundation of a character different from what is merely mechanical addition.

It is our habit of assuming that we are dealing with aggregates of mechanical and exclusive things, standing in no higher relationship than that of causes and effects external to one another, that has caused confusion. The tendency to assume that the category appropriate to things or substances is sufficient for the representation of all phases of our experience of the actual, has been responsible for the genesis of this habit. Miss Follett's task has been to bring unconscious assumptions of this kind to light and to scrutiny, and this she has sought to do simply by testing them against the facts of life and their background.

For her the true state does not demand a merely submissive allegiance, for it is the outcome of a spontaneous and instinctive process of unifying manifold interests. Nor need it in its activities supersede those of subordinate groups, such as trade unions, whose functions are different from its own, while they can yet be fitted into their places in a larger entirety. Every legitimate interest can not only be recognised but can be regarded with satisfaction. If I am discontented with the policy of the state I can seek to change it. For I am a member of the whole with a title to an integral function and voice in it. No abstract principle can be laid down for the solution of situations in which dissatisfaction arises. For the facts are usually highly individual. And the state is no static unit. For it is not an arbitrary creation; "It is a process; a continual self-modification to express its different stages of growth in which each and all must be so flexible that continual change of form is twin-fellow of continual growth." The stability of the state depends on continuity of broad national purpose, and, consistently with that continuity and the stability resulting from it, there is room for infinite modification in internal institutions. The state is made, not by external acts, but by the continuous thought and action of the people who live its life. In this sense it is never perfect for it is a process that remains always unbroken in creative activity.

The practical lesson of all this may be expressed in Miss Follett's own words: — "Neighbourhood education and neighbourhood organisation is then the pressing problem of 1918. All those who are looking towards a real democracy, not the pretence of one which we have now, feel that the most imminent of our needs is the awakening and invigorating, the educating and organising of the local unit. All those who in the humblest way, in settlement or community centre, are working for this, are working at the greatest political problem of the twentieth century." Knowledge is from this point of view indeed power, and here is a method for systematically acquiring and imparting the knowledge requisite for political life. She concludes a chapter on this subject in fervent words: — "This is the way we must understand an individual allegiance. I live for ever the individual life. As an individual I am the undivided one, as the group-I, I am again the undivided one, as the state-I, I am the undivided one — I am always and for ever the undivided one, mounting from height to height, always mounting, always the whole of me mounting."

"The great lesson of the group process," says Miss Follett towards the end of the book, "is that particularism, however magnified, is no longer possible. There is no magic by which selfishness becomes patriotism the moment we can invoke the nation. The change must be this: as we now see that a nation cannot be healthy and virile if it is merely protecting the rights of its members, so we must see that we can have no sound condition of world affairs merely by the protection of each individual nation — that is the old theory of individual rights. Each nation must play its part in some larger whole. Nations have fought for national rights." "What raises this war to a plane never reached by any war before is that the Allies are not fighting for national rights. As long as history is read the contribution of America to the Great War will be told as America's taking her stand squarely and responsibly on the position that national particularism was in 1917 dead."

If I read aright the record of the constitutional issues which are to-day being discussed throughout the United States, this remains profoundly true. That a great nation should examine these questions critically and in detail seems to me as natural as it is necessary, and in no sense to be in conflict with the full recognition of the principle that her people have definitely taken their stand on what goes beyond national particularism. It is by the fullest and freest discussion and debate, and by this means alone, that a true national purpose can be evolved and brought to clarity and full fruition.

I now pass to the second object with which "The New State" is written. It is to show how, the state being non-mechanical and capable of self-development, its self-development can be best accomplished. The answer of the authoress is that the question is ultimately one of education in the largest sense. She does not deal with education as a general subject. She confines herself to the capacity which the individual, with the ability for a larger life as a citizen in the state about which she writes, can make that life actual. How is democracy to be improved? How are we to reach something with a deeper significance than a majority obtained in the ballot boxes by mere mechanical and narrow party organisation? To this her answer is that no government will be really successful or endure which does not rest on the individual on his better side, and that this better side is to be reached neither by sending more people to the poll nor by sending them there more frequently. For to do so is to effect no real deliverance from particularism, nor is genuine union to be got by simply collecting a crowd. It is only by a sufficiency of intelligent discussion and by the evolution of common purpose in diverse forms of group life that the capacity of the individual citizen can be called forth. That individual is always potentially more than he knows himself to be. He is no passive element in an assemblage. He can create, and this he does best when joining with others to form a real whole of opinion and action, a living group, in which he can develop his personality. The first need of democracy is therefore training for citizenship, which must be trained for as we train to develop other capacities.

It appears that in the United States a beginning has been made in the organisation of the group training which is thus requisite. As there are many relations in which men stand to each other, so training in more than one form of association is necessary. In a particular town there may be a group, with a character resembling the Whitley Council in Great Britain, in which employers and workmen voluntarily meet and discuss the conditions of industrial life. Injustice and imagined injustice are equally found in the majority of cases to have resulted from want of knowledge and not from evil purpose. A common general opinion is developed which tends to settle such disputes as remain, and capital and labour may thus come to understand and interpret aright each other's claims. The sense of a set of common functions in industry can so grow.

Next door to the industrial group and in the same town there may be a health group. As I write I have before me the papers relating to an organisation of this kind in Cincinnati. We are familiar with something of the same sort in my own country. Our health committees are organised for the same end, and they are partially recognised by the State and by the Local Authorities, and receive some assistance. But the movement is still in its infancy, and it has not so far been practicable to put it adequately on a democratic basis, instead of trusting to the energies of individuals to run it.

In Cincinnati, where the name used for the group is "social unit," this is defined as being "a group of people living in the same neighbourhood, and organised to give and receive community service." The plan of work goes on to state that "the same principle of group organisation will be applied to the social work, the nursing, the statistical work, etc., as well as to the gradual building up of an advisory council composed of men and women from other occupational groups in the community. For example, in social work, formulation of plans and directions of policies will rest in city committees of social experts, elected by their fellow-members and united through their heads in a social council, of which the Superintendent of Public Welfare will be a member. . . . In summary the unit plan aims at three things: to organise the people of a limited district democratically, so that they can get a clear idea of what their common needs are, and what they think ought to be done about them; to organise democratically the specialists of the neighbourhood and of the city so that the highest skill and experience can be applied to meeting the needs disclosed, and to bind the people and the technically skilled groups together in such a way that the people can tell the specialists what they want done, and the specialists can point out how to do it, submitting plans, programmes, and policies to the people for their approval. To put it another way, the plan is an attempt to bring efficiency to democracy."

This is an illustration of the principle set forth in "The New State" for the building up of an enlightened general opinion, a principle which is meant, however, to have a far wider application than it has as yet obtained in Cincinnati and the other cities which have partially applied it. In particular the principle is capable of application to the relations between Labour and Capital. The British Whitley Council plan is capable of great extension. So soon as employers learn that their workmen are now insisting on having a voice as to the conditions under which they work, and that this does not mean interference with expert direction of higher policy, progress of this kind may become rapid. Such progress has already begun to show itself, both in the United States and in Great Britain. There is indeed a broad political and economic question raised. There is a growing sense that those who do constructive work, whether as hand workers or as brain workers, should no longer be wholly under the domination of those whose sole aim is to make money. The true purpose of industry is being felt by an increasing number to be the provision, not so much of mere dividends, as of service from which the community as a whole may derive benefit. The function of capital is becoming recognised to be that of a means rather than that of an end; to assist and to develop the labour of human beings, rather than to use human beings to serve it. Economic activity should always be carried on consistently with the greatest social purposes, and its rewards should be, as far as possible, rewards for real service rendered whether by hand or by brain.

It is this conception of the duty and station of the members of the state that is becoming more and more prominent in both the New World and the Old. It is the outcome of increasing reflective power in the working classes, and its neglect in the past has been the most fertile of the sources of industrial unrest. Mere profit-sharing does not suffice to-day. The desire is for the status of free men, co-operating in the discharge of a general obligation. An individual is not the less free because he must work hard. But his freedom in his toil consists in this, that he knows why he toils and that he does so as a member of his community. If he has the sense that he does what he does as what he owes to himself, and not merely to another who can compel him, the best kind of man will not only work hard but he will work willingly. He does not even ask that he should have the same share as others more fortunate in this respect. What he wishes to feel is that he is a free citizen and respected as such. Poor and rich are alike in this quality, more than those who come in contact with only one or the other are apt to suppose. The gloom which bases itself on the supposed absence of justice is carried too far. Those who talk so forget that it is not by bread alone that man wishes to live. Whether the duties which are allocated are those of the physical toiler or of the brain worker, the best of all look for their reward in a sense gained which is of a spiritual character. There is a fine passage in the second series of Mr. Bosanquet's Gifford Lectures,[1] which points to the deeper-lying principle on which this conclusion rests. "If we are arranging any system or enterprise of a really intimate character for persons closely united in mind and thoroughly penetrated with the spirit of the whole — persons not at arm's length to one another — all the presumptions of individualistic justice at once fall to the ground. We do not give the 'best' man the most comfort, the easiest task, or even, so far as the conduct of the enterprise is concerned, the highest reward. We give him the greatest responsibility, the severest toil and hazard, the most continuous and exacting toil and self-sacrifice. It is true and inevitable, for the reasons we have pointed out as affecting all finite life, that in a certain way and degree honour and material reward do follow on merit in this world. They follow, we may say, mostly wrong; but the world, in its rough working, by its own rough and ready standards, thinks it necessary to attempt to appraise the finite individual unit; this is, in fact, the individualistic justice, which, when we find it shattered and despised by the Universe, calls out the pessimism we are discussing. But the more intimate and spiritual is the enterprise, the more does the true honour and reward restrict itself to what lives —

> 'In those pure eyes
> And perfect witness of all-judging Love.'

Under an order of things that has now passed away it was easier to find room for freedom in this attitude than it is in our time. Production on an enormous scale, the use of machinery at every turn, and the magnitude of output, have all tended to separate capital from labour, and to create rival organisations with uniform and monotonous work for the individual worker, especially in the case of labour. We have moved away from the state of things in which the workman began and carried to its completion the production of each

[1] The Value and Destiny of the Individual, p. 153.

particular article. It was inevitable that it should be so.
But with the change his pride of paternity is gone. His piece
of work is no longer his own, in idea and execution, as it was
in the old days. It is more difficult for him to feel that his
activity is directed to an end complete in itself, in which quality
can count. His service is to-day much more directed to an
end that does not appeal to him, contributing merely one
particle to a huge aggregate in which its character, and his
own intellect, is lost out of sight. We have consequently a
far more difficult problem to deal with when we endeavour
to make his sense of self-respect keep pace with his growing
enlightenment on the question of what his life ought to be.

Change of a considerable kind in the general organisation
which prevails to-day appears to be slowly becoming unavoid-
able, if industrial and social unrest is not to increase with
that increasing spread of knowledge which is inevitable and
is already in progress and which all right-minded people must
welcome. Democracy will doubtless solve this problem for
itself, the only way in which it can be really solved, and the
practical question is whether this is to be done by sudden
and violent effort, such as is being called for by the impatient,
or by methods that are progressive and gradual in their un-
hasting yet unresting gentleness, yet not on that account the
less efficient. If the latter alternative is to become the order
of the day there is something else required than simple organisation of the democracy. This further requisite is indicated,
if not dwelt on in detail, in Miss Follett's book. I am not sure
that in what I am going to refer to we are not, on this side of
the Atlantic, at least as far on in our commencement of the
solution of the further problem as are the people of the United
States. But it is evident that both peoples are becoming conscious of a new social question, if slowly, yet profoundly.

What I refer to is the necessity of education in a larger
meaning of the word. Education is looked on popularly as a
dull topic. So it is in some of its aspects, but only if the sense
of the word is unduly confined. The name does not signify
merely what we are familiar with in the training of youth.
That is a most important national concern, but it does not

occupy all the ground. Its purpose is, by instruction given to those who have not yet developed full freedom or full personality, to inculcate what is required for such development. Consequently the position of the teacher has to be one of authority. What he lays down must in the main be accepted as the truth. It, therefore, implies a standard in the main external to the mind which is confronted with it. It is assumed that a defined result, rather than the method of attaining it, or the spirit of the search after it, is what matters.

Now in the case of the University student of the higher type this is different. He comes with a good deal of knowledge, normally gained in the secondary school, and with considerable experience of life. He is already to a considerable extent an educated adult. What he comes for is to receive a new inspiration. His professor does not stand over him in a relationship of external authority. Student and teacher are comrades on a journey of discovery on which both recognise that there is no finality, and that what signifies is not a body of rigid and complete truth, for there is none such, but the search after truth, and the expansion and freedom of spirit which such search gives. The relationship at this later stage, where the education is that of the adult, is a fresh one, and it presupposes a considerable amount of mental and spiritual experience as already possessed by the student. But such teaching has a creative effect. It brings to birth in the best student a new discovery of how much he can become that he is not yet. He has a nascent sense of a freedom that he did not before possess, and his outlook on life becomes enlarged in a new fashion. The best in literature, in science, in philosophy, in art, in public life, and in religion, is now fully opened to him, and he can commune with the great souls that have expressed themselves throughout history as though they were his living teachers. The importance of his new gift is one that is difficult to exaggerate. He is an individual who takes his place in the whole that society constitutes with enlarged relations and capacities for good.

The problem which is occupying some of us in Great Britain is how to extend the range of such training, and the enlarge-

ment of the spirit which follows on it, to the working classes.
We now think that this has been demonstrated to be possible.
If it is possible, then there lies in front a new avenue towards
a state of society in which unrest will be, not abolished, but
converted into a discontent of a new order, the discontent of
the individual with limitations for which he himself, and not
circumstances, will have the responsibility. For the really
educated man works himself out of adverse conditions. He
and his educated neighbours combine in a rational fashion
to re-fashion general opinion and the conditions which are
there just because general opinion has let them be there.

Let us therefore give to the working classes as freely as can
be of the water of this priceless fountain. They are just like
the rest of society, and are inspired by the same ideals. The
point is how to make the highest ideals prominent and to
develop these among them. For it is the most spiritual that
is the most real and most compelling, with them as with us.

I have seen a good deal of the Labour movement over here.
I have intimate and valued friends among its leaders. I have
addressed a good many Labour meetings. And this has struck
me. Those who assemble in them think just as the rest of us
do. They feel keenly when they are excluded from what is
best, but their desire is to live along with us the lives of good
citizens if we will only let them. Good citizens they cannot
fully become while we deny them the higher blessings of citizenship. It is this denial that gives rise to violent language. The
agitations for nationalisation, for better housing, for higher
wages, for shorter hours of work, are just the expressions of
the real demand which if larger is gentler. If we can give them
the full education they desire, then a larger and more enlightened society at a more uniform level will put these things
right. Service to others will be more evenly rewarded, and the
conditions of life will gradually become more nearly equal-
ised. There will be in any case reasonable hope for the
attainment of such a result. The methods to-day prescribed
for attaining the ends which Labour sets before itself will
gradually be superseded, as the ends to which they have been
directed become attained. Capital will no longer dominate.

It will still be there but as progressively being endowed with a new function in the interests of society, and its owners will be rewarded, not merely for the accident of possession, but on the basis of what they do for those in conjunction with whom they work. The great organiser may continue to be paid a great wage, for his service may be as irreplaceable as it is priceless. But when it is so it will be in accordance with general assent to its being so. Individual talent must command individual reward. Even Bolshevist Russia appears to have now discovered this. Probably nine industries out of ten will be found to be so dependent on this talent as to be incapable of anything like nationalisation, notwithstanding the fact that there are conditions which must be observed in the general interest. Yet there may remain other industries which can be and ought to be national, just as navies and postal services are. They may require a new and very high class of state servants to be trained for their management for the public, men whose position must be made to correspond with the sense of duty to the state required of them. But there should be available in the provision of such service a new and as yet untapped reservoir of democratic talent to draw on, which so far has not yet been constructed.

I am impressed, so far as my observation has gone, with the moderation of the working classes when they are taken into counsel and trusted, even when they are suffering under hardships which they hold to be preventable. The loud and discordant voices, whether expressed at meetings or in print, turn out to represent those of a minority. The majority desire far-reaching reform, but they would rather have it quietly, and so avoid the risk of confusion and consequent failure. The way to meet them seems to be to act on the principle on which the Reform Bill was conceded over here in 1832, and in which the demands of the Chartists were gradually met a little later on. This principle was that of the Whigs, a body of men who were very shrewd, even where they do not seem to us to have been very intelligent according to the standards of our time. It was by their resolute refusal to bolt and bar doors that the application of the battering ram was avoided. They were always ready to discuss things on the assumption that the political truth to which they had been accustomed could never have been more than relative truth. Nothing stands still in political thought, any more than in thought of other kinds.

But I have not referred to these things in order to speculate on the future of political institutions. About these there will be many varieties of opinion and much divergence of method. What I am insisting on is the principle of relativity in political thought, and that its co-ordinates of reference are ever varying. It is with the hope of getting a larger outlook, the result of a more intelligent public opinion, that I am suggesting here the advisability of a great and systematic stimulation of the self-education of the adult working-class population, and I will, before concluding, draw attention very briefly to how we are attempting in my own country to initiate this stimulation.[1]

The adult son or daughter of the well-to-do citizen can only be adequately educated further in a university atmosphere, and so also the working people can only receive adequately the stimulus of education of the same kind through the personality of a first-rate university teacher. Personality counts for much in this connection. The universities must therefore be primarily entrusted with this new mission. They must be encouraged to train teachers of a quality as high as that of their best tutors for their internal purposes, who will devote themselves to this new and extra-mural work. For the class of teacher of this kind a profession is thus opened as real as that of the clergymen whom the old universities over here used to train in such large numbers. It is an attractive mission. The tutor may go for three or four years' work among the new class of students, and ought then to return within the walls of his university for study and research, so that he may

---

[1] For fuller information on this subject see "University Tutorial Classes; a Study in the Development of Higher Education among Working Men and Women" by Albert Mansbridge (1913), and The Report to the Government of the Master of Balliol's Committee on Adult Education in 1919 (Cmd. 321), as well as, from the point of view of Labour, "The Education of the Citizen," by Arthur Greenwood.

return to his work refreshed. The cost to the state is small, and already some provision has been made here for a new communal service which promises to have a most valuable future. Oxford has been particularly active in the movement.

In his book on "Nationality and Government" Mr. A. E. Zimmern, after defining education as, not simply experience, but experience *interpreted*, goes on, in the chapter on Education, social and national, to say this: "Few parts of Industrial England can appear more depressing at first sight to the casual visitor than the string of overlapping villages now comprised in the new County Borough of Stoke-on-Trent and known as the Five Towns. Smoke and slag-heaps have done their best to mar the appearance of a once beautiful countryside; nor have the towns themselves yet been able to do much to remedy the confusion and ugliness inseparable from nineteenth-century industrialism.

"Yet, a few weeks ago, addressing an audience of miners in a village schoolroom on one of the ridges overlooking this vale of smoke, a distinguished student of Sixteenth Century England spoke of what he termed the revival of humanism in the England of to-day. 'Early in the sixteenth century,' he said, 'a great educational movement arose in Europe and penetrated to England. Men felt that new worlds were opening up before their eyes, that there were great kingdoms of the mind to be overrun and possessed. In those days there was a great Dutch scholar named Erasmus. He came to England to meet his fellow scholars. He went to the seats of knowledge, to Oxford and to Cambridge, where the new learning was at home. If Erasmus were to come to England on such a mission to-day, do you know,' he asked the miners, 'where he would be directed to come? *He would be taken to the Potteries.*' The miners looked surprised. Some of them had been in the pit all day; others were going down on the night shift; but that so much importance should be attached to their natural human desire to meet at regular intervals for an evening's tussle at economics seemed strange to them. Their tutor, for whom the regular five miles' missionary journey up the hill at the end of his own day's work was more of a strain than

he let them know, was, however, glad to feel that his work
linked him with the great scholars of the past."

This kind of extra-mural university teaching is to-day
being given by most of our universities and in different parts
of the country. There is no restriction on the number or character of the subjects. What is offered consists not in disjointed
lectures but in systematic courses, on which is built the encouragement of investigation by the students themselves, distributed into groups for the purpose. Philosophy, Economics,
History, Literature, Art, Music, Science, all have their places,
and care is taken to avoid prejudice on the part of the men due
to the exclusion of particular standpoints. Discussion is
therefore trusted for bringing out the relative merits of doctrines. Each class, consisting of about twenty-five, lasts for
about two hours, the first of which is occupied with exposition,
and the second with the discussions to which the workmen
attach much importance.

What I have sketched represents the best form of what is
actually taking place. The system has been organised in a
fair number of places by the various universities. But it is
still in its infancy, and some of us will not be satisfied until
it has spread all over our country, while at least maintaining
its level and quality. It is for the state to give it recognition
as of an importance as great as that of the education of the
youth of the nation. For an educated democracy would gradually become a democracy inspired as the people of to-day are
not yet inspired. Its capacity for the estimation of *values*
would be heightened, and so would be its power of judging
about the means to its ends. It is fuller knowledge alone
that can be trusted to make a people conscious of the immensi-
ties of the difficulties of self-government,

> "And apprise it if pursuing
> Or the right way or the wrong way
> To its triumph or undoing."

It is also such knowledge alone that can render it fully
aware of "the little done; the undone vast," and awaken in it
that "divine discontent" which the spectacle of unrealised
standards around must awaken before a remedy is practicable.

A great educational change of this kind, if made throughout a country, ought to tend to change the temper, not merely of the working classes, but of the whole community, and to change it for the better. It is from ignorance that the bulk of injustice springs, and knowledge treats injustice gently because it has latent in it a spiritual power of getting rid of it. Such knowledge cannot but double the efficacy of Miss Follett's principle of group organisation. Indeed it is hardly separable from it, and she herself treats the matter as itself falling within the domain of national education.

It is to the self-organisation of the citizens of the state in groups formed for the several purposes of social life that some of us are coming to look more and more in the interests of democracy in the future. The individual citizens dare not, if the organisation is to be a reality, allow their intellectual and spiritual education to stand still after any period of life. The striving for the larger outlook resulting from fuller knowledge, if it is encouraged in childhood, must not be allowed to cease before the end of life. As Goethe makes Faust in his last days declare,

"He only gains and keeps his life and freedom
Who daily strives to conquer them anew."

In reform there is finality no more than there is in truth in general, of which reform is only an example. It is in the quality reached in the striving itself, and not in a result, apparently but not really to be attained once for all, that we may profitably seek to satisfy our desire for the sense of something accomplished.

If I have interpreted her book aright this appears to me to be an inference to be drawn from Miss Follett's results. But whether or not she would accept my inference in this very general form, I am persuaded that the principles relative to the future of the state, set by her before the public in the scientific and systematic fashion which is characteristic of her volume, ought to influence opinion deeply, not only in her country but in my own.

HALDANE

LONDON, *April*, 1920

CONTENTS

PART III

GROUP ORGANIZATION DEMOCRACY'S
METHOD

1. THE NEIGHBORHOOD GROUP

2. THE OCCUPATIONAL GROUP

CONTENTS

PART IV

THE DUAL ASPECT OF THE GROUP:
A UNION OF INDIVIDUALS, AN INDIVIDUAL IN A LARGER UNION

THE NEW STATE

THE NEW STATE

O UR political life is stagnating, capital and labor are virtually at war, the nations of Europe are at one another's throats — because we have not yet learned how to live together. The twentieth century must find a new principle of association. Crowd philosophy, crowd government, crowd patriotism must go. The herd is no longer sufficient to enfold us.

Group organization is to be the new method in politics, the basis of our future industrial system, the foundation of international order. Group organization will create the new world we are now blindly feeling after, for creative force comes from the group, creative power is evolved through the activity of the group life.

We talk about the evils of democracy. We have not yet tried democracy. Party or "interests" govern us with some fiction of the "consent of the governed" which we say means democracy. We have not even a conception of what democracy means. That conception is yet to be forged out of the crude ore of life.

We talk about the tragedy of individualism. The individual we do not yet know, for we have no methods to release the powers of the individual. Our particularism — our *laissez-faire*, our every-man-for-his-own-interests — has little to do with true individualism, that is, with the individual as consciously responsible for the life from which he draws his breath and to which he contributes his all.

3

Politics do not need to be "purified." This thought is leading us astray. Politics must be vitalized by a new method. "Representative government," party organization, majority rule, with all their excrescences, are dead-wood. In their stead must appear the organization of non-partisan groups for the begetting, the bringing into being, of common ideas, a common purpose and a collective will.

Government by the people must be more than the phrase. We are told — The people should do this, the people should do that, the people must be given control of foreign policy, etc. etc. But all this is wholly useless unless we provide the procedure within which the people *can* do this or that. What does the "sovereign will" of the people amount to unless it has some way of operating? Or have we any "sovereign will?" There is little yet that is practical in "practical politics."

But method must not connote mechanics to any mind. Many of us are more interested in the mechanism of life than in anything else. We keep on putting pennies in the slot from sheer delight in seeing something come out at the other end. All this must change. Machines, forms, images, moulds — all must be broken up and the way prepared for our plastic life to find plastic expression. The principle of democracy may be the underlying unity of men, the method of democracy must be that which allows the quickest response of our daily life to the common faith of men.

Are we capable of a new method? Can the inventive faculty of the American people be extended from mechanical things to political organization? There is no use denying that we are at a crisis in our history. Whether that crisis is to abound in acute moments which will largely wreck us, or whether we are going to be wise enough to make the necessary political and social adjustments — that is the crucial question which faces America to-day.

Representative government has failed. It has failed because it was not a method by which men could govern themselves. Direct government is now being proposed. But direct government will never succeed if (1) it is operated from within the party organization as at present, or (2) if it consists merely in counting all the votes in all the ballot-boxes. Ballot-box democracy is what this book is written to oppose.

No government will be successful, no government will endure, which does not rest on the individual, and no government has yet found the individual. Up to the present moment we have never seen the individual. Yet the search for him has been the whole long striving of our Anglo-Saxon history. We sought him through the method of representation and failed to find him. We sought to reach him by extending the suffrage to every man and then to every woman and yet he eludes us. Direct government now seeks the individual; but as we have not found him by sending more men to the ballot-box, so we shall not find him by sending men more often to the ballot-box. Are our constitutional conventions to sit and congratulate themselves on their progressive ideas while they are condemning us to a new form of our old particularism? The ballot-box! How completely that has failed men, how completely it will fail women. Direct government as at present generally understood is a mere phantom of democracy. Democracy is not a sum in addition. Democracy is not brute numbers; it is a genuine union of true individuals. The question before the American people to-day is — How is that genuine union to be attained, how is the true individual to be discovered? The party has always ignored him; it wants merely a crowd, a preponderance of votes. The early reform associations had the same aim. Both wanted voters not men. It makes little difference whether we follow the boss or follow the good government associations, this is all herd life — "following the lead" — democracy means a wholly different kind of existence. To follow means to murder the individual, means to kill the only force in the world which can make the Perfect Society — democracy depends upon the creative power of every man.

We find the true man only through group organization. The potentialities of the individual remain potentialities until they are released by group life. Man discovers his true nature, gains his true freedom only through the group. Group organization must be the new method of politics because the modes by which the individual can be brought forth and made effective are the modes of practical politics.

But who is the individual we have been seeking, who is the individual we are to find within the group? Certainly not the particularist individual. Every man to count as one? That was once our slogan. Now we have relegated it to a mechanical age. To-day we see that every man must count for infinitely more than one because he is not part of a whole, a cog in a machine, not even an organ in an organism, but from one point of view the whole itself. A man said to me the other day, "That is not democracy, that is mysticism." But why mysticism? It is our daily life as lived from hour to hour. We join with one group of men at work, with another at play, another in our civic committee, another in our art club. Man's life is one of manifold relatings. His vote at the polls must express not his particularist self, but the whole complex of his related life, must express as much of the whole as these multiple relations have brought into existence for him, through him. I find my expression of the whole-idea, the whole-will, through my group life. The group must always dictate the modes of activity for the individual. We must put clearly before us the true individual with his infinite relations, expressing his infinite relations, as the centre of politics, as the meaning of democracy. The first purpose of genuine politics is to make the vote of every man express the All at his special coign of outlook. In every man is the potentiality of such expression. To call it forth is the aim of all training, the end sought by all modes of real living.

Thus group organization releases us from the domination of mere numbers. Thus democracy transcends time and space, it can never be understood except as a spiritual force. Majority rule rests on numbers; democracy rests on the well-grounded assumption that society is neither a collection of units nor an organism but a network of human relations. Democracy is not worked out at the polling-booths; it is the bringing forth of a genuine collective will, one to which every single being must contribute the whole of his complex life, as one which every single being must express the whole of at one point. Thus the essence of democracy is creating. The technique of democracy is group organization. Many men despise politics because they see that politics manipulate, but make nothing. If politics are to be the highest activity of man, as they should be, they must be clearly understood as creative.

What is there inherent in the group which gives it creative power? The activity which produces the true individual is at the same time interweaving him and others into a real whole. A genuine whole has creative force. Does this seem "mystical?" The power of our corporations depends upon this capability of men to interknit themselves into such genuine relations that a new personality is thereby evolved. This is the "real personality" of modern legal theory. Are our company directors and corporation lawyers usually mystics?

The seeing of self as, with all other selves, creating, demands a new attitude and a new activity in man. The fallacy of self-and-others fades away and there is only self-in-and-through-others, only others so firmly rooted in the self and so fruitfully growing there that sundering is impossible. We must now enter upon modes of living commensurate with this thought.

What American politics need to-day is positive principles. We do not want to "regulate" our trusts, to "restrain" our bosses. The measure of our progress is never what we give up, but what we add. It may be necessary to prune the garden, but we do not make a pile of the dead branches and take our guests to see them as evidence of the flourishing state of the garden.

The group organization movement means the substitution of intention for accident, of organized purpose for scattered desire. It rests on the solid assumption that this is a man-made not a machine-made world, that men and women are capable of constructing their own life, and that not upon socialism or any rule or any order or any plan or any utopia can we rest our hearts, but only on the force of a united and creative citizenship.

We are asking for group organization in order to leap at once from the region of theory, of which Americans are so fond, to a practical scheme of living. We hear a good deal of academic talk about "the functioning of the social mind"; what does it all amount to? We have no social mind yet, so we have no functioning of the social mind. We want the directive force of consciously integrated thought and will. All our ideas of conscious self-determination lead us to a new method: it is not merely that we must be allowed to govern ourselves, we must learn how to govern ourselves; it is not only that we must be given "free speech," we must learn a speech that is free; we are not given rights, we create rights; it is not only that we must invent machinery to get a social will expressed, we must invent machinery that will get a social will created.

Politics have one task only — to create. To create? But what are politics to create? The state? The state is now discredited in many quarters. The extremists cry, "The state is dead, Down with the state." And it is by no means the extremists alone who are saying that our present state has played us false and that therefore we are justified in abolishing it. An increasing number of men are thinking what one writer has put into words, "We have passed from the *régime* of the state to that of the groups." We must see if it is necessary to abolish the state in order to get the advantage of the group.

Many trickles have gone to feed the stream of reaction against the state: (1) an economic and industrial progress which demands political recognition, which demands that labor have a share in political power, (2) the trend of philosophic thought towards pluralism and the whole anti-intellectualistic tendency, (3) a progressive legal theory of the "real personality" of groups, (4) a growing antagonism to the state because it is supposed to embody the crowd mind: our electorate is seen as a crowd hypnotized by the party leaders, big words, vague ideas and loose generalizations, (5) our life of rapidly increasing intercourse has made us see our voluntary associations as real and intimate, the state as something remote and foreign to us, and (6) the increasing alignment before the war of interests across state lines.

Every one of these reasons has force. Almost any one of these reasons is sufficient to turn political theory into new channels, seeking new currents of political life.

Yet if our present state is taken from us and we are left with our multiple group life, we are at once confronted with many questions. Shall the new state be based on occupational groups or neighborhood groups? Shall they form a unifying or a plural state? Shall the group or the individual be the basis of politics? The pluralist gives us the group as the unit of politics, but most of the group theories of politics are as entirely particularistic as the old "individualistic" theories; our particularism is merely transferred from the individual to the group.

Pluralism is the most vital trend in political thought to-day, but there are many dangers lurking in pluralism as at present understood. The pluralists apotheosize the group; the average American, on the other hand, is afraid of the group because he thinks of it chiefly in the form of corporation and trust. Both make the same mistake: both isolate the group. The group *in relation* must be the object of our study if that study is to be fruitful for politics. The pluralists have pointed out diversity but no pluralist has yet answered satisfactorily the question to which we must find an answer — What is to be done with this diversity?

Some of the pluralists tend to lose the individual in the group; others, to abandon the state for the group. But the individual, the group, the state — they are all there to be reckoned with — we cannot ignore or minimize any one. The relation of individual to group, of group to group, of individual and group to state — the part that labor is to have in the new state — these are the questions to the consideration of which this book is directed.

This book makes no attempt, however, to construct the new state, only to offer certain suggestions. But before the details of a new order are even hinted at, we must look far enough within for our practical suggestions to have value. In Part I we shall try to find the fundamental principles which must underlie the new state; in Part II we shall see how far they are expressed in present political forms; in Part III we shall consider how they can be expressed. When they are fully expressed, then we shall have the true Federal State, then we shall see appearing the World State.

To sum up this Introduction: The immediate problem of political science is to discover the method of self-government. Industrial democracy, the self-government of smaller nations, the "sovereignty" of an International League, our own political power, — how are these to be attained? Not by being "granted" or "conferred." Genuine control, power, authority are always a growth. Self-government is a psychological process. It is with that psychological process that this book is largely concerned. To free the way for that process is the task of practical politics.

New surges of life are pounding at circumference and centre; we must open the way for their entrance and onflow. To-day the individual is submerged, smothered, choked by the crowd fallacy, the herd theory. Free him from these, release his energies, and he with all other Freemen will work out quick, flexible, constantly changing forms which shall respond sensitively to every need.

Under our present system, social and economic changes necessary because of changing social and economic conditions cannot be brought about. The first reform needed in our political practice is to find some method by which the government shall continuously represent the people. No state can endure unless the political bond is being forever forged anew. The organization of men in small local groups gives opportunity for this continuous political activity which ceaselessly creates the state. Our government forms cannot be fossils from a dead age, but must be sensitive, mobile channels for the quick and quickening soul of the individual to flow to those larger confluences which finally bring forth the state. Thus every man *is* the state at every moment, whether in daily toil or social intercourse, and thus the state itself, leading a myriad-membered life, is expressing itself as truly in its humblest citizen as in its supreme assembly.

The principle of modern politics, the principle of creative citizenship, must predominantly and preëminently body itself and be acknowledged by every human being. Then will "practical politics" be for the first time practical.

A few words of explanation seem necessary. I have no bibliography simply because any list of references which I could give would necessarily be a partial one since much of this book has come by wireless. Besides all that is being written definitely of a new state, the air to-day is full of the tentative, the partial, the fragmentary thought, the isolated flash of insight from some genius, all of which is being turned to the solution of those problems which, from our waking to our sleeping, face us with their urgent demand. I am here trying to show the need of a wide and systematic study of these problems, not pretending to be able to solve them. Much interweaving of thought will be necessary before the form of the new state appears to us.

Moreover, I have not traced the strands of thought which have led us to our present ideas. That does not mean that I do not recognize the slow building up of these ideas or all our indebtedness to the thinkers of the past. I speak of principles as "new" which we all know were familiar to Aristotle or Kant and are new to-day only in their application.

The word new is so much used in the present day
— New Freedom, New Democracy, New Society etc.
— that it is perhaps well for us to remind ourselves what
we mean by this word.   We are using the word new partly
in reaction to the selfishness of the nineteenth century,
in reaction to a world which has culminated in this
war, but more especially in the sense of the live, the
real, in contrast to the inert, the dead.   It is not a time
distinction — the "new" (the vital) claims fellowship
with all that is "new" (vital) in the past.   When we
speak of the "New" Freedom we mean all the reality
and truth which have accumulated in all the conceptions of freedom up to the present moment.   The "New"
Society is the "Perfect Society."   The "New" Life
is the Vita Nuova, "when spring came to the heart of
Italy."

It is I hope unnecessary to explain that in my frequent
use of the term "the new psychology," I am not referring
to any definitely formulated body of thought;   there
are no writers who are expounding the new psychology
as such.   By the "new psychology" I mean something
now in the making: I mean partly that group psychology which is receiving more attention and gaining more
influence every day, and partly I mean simply that feeling out for a new conception of *modes of association*
which we see in law, economics, ethics, politics, and
indeed in every department of thought.   It is a short
way of saying that we are now looking at things not as
entities but in relation.   When our modern jurists
speak of the growing emphasis upon relation rather
than upon contract — they are speaking of the "new
psychology."

There is, however, another and very important aspect
of contemporary psychology closely connected with
this one of relation.   We are to-day seeking to under-

stand the sources of human motives,[1] and then to free
their channels so that these elemental springs of human
activity (the fundamental instincts of man) shall not
be dammed but flow forth in normal fashion, for normal
man is constructive. A few years ago, for instance, we
were satisfied merely to condemn sabotage and re-
pudiation of law; now we are trying to discover the
cause of this deviation from the normal in order to see
if it can be removed. This necessity for the understanding of the nature and vital needs of men has not
yet reached full self-consciousness, but appears in diverse
forms: as the investigation of the I. W. W., as a study
of "Human Nature in Politics," an examination of "The
Great Society," as child-study, as Y. M. C. A. efforts
to nourish all sides of men at the front, etc. etc. To-day
the new psychology speaks in many voices. Soon we
may hope for some unified formulation of all this varied
and scattered utterance. Soon we may hope also that
the connection will be made between this aspect of contemporary psychology and the group psychology upon
which this book is mainly founded.[2]

I wish to add my reason for giving quotations from
many writers whose names I have not cited. This
has been chiefly because often the sentence or phrase
quoted taken away from all context does not give a fair
idea of the writer's complete thought, and I have used
it not in an attempt to refute these writers, but merely
as illustrating certain tendencies to which we are all
more or less subject at present. Many of the writers
with whom I have disagreed in some particular have
been in the main my teachers and guides.

A certain amount of repetition has seemed necessary
in order to look at the same idea from a number of angles
and to make different applications of the same principle.

[1] See William McDougall, Social Psychology.

From a few friends I have received much help. My thanks are especially due to my teacher and counsellor of many years, Miss Anna Boynton Thompson, who went over the first copy of the manuscript with me and gave to it the most careful consideration and criticism, offering constantly invaluable suggestion and advice; to her unflagging and most generous help the final form owes more than I can quite express. The inception of the book is due to my friends and fellow-workers, Mrs. Louis Brandeis, Mrs. Richard Cabot and Mr. Arthur Woodworth, as also much of its thought to the stimulus of "group" discussion with them. Mrs. Charles W. Mixter, Professor Albert Bushnell Hart, Professor H. A. Overstreet, Professor W. Ernest Hocking and Mr. Roscoe Pound have read the manuscript in full or in part and have given me many valuable suggestions. I owe to my friend, Miss Isobel L. Briggs, daily help, advice and encouragement in the development of the book, and the revision of manuscript and proofs.

[2] I have also taken it for granted that "the new psychology" would be generally understood to include some of the interpretations of the results of recent biological research given by behaviorists and Freudian psychologists.

Part I

THE GROUP PRINCIPLE

I

THE GROUP AND THE NEW PSYCHOLOGY

POLITICS must have a technique based on an understanding of the laws of association, that is, based on a new and progressive social psychology. Politics alone should not escape all the modern tendency of scientific method, of analysis, of efficiency engineering. The study of democracy has been based largely on the study of institutions; it should be based on the study of how men behave together. We have to deal, not with institutions, or any mechanical thing, or with abstract ideas, or "man," or anything but just men, ordinary men. The importance of the new psychology is that it acknowledges man as the centre and shaper of his universe. In his nature all institutions are latent and perforce must be adapted to this nature. Man not things must be the starting point of the future.

But man in association, for no man lives to himself. And we must understand further that the laws of association are the laws of the group. We have long been trying to understand the relation of the individual to society; we are only just beginning to see that there is no "individual," that there is no "society." It is not strange, therefore, that our efforts have gone astray, that our thinking yields small returns for politics. The old psychology was based on the isolated individual as the unit, on the assumption that a man thinks, feels and judges independently. Now that we know that there is no such thing as a separate ego, that individuals are created by reciprocal interplay, our whole study of psychology is being transformed.

19

Likewise there is no "society" thought of vaguely as the mass of people we see around us. I am always in relation not to "society" but to some concrete group. When do we ever as a matter of fact think of "society"? Are we not always thinking of our part in our board of directors or college faculty, in the dinner party last night,[1] in our football team, our club, our political party, our trade-union, our church? Practically "society" is for every one of us a number of groups. The recognition of this constitutes a new step in sociology analogous to the contribution William James made in regard to the individual. James brought to popular recognition the truth that since man is a complex of experiences there are many selves in each one. So society as a complex of groups includes many social minds. The craving we have for union is satisfied by group life, groups and groups, groups ever widening, ever unifying, but always groups. We sometimes say that man is spiritually dependent upon society; what we are referring to is his psychic relation to his groups. The vital relation of the individual to the world is through his groups; they are the potent factors in shaping our lives.

Hence social psychology cannot be the application of the old individual psychology to a number of people. A few years ago I went to a lecture on "Social Psycology," as the subject was announced. Not a word was said except on the nervous systems and other aspects of individual psychology, but at the last moment the lecturer told us that had there been time he would have applied what he had said to social conditions! It reminded me of the mental processes of the man who, when he wanted to know something about Chinese metaphysics, first looked up China in the encyclopedia and

[1] Probably by no means a group, but tending in some instances in that direction, as in the discussion or conference dinners now so common.

then metaphysics and put them together. The new psychology must take people with their inheritance, their "tendencies," their environment, and then focus its attention on their interrelatings. The most careful laboratory work must be done to discover the conditions which make these interrelatings possible, which make these interrelatings fruitful.

Some writers make "socially minded" tendencies on the part of individuals the subject of social psychology, but such tendencies belong still to the field of individual psychology. A social action is not an individual initiative with social application.[1] Neither is social psychology the determination of how far social factors determine the individual consciousness. Social psychology must concern itself primarily with the *interaction* of minds.

Early psychology was based on the study of the individual; early sociology was based on the study of society. But there is no such thing as the "individual," there is no such thing as "society"; there is only the group and the group-unit — the social individual. Social psychology must begin with an intensive study of the group, of the selective processes which go on within it, the differentiated reactions, the likenesses and unlikenesses, and the spiritual energy which unites them.

The acceptance and the living of the new psychology will do away with all the progeny of particularistic psychology: consent of the governed, majority rule, external leadership, industrial wars, national wars etc. From the analysis of the group must come an understanding of collective thought and collective feeling, of the common will and concerted activity, of the true nature of free-

[1] The old definition of the word social has been a tremendous drag on politics. Social policies are not policies for the good of the people but policies created by the people, etc. etc. We read in the work of a continental sociologist, "When a social will is born in the brain of a man," but a social will never is born in the brain of a man.

dom, the illusion of self-and-others, the essential unity of men, the real meaning of patriotism, and the whole secret of progress and of life as a genuine interpenetration which produces true community.

All thinking men are demanding a new state. The question is — What form shall that state take? No one of us will be able to give an answer until we have studied men in association and have discovered the laws of association. This has not been done yet, but already we can see that a political science which is not based on a knowledge of the laws of association gained by a study of the group will soon seem the crudest kind of quackery. Syndicalism, in reaction to the so-called "metaphysical" foundation of politics, is based on "objective rights," on function, on its conception of modes of association which shall emphasize the object of the associated and not the relation of the associated to one another. The new psychology goes a step further and sees these as one, but how can any of these things be discussed abstractly? Must we not first study men in association? Young men in the hum of actual life, practical politicians, the members of constitutional conventions, labor leaders — all these must base their work on the principles of group psychology.

The fundamental reason for the study of group psychology is that no one can give us democracy, we must learn democracy. To be a democrat is not to decide on a certain form of human association, it is to learn how to live with other men. The whole labor movement is being kept back by people not knowing how to live together much more than by any deliberate refusal to grant justice. The trouble with syndicalism is that its success depends on group action and we know almost nothing of the laws of the group.

I have used group in this book with the meaning of

men associating under the law of interpenetration as opposed to the law of the crowd—suggestion and imitation. This may be considered an arbitrary definition, but of course I do not care about the names, I only want to emphasize the fact that men meet under two different sets of laws. Social psychology may include both group psychology and crowd psychology, but of these two group psychology is much the more important. For a good many years now we have been dominated by the crowd school, by the school which taught that people met together are governed by suggestion and imitation, and less notice has been taken of all the interplay which is the real social process that we have in a group but not in a crowd. How men behave in crowds, and the relation of the crowd conception of politics to democracy, will be considered in later chapters. While I recognize that men are more often at present under the laws of the crowd than of the group, I believe that progress depends on the group, and, therefore, that the group should be the basis of a progressive social psychology. The group process contains the secret of collective life, it is the key to democracy, it is the master lesson for every individual to learn, it is our chief hope for the political, the social, the international life of the future.[1]

[1] This is essentially the process by which sovereignty is created. Therefore chapters II–VI on The Group Process are the basis of the conception of sovereignty given in Part III and of the relation of that conception to the politics of reconstruction.

II

THE GROUP PROCESS: THE COLLECTIVE IDEA

L ET us begin at once to consider the group process. Perhaps the most familiar example of the evolving of a group idea is a committee meeting. The object of a committee meeting is first of all to create a common idea. I do not go to a committee meeting merely to give my own ideas. If that were all, I might write my fellow-members a letter. But neither do I go to learn other people's ideas. If that were all, I might ask each to write me a letter. I go to a committee meeting in order that all together we may create a group idea, an idea which will be better than any one of our ideas alone, moreover which will be better than all of our ideas added together. For this group idea will not be produced by any process of addition, but by the interpenetration of us all. This subtle psychic process by which the resulting idea shapes itself is the process we want to study.

Let us imagine that you, I, A, B and C are in conference. Now what from our observation of groups will take place? Will you say something, and then I add a little something, and then A, and B, and C, until we have together built up, brick-wise, an idea, constructed some plan of action? Never. A has one idea, B another, C's idea is something different from either, and so on, but we cannot add all these ideas to find the group idea. They will not add any more than apples and chairs will add. But we gradually find that our problem can be

24

solved, not indeed by mechanical aggregation, but by the subtle process of the intermingling of all the different ideas of the group. A says something. Thereupon a thought arises in B's mind. Is it B's idea or A's? Neither. It is a mingling of the two. We find that A's idea, after having been presented to B and returned to A, has become slightly, or largely, different from what it was originally. In like manner it is affected by C and so on. But in the same way B's idea has been affected by all the others, and not only does A's idea feel the modifying influence of each of the others, but A's ideas are affected by B's relation to all the others, and A's plus B's are affected by all the others individually and collectively, and so on and on until the common idea springs into being.

We find in the end that it is not a question of my idea being supplemented by yours, but that there has been evolved a composite idea. But by the time we have reached this point we have become tremendously civilized people, for we have learned one of the most important lessons of life: we have learned to do that most wonderful thing, to say "I" representing a whole instead of "I" representing one of our separate selves. The course of action decided upon is what we all together want, and I see that it is better than what I had wanted alone. It is what *I* now want. We have all experienced this at committee meetings or conferences.

We see therefore that we cannot view the content of the collective mind as a holiday procession, one part after another passing before our mental eyes; every part is bound up with every other part, every tendency is conditioned by every other tendency. It is like a game of tennis. A serves the ball to B. B returns the serve but his play is influenced as largely by the way the ball has been served to him as it is by his own method of return. A senas the ball back to B, but his return is made up of his own play plus the way in which the ball has been played to him by B plus his own original serve. Thus in the end does action and reaction become inextricably bound up together.

I have described briefly the group process. Let us consider what is required of the individual in order that the group idea shall be produced. First and foremost each is to do his part. But just here we have to get rid of some rather antiquated notions. The individual is not to facilitate agreement by courteously (!) waiving his own point of view. That is just a way of shirking. Nor may I say, "Others are able to plan this better than I." Such an attitude is the result either of laziness or of a misconception. There are probably many present at the conference who could make wiser plans than I alone, but that is not the point, we have come together each to give something. I must not subordinate myself, I must affirm myself and give my full positive value to that meeting.

And as the psychic coherence of the group can be obtained only by the full contribution of every member, so we see that a readiness to compromise must be no part of the individual's attitude. Just so far as people think that the basis of working together is compromise or concession, just so far they do not understand the first principles of working together. Such people think that when they have reached an appreciation of the necessity of compromise they have reached a high plane of social development; they conceive themselves as nobly willing to sacrifice part of their desire, part of their idea, part of their will, in order to secure the undoubted benefit of concerted action. But compromise is still on the same plane as fighting. War will continue — between capital and labor, between nation and nation — until we relinquish the ideas of compromise and concession.[1]

But at the same time that we offer fully what we have to give, we must be eager for what all others have to give. If I ought not to go to my group feeling that I must give up my own ideas in order to accept the opinions of others, neither ought I to go to force my ideas upon others. The "harmony" that comes from the domination of one man is not the kind we want. At a board of directors' meeting once Mr. E. H. Harriman said, "Gentlemen, we must have coöperation. I insist upon it." They "coöperated" and all his motions were put through. At the end of the meeting some one asked Mr. Harriman to define coöperation. "Oh, that's simple," he said, "do as I say and do it damned quick."

There are many people who conscientiously go to their group thinking it their duty to impose their ideas upon others, but the time is coming soon when we are going to see that we have no more right to get our own way by persuading people than by bullying or bribing them. To take our full share in the synthesis is all that is legitimate.[2]

Thus the majority idea is not the group idea. Suppose I belong to a committee composed of five: of A, B, C, D and myself. According to the old theory of my duties as a committee member I might say, "A

[1] This is the heart of the latest ethical teaching based on the most progressive psychology: between two apparently conflicting courses of action, a and b, a is not to be followed and b suppressed, nor b followed and a suppressed, nor must a compromise between the two be sought, but the process must always be one of integration. Our progress is measured by our ability to proceed from integration to integration.

[2] This statement may be misunderstood unless there is borne in mind at the same time: (1) the necessity for the keenest individual thinking as the basis of group thinking, and (2) that every man should maintain his point of view until it has found its place in the group thought, that is, until he has been neither overruled nor absorbed but integrated.

agrees with me, if I can get B to agree with me that
will make a majority and I can carry my point." That
is, we five can then present this idea to the world as our
group idea.   But this is not a group idea, although it
may be the best substitute we can get for the moment.
To a genuine group idea every man must contribute
what is in him to contribute.   Thus even the passing
of a unanimous vote by a group of five does not prove
the existence of a group idea if two or three (or even one)
out of indifference or laziness or prejudice, or shut-upness,
or a misconception of their function, have not added
their individual thought to the creation of the group
thought.   No member of a group which is to create can
be passive.   All must be active and constructively active.

It is not, however, to be constructively active merely
to add a share: it must be a share which is related to and
bound up with every other share.   And it must be given
in such a way that it fits in with what others are giving.
Some one said to me the other day, "Don't you think
Mr. X talks better than anyone else in Boston?"   Well
the fact is that Mr. X talks so well that I can never talk
with him.   Everything he says has such a ring of finality, is such a rounding up of the whole question, that it
leaves nothing more to be said on the subject.   This is
particularly the kind of thing to be avoided in a committee meeting or conference.

There are many people, moreover, who want to score,
to be brilliant, rather than to find agreement.   Others
come prepared with what they are going to say and
either this has often been said long before they get a
chance to speak, or, in any case, it allows no give-and-
take, so they contribute nothing; when we really learn
the process our ideas will be struck out by the interplay.
To compare notes on what we have thought separately
is not to think together.

I asked a man once to join a committee I was organizing and he replied that he would be very glad to come and give his advice. I didn't want him — and didn't have him. I asked another man and he said he would like very much to come and learn but that he couldn't contribute anything. I didn't have him either — I hadn't a school. Probably the last man thought he was being modest and, therefore, estimable. But what I wanted was to get a group of people who would deliberately work out a thing together. I should have liked very much to have the man who felt that he had advice to give if he had had also what we are now learning to call the social attitude, that is, that of a man willing to take his place in the group, no less and no more. This definition of social attitude is very different from our old one — the willingness to give; my friend who wanted to come and give advice had that, but that is a crude position compared with the one we are now advocating.

It is clear then that we do not go to our group — trade-union, city council, college faculty — to be passive and learn, and we do not go to push through something we have already decided we want. Each must discover and contribute that which distinguishes him from others, his difference. The only use for my difference is to join it with other differences. The unifying of opposites is the eternal process.[1] We must have an imagination which will leap from the particular to the universal. Our joy, our satisfaction, must always be in the more inclusive aspect of our problem.

We can test our group in this way: do we come together to register the results of individual thought,

---

[1] We must not of course confuse the type of unifying spoken of here (an integration), which is a psychological process, with the "reconciliation of opposites," which is a logical process.

to compare the results of individual thought in order to make selections therefrom, or do we come together to create a common idea? Whenever we have a real group something new *is* actually created. We can now see therefore that the object of group life is not to find the best individual thought, but the collective thought. A committee meeting isn't like a prize show aimed at calling out the best each can possibly produce and then the prize (the vote) awarded to the best of all these individual opinions. The object of a conference is not to get at a lot of different ideas, as is often thought, but just the opposite — to get at one idea. There is nothing rigid or fixed about thoughts, they are entirely plastic, and ready to yield themselves completely to their master — the group spirit.[1]

I have given some of the conditions necessary for collective thinking. In every governing board — city councils, hospital and library trustees, the boards of colleges and churches, in business and industry, in directors' meetings — no device should be neglected which will help to produce joint rather than individual thinking. But no one has yet given us a scientific analysis of the conditions necessary or how to fulfil them. We do not yet know, for instance, the best number to bring out the group idea, the number, that is, which will bring out as many differences as possible and yet form a whole or group. We cannot guess at it but only get it through scientific experiments. Much laboratory work has to be done. The numbers on Boards of Education, on Governors' Commissions, should be determined by psychological as well as by political reasons.

Again it is said that private sessions are undemocratic.

---

[1] I am sometimes told that mine is a counsel of perfection only to be realized in the millenium, but we cannot take even the first step until we have chosen our path.

If they contribute to true collective thinking (instead of efforts to dazzle the gallery), then, in so far, they are democratic, for there is nothing in the world so democratic as the production of a genuine group will.

Mr. Gladstone must have appreciated the necessity of making conditions favorable to joint thinking, for I have been told that at important meetings of the Cabinet he planned beforehand where each member should sit.

The members of a group are reciprocally conditioning forces none of which acts as it would act if any one member were different or absent. You can often see this in a board of directors: if one director leaves the room, every man becomes slightly different.

When the conditions for collective thinking are more or less fulfilled, then the expansion of life will begin. Through my group I learn the secret of wholeness.[1] The inspiration of the group is proportionate to the degree in which we do actually identify ourselves with the whole and think that *we* are doing this, not Mr. A and Mr. B and I, but we, the united we, the singular not the plural pronoun we. (We shall have to write a new grammar to meet the needs of the times, as non-Euclidean geometries are now being published.) Then we shall no longer have a feeling of individual triumph, but feel only elation that the group has accomplished something. Much of the evil of our political and social life comes from the fact that we crave personal recognition and personal satisfaction; as soon as our greatest satisfaction is group satisfaction, many of our present problems will disappear. When one thinks of one's self as part of a group, it means keener moral perceptions,

[1] The break in the English Cabinet in 1915, which led to the coalition Cabinet, came when both Kitchener and Churchill tried to substitute individual for group action.

greater strength of will, more enthusiasm and zest in life. We shall enjoy living the social life when we understand it; the things which we do and achieve together will give us much greater happiness than the things we do and achieve by ourselves. It has been asked what, in peace, is going to take the place of those songs men sing as they march to battle which at the same time thrill and unite them. The songs which the hearts of men will sing as they go forward in life with one desire — the song of the common will, the social will of man.

Men descend to meet? This is not my experience. The *laissez-aller* which people allow themselves when alone disappears when they meet. Then they pull themselves together and give one another of their best. We see this again and again. Sometimes the ideal of the group stands quite visibly before us as one which none of us is quite living up to by himself. We feel it there, an impalpable, substantial thing in our midst. It raises us to the nth power of action, it fires our minds and glows in our hearts and fulfils and actuates itself no less, but rather on this very account, because it has been generated only by our being together.

III

THE GROUP PROCESS: THE COLLECTIVE IDEA
(CONTINUED)

WHAT then is the essence of the group process by which are evolved the collective thought and the collective will? It is an acting and reacting, a single and identical process which brings out differences and integrates them into a unity. The complex reciprocal action, the intricate interweavings of the members of the group, is the social process.

We see now that the process of the many becoming one is not a metaphysical or mystical idea; psychological analysis shows us how we can at the same moment be the self and the other, it shows how we can be forever apart and forever united. It is by the group process that the transfiguration of the external into the spiritual takes place, that is, that what seems a series becomes a whole. The essence of society is difference, related difference. "Give me your difference" is the cry of society to-day to every man.[1]

But the older sociology made the social mind the consciousness of likeness. This likeness was accounted for by two theories chiefly: the imitation theory and the like-response-to-like-stimuli theory. It is necessary to consider these briefly, for they have been gnawing at the roots of all our political life.

To say that the social process is that merely of the spread of similarities is to ignore the real nature of the collective thought, the collective will. Individual ideas

[1] Free speech is not an "individual" right; society needs every man's difference.

do not become social ideas when communicated. The difference between them is one of kind. A collective thought is one evolved by a collective process. The essential feature of a common thought is not that it is held in common but that it has been produced in common.

Likewise if every member of a group has the same thought, that is not a group idea: when all respond simultaneously to the same stimulus, it cannot be assumed that this is in obedience to a collective will, When all the men in a street run round the corner to see a procession, it is not because they are moved by a collective thought.

Imitation indeed has a place in the collective life, it is one of the various means of coadaptation between men, but it is only a part and a part which has been fatally overemphasized.[1] It is one of the fruits of particularism. "Imitation" has been made the bridge to span the gap between the individual and society, but we see now that there is no gap, therefore no bridge is necessary.

The core of the social process is not likeness, but the harmonizing of difference through interpenetration.[2] But to be more accurate, similarity and difference can not be opposed in this external way — they have a vital connection. Similarities and differences make up the differentiated reactions of the group; that is what con-

---

[1] It has been overemphasized in two ways: first, many of the writers on imitation ignore the fact that the other law of association, that of interpenetrating, is also in operation in our social life, as well as the fact that it has always been the fundamental law of existence; secondly, they speak as if it were *necessary* for human beings to be under the law of imitation, not that it is merely a stage in our development.

[2] This is the alpha and omega of philosophical teaching: Heraclitus said, "Nature desires eagerly opposites and out of them it completes its harmony, not out of similars." And James, twenty-four hundred years later, has given his testimony that the process of life is to "compenetrate."

stitutes their importance, not their likeness or unlikeness as such. I react to a stimulus: that reaction may represent a likeness or an unlikeness. Society is the unity of these differentiated reactions. In other words the process is not that merely of accepting or rejecting, it is bound up in the interknitting. In that continuous coördinating which constitutes the social process both similarity and difference have a place. Unity is brought about by the reciprocal adaptings of the reactions of individuals, and this reciprocal adapting is based on both agreement and difference.

To push our analysis a little further, we must distinguish between the given similarity and the achieved similarity. The common at any moment is always the given: it has come from heredity, biological influences, suggestion and imitation, and the previous workings of the law of interpenetration. All the accumulated effect of these is seen in our habits of thinking, our modes of living. But we cannot rest in the common. The surge of life sweeps through the given similarity, the common ground, and breaks it up into a thousand differences. This tumultuous, irresistible flow of life is our existence: the unity, the common, is but for an instant, it flows on to new differings which adjust themselves anew in fuller, more varied, richer synthesis. The moment when similarity achieves itself as a composite of working, seething forces, it throws out its myriad new differings. The torrent flows into a pool, works, ferments, and then rushes forth until all is again gathered into the new pool of its own unifying.

This is the process of evolution. Social progress is to be sure coadapting, but coadapting means always that the fresh unity becomes the pole of a fresh difference leading to again new unities which lead to broader and broader fields of activity.

Thus no one of course undertakes to deny the obvious fact that in order to have a society a certain amount of similarity must exist. In one sense society rests on likeness: the likeness between men is deeper than their difference. We could not have an enemy unless there was much in common between us. With my friend all the aims that we share unite us. In a given society the members have the same interests, the same ends, in the main, and seek a common fulfilment. Differences are always grounded in an underlying similarity. But all this kind of "similarity" isn't worth mentioning because we *have* it. The very fact that it is common to us all condemns it from the point of view of progress. Progress does not depend upon the similarity which we *find* but upon the similarity which we *achieve*.

This view of the social process gives us individual responsibility as to the central fact of life because it demands that we grow our own like-mindedness. To-day we are basing all our hopes not on the given likeness but the created unity. To rest in the given likeness would be to annihilate social progress. The organization of industry and the settlement of international relations must come under the domination of this law. The Allies are fighting to-day with one impulse, one desire, one aim, but at the peace table many differences will arise between them. The progress of the whole world at that moment will depend upon the "similarity" we can create. This "similarity" will consist of all we now hold in common and also, of the utmost importance for the continuance of civilization, upon our ability to unify our differences. If we go to that peace table with the idea that the new world is to be based on that community of interest and aim which now animates us, the disillusion will be great, the result an overwhelming failure.

Let us henceforth, therefore, use the word unifying

instead of similarity to represent the basis of association. And let us clearly understand that unifying is a process involving the continuous activity of every man. To await "variation-giving" individuals would be to make life a mere chance. We cannot wait for new ideas to appear among us, we must ourselves produce them. This makes possible the endless creation of new social values. The old like-minded theory is too fortuitous, too passive and too negative to attract us; creating is the divine adventure.

Let us imagine a group of people whom we know. If we find the life of that group consisting chiefly of imitation, we see that it involves no activity of the real self but crushes and smothers it. Imitation condemns the human race. Even if up to the present moment imitation has been a large factor in man's development, from this moment on such a smothering of all the forces of life must cease.

If we have, however, among this group "like-response," that is if there spring up like thoughts and feelings, we find a more dignified and worthy life — fellowship claims us with all its joys and its enlargement of our single self. But there is no progress here. We give ourselves up to the passive enjoyment of that already existing. We have found our kindred and it comforts us. How much greater enhancement comes from that life foreshadowed by the new psychology where each one is to go forth from his group a richer being because each one has taken and put into its right membership all the vital differences of all the others. The like-mindedness which is now to be demanded of us is the like-mindedness which is brought about by the enlargement of each by the inflowing of every other one. Then I go forth a new creature. But to what do I go forth? Always to a new group, a new "society." There is no end to this process. A new being springs forth from every fresh contact. My nature opens and opens to thousands of new influences. I feel countless new births. Such is the glory of our common every-day life.

Imitation is for the shirkers, like-mindedness for the comfort lovers, unifying for the creators.

The lesson of the new psychology is then: Never settle down within the theory you have chosen, the cause you have embraced; know that another theory, another cause exists, and seek that. The enhancement of life is not for the comfort-lover. As soon as you succeed — real success means something arising to overthrow your security.

In all the discussion of "similarity" too much importance has been put upon analogies from the animal world.[1] We are told, for instance, and important conclusions are drawn in regard to human society, that the gregarious instinct of any animal receives satisfaction only through the presence of animals similar to itself, and that the closer the similarity the greater the satisfaction. True certainly for animals, but it is this fact which keeps them mere animals. As far as the irrational elements of life give way to the rational, interpenetration becomes the law of association. Man's biological inheritance is not his only life. And the progress of man means that this inheritance shall occupy a less and less important place relatively.

It has been necessary to consider the similarity theory, I have said, because it has eaten its way into all our thought.[2] Many people to-day seem to think that prog-

[1] Also the group-units of early societies are studied to the exclusion of group-units within modern complex society.

[2] Even some of our most advanced thinking, which repudiates the like-minded theory and takes pains to prove that imitation is not an instinct, nevertheless falls into some of the errors implicit in the imitation theory.

ress depends upon a number of people all speaking loudly together. The other day a woman said to me that she didn't like the *Survey* because it has on one page a letter from a conservative New York banker and on another some radical proposal for the reconstruction of society; she said she preferred a paper which took one idea and hammered away on that. This is poor psychology. It is the same reasoning which makes people think that certain kindred souls should come together, and then by a certain intensified thinking and living together some noble product will emerge for the benefit of the world. Such association is based on a wrong principle. However various the reasons given for the non-success of such experiments as Brook Farm, certain religious associations, and certain artistic and literary groups who have tried to live together, the truth is that most of them have died simply of non-nutrition. The bond created had not within it the variety which the human soul needs for its nourishment.

Unity, not uniformity, must be our aim. We attain unity only through variety. Differences must be integrated, not annihilated, nor absorbed.[1] Anarchy means unorganized, unrelated difference; coördinated, unified difference belongs to our ideal of a perfect social order. We don't want to avoid our adversary but to "agree with him quickly"; we must, however, learn the technique of agreeing. As long as we think of difference as that

---

[1] When we come in Part III to consider the group process in relation to certain political methods now being proposed, we shall find that part of the present disagreement of opinion is verbal. I therefore give here a list of words which can be used to describe the genuine social process and a list which gives exactly the wrong idea of it. Good words: integrate, interpenetrate, interpermeate, compenetrate, compound, harmonize, correlate, coördinate, interweave, reciprocally relate or adapt or adjust, etc. Bad words: fuse, melt, amalgamate, assimilate, weld, dissolve, absorb, reconcile (if used in Hegelian sense), etc.

which divides us, we shall dislike it; when we think of it as that which unites us, we shall cherish it. Instead of shutting out what is different, we should welcome it because it is different and through its difference will make a richer content of life. The ignoring of differences is the most fatal mistake in politics or industry or international life: every difference that is swept up into a bigger conception feeds and enriches society; every difference which is ignored feeds *on* society and eventually corrupts it.

Heterogeneity, not homogeneity, I repeat, makes unity. Indeed as we go from groups of the lower types to groups of the higher types, we go from those with many resemblances to those with more and more striking differences. The higher the degree of social organization the more it is based on a very wide diversity among its members. The people who think that London is the most civilized spot in the world give as evidence that it is the only city in which you can eat a bun on a street corner without being noticed. In London, in other words, difference is expected of us. In Boston you cannot eat a bun on the street corner, at least not without unpleasant consequences.

Give *your* difference, welcome *my* difference, unify *all* difference in the larger whole — such is the law of growth. The unifying of difference is the eternal process of life — the creative synthesis, the highest act of creation, the at-onement. The implications of this conception when we come to define democracy are profound.

And throughout our participation in the group process we must be ever on our guard that we do not confuse differences and antagonisms, that diversity does not arouse hostility. Suppose a friend says something with which I do not agree. It may be that instantly I feel antagonistic, feel as if we were on opposite

sides, and my emotions are at once tinged with some
of the enmity which being on opposite sides usually
brings. Our relations become slightly strained, we
change the subject as soon as possible, etc. But suppose
we were really civilized beings, then we should think:
"How interesting this is, this idea has evidently a larger
content than I realized; if my friend and I can unify
this material, we shall separate with a larger idea than
either of us had before." If my friend and I are always
trying to find the things upon which we agree, what is
the use of our meeting? Because the consciousness of
agreement makes us happy? It is a shallow happiness,
only felt by people too superficial or too shut-up or too
vain to feel that richer joy which comes from having
taken part in an act of creation — created a new thought
by the uniting of differences. A friendship based on
likenesses and agreements alone is a superficial matter
enough. The deep and lasting friendship is one capable
of recognizing and dealing with all the fundamental differences that must exist between any two individuals,
one capable therefore of such an enrichment of our
personalities that together we shall mount to new heights
of understanding and endeavor. Some one ought to
write an essay on the dangers to the soul of congeniality.
Pleasant little glows of feeling can never be fanned into
the fire which becomes the driving force of progress.

In trying to explain the social process I may have
seemed to over emphasize difference as difference. Difference as difference is non-existent. There is only
difference which carries within itself the power of unifying. It is this latent power which we must forever and
ever call forth. Difference in itself is not a vital force,
but what accompanies it is — the unifying spirit.

Throughout my description of the group process I
have taken committee-meetings, conferences etc. for

illustration, but really the object of every associating with others, of every conversation with friends, in fact, should be to try to bring out a bigger thought than any one alone could contribute. How different our dinner parties would be if we could do this. And I mean without too labored an effort, but merely by recognizing certain elementary rules of the game. Creation is always possible when people meet; this is the wonderful interest of life. But it depends upon us so to manage our meetings that there shall be some result, not just a frittering away of energy, unguided because not understood. All our private life is to be public life. This does not mean that we cannot sit with a friend by our fireside; it does mean that, private and gay as that hour may be, at the same time that very intimacy and lightness must in its way be serving the common cause, not in any fanciful sense, but because there is always the consciousness of my most private concerns as tributary to the larger life of men. But words are misleading: I do not mean that we are always to be thinking about it — it must be such an abiding sense that we never think of it.

Thus the new psychology teaches us that the core of the group process is creating. The essential value of the new psychology is that it carries enfolded within it the obligation upon every man to live the New Life. In no other system of thought has the Command been so clear, so insistent, so compelling. Every individual is necessary to the whole. On the other hand, every member participates in that power of a whole which is so much greater than the addition of its separate forces. The increased strength which comes to me when I work with others is not a numerical thing, is not because I feel that ten of us have ten times the strength of one. It is because all together we have struck out a new power in the universe. Ten of us may have ten,

or a hundred, or a thousand times the strength of one
— or rather you cannot measure it mathematically at
all.

The law of the group is not arbitrary but intrinsic.
Nothing is more practical for our daily lives than an
understanding of this. The group-spirit is the pillar of
cloud by day and of fire by night — it is our infallible
guide — it is the Spirit of democracy. It has all our
love and all our devotion, but this comes only when we
have to some extent identified ourselves with It, or
rather perhaps indentified It with all our common,
every-day lives. We can never dominate another or
be dominated by another; the group-spirit is always our
master.

IV

THE unification of thought, however, is only a part of the social process. We must consider, besides, the unification of feeling, affection, emotion, desire, aspiration — all that we are. The relation of the feelings to the development of the group has yet to be sufficiently studied. The analysis of the group process is beginning to show us the origin and nature of the true sympathy. The group process is a rational process. We can no longer therefore think of sympathy as "contagion of feeling" based on man's "inherited gregarious instinct." But equally sympathy cannot belong to the next stage in our development — the particularistic. Particularistic psychology, which gave us ego and alter, gave us sympathy going across from one isolated being to another. Now we begin with the group. We see in the self-unifying of the group process, and all the myriad unfoldings involved, the central and all-germinating activity of life. The group creates. In the group, we have seen, is formed the collective idea, "similarity" is there achieved, sympathy too is born within the group — it springs forever from interrelation. The emotions I feel when apart belong to the phantom ego; only from the group comes the genuine feeling *with* — the true sympathy, the vital sympathy, the just and balanced sympathy.

From this new understanding of sympathy as essentially involved in the group process, as part of the generating activity of the group, we learn two lessons: that sympathy cannot antedate the group process, and that it must not be confused with altruism. It had been

44

thought until recently by many writers that sympathy came before the social process. Evidences were collected among animals of the "desire to help" other members of the same species, and the conclusion drawn that sympathy exists and that the result is "mutual aid." But sympathy cannot antedate the activity. We do not however now say that there is an "instinct" to help and then that sympathy is the result of the helping; the feeling and the activity are involved one in the other.

It is asked, Was Bentham right in making the desire for individual happiness the driving force of society, or was Comte right in saying that love for our fellow creatures is as "natural" a feeling as self-interest? Many such questions, which have long perplexed us, will be answered by a progressive social psychology. The reason we have found it difficult to answer such questions is because we have thought of egoistic or altruistic feelings as preëxisting; we have studied action to see what precedent characteristics it indicated. But when we begin to see that men possess no characteristics apart from the unifying process, then it is the process we shall study.

Secondly, we can no longer confuse sympathy and altruism. Sympathy, born of our union, rises above both egoism and altruism. We see now that a classification of ego feelings and alter feelings is not enough, that there are always whole feelings to be accounted for, that true sympathy is sense of community, consciousness of oneness. I am touched by a story of want and suffering, I send a check, denying myself what I have eagerly desired in order to do so, — is that sympathy? It is the old particularistic sympathy, but it is not the sympathy which is a group product, which has come from the actual intermingling of myself with those who are in want and suffering. It may be that I do more harm than good with my check because I do not really know what the situation demands. The sympathy which springs up within the group is a productive sympathy.

But, objects a friend, if I meet a tramp who has been drinking whiskey, I can feel only pity for him, I can have no sense of oneness. Yes, the tramp and I are bound together by a thousand invisible bonds. He is a part of that society for which I am responsible. I have not been doing my entire duty; because of that a society has been built up which makes it possible for that tramp to exist and for whiskey drinking to be his chief pleasure.

A good illustration of both the errors mentioned — making sympathy antedate the group process and the confusion of sympathy and altruism — we see frequently in the discussion of coöperation in the business world. The question often asked, "Does modern coöperation depend upon self-interest or upon sympathy?" is entirely misleading as regards the real nature of sympathy. Suppose six manufacturers meet to discuss some form of union. There was a time when we should have been told that if each man were guided entirely by what would benefit his own plant, trusting the other five to be equally interested each in his own, thereby the interest of all would be evolved. Then there came a time when many thinkers denied this and said, "Coöperation cannot exist without some feeling of altruism; every one of those manufacturers must go to the meeting with the feeling that the interests of the other five should be considered as well as his own; he must be guided as much by sympathy as by self-interest." But we are now beginning to think that what these men need most is not altruistic feelings, but a consciousness of themselves as a new unit and a realization of the needs of that unit. The process of forming this new unit generates such realization which is sympathy. This true sympathy, therefore, is not a vague sentiment they bring with them; it springs from their meeting to be in its turn a vital factor in their meeting. The needs of that new unit may be so different from that of any one of the manufacturers alone that altruistic feelings might be wasted! The new ethics will never preach alter feelings but whole feelings. Sympathy is a whole feeling; it is a recognition of oneness. Perhaps social psychology has no more interesting task than to define for us that true sympathy which is now being born in a society which is shedding its particularistic garments and clothing itself in the mantle of wholeness.

To sum up: sympathy is not pity, it is not benevolence, it is one of the goals of the future, it cannot be actualized until we can think and feel together. At present we confuse it with altruism and all the particularist progeny, but sympathy is always a group product; benevolence, philanthropy, tenderness, fervor, ardor, pity, may be possible to me alone, but sympathy is not possible alone. The particularist stage has been necessary to our development, but we stand now on the threshold of another age: we see there humanity consciously generating its own activity, its own purpose and all that it needs for the accomplishment of that purpose. We must now fit ourselves to cross that threshold. Our faces have turned to a new world; to train our footsteps to follow the way is now our task.

This means that we must live the group life. This is the solution of our problems, national and international. Employers and employed cannot be exhorted to feel sympathy one for the other; true sympathy will come only by creating a community or group of employers and employed. Through the group you find the details, the filling-out of Kant's universal law. Kant's categorical imperative is general, is empty; it is only a blank check. But through the life of the group we learn the content of universal law.

V

THE GROUP PROCESS: THE COLLECTIVE WILL

FROM the group process arise social understanding and true sympathy. At the same moment appears the social will which is the creative will. Many writers are laying stress on the *possibilities* of the collective will; what I wish to emphasize is the necessity of *creating* the collective will. Many people talk as if the collective will were lying round loose to be caught up whenever we like, but the fact is we must go to our group and see that it is brought into existence.

Moreover, we go to our group to learn the process. We sometimes hear the advantages of collective planning spoken of as if an act of Congress or Parliament could substitute collective for individual planning! But it is only by doing the deed that we shall learn this doctrine. We learn how to create the common will in our groups, and we learn here not only the process but its value. When I can see that agreement with my neighbor for larger ends than either of us is pursuing alone is of the same essence as capital and labor learning to think together, as Germany and the Allies evolving a common will, then I am ready to become a part of the world process. To learn how to evolve the social will day by day with my neighbors and fellow-workers is what the world is demanding of me to-day. This is getting into the inner workshop of democracy.

Until we learn this lesson war cannot stop, no constructive work can be done. The very essence and substance of democracy is the creating of the collective will. Without this activity the forms of democracy are useless, and the aims of democracy are always unfulfilled. Without this activity both political and industrial democracy must be a chaotic, stagnating, self-stultifying assemblage. Many of the solutions offered to-day for our social problems are vitiated by their mechanical nature, by assuming that if society were given a new form, the socialistic for instance, what we desire would follow. But this assumption is not true. The deeper truth, perhaps the deepest, is that *the will to will the common will* is the core, the germinating centre of that large, still larger, ever larger life which we are coming to call the true democracy.

VI

WE have seen that the common idea and the common will are born together in the social process. One does not lead to the other, each is involved in the other. But the collective thought and the collective will are not yet complete, they are hardly an embryo. They carry indeed within themselves their own momentum, but they complete themselves only through activity in the world of affairs, of work, of government. This conception does away with the whole discussion, into which much ardor has gone, of the priority of thought or action in the social life. There is no order. The union of thought and will and activity by which the clearer will is generated, the social process, is a perfect unity.

We see this in our daily life where we do not finish our thought, construct our will, and then begin our actualizing. Not only the actualizing goes on at the same time, but its reactions help us to shape our thought, to energize our will. We have to digest our social experience, but we have to have social experience before we can digest it. We must learn and build and learn again through the building, or we must build and learn and build again through the learning.

We sit around the council table not blank pages but made up of all our past experiences. Then we evolve a so-called common will, then we take it into the concrete world to see if it will work. In so far as it does work, it proves itself; in so far as it does not, it generates the necessary idea to make it "common." Then again we

50

test and so on and so on. In our work always new and necessary modifications arise which again in actualizing *themselves*, again modify themselves. This is the process of the generation of the common will. First it appears as an ideal, secondly it works itself out in the material sphere of life, thereby generating itself in a new form and so on forever and ever. All is a-making. This is the process of creating the absolute or Good Will. To elevate General Welfare into our divinity makes a golden calf of it, erects it as something external to ourselves with an absolute nature of its own, whereas it is the ever new adjusting of ever new relatings to one another. The common will never finds perfection but is always seeking it. Progress is an infinite advance towards the infinitely receding goal of infinite perfection.

How important this principle is will appear later when we apply these ideas to politics. Democratic ideals will never advance unless we are given the opportunity of constantly embodying them in action, which action will react on our ideals. Thought and will go out into the concrete world in order to generate their own complete form. This gives us both the principle and the method of democracy. A democratic community is one in which the common will is being gradually created by the civic activity of its citizens. The test of democracy is the fulness with which this is being done. The practical thought for our political life is that the collective will exists only through its self-actualizing and self-creating in new and larger and more perfectly adjusted forms.

Thus the unity of the social process becomes clear to us. We now gain a conception of "right," of purpose, of loyalty to that purpose, not as particularistic ideas but as arising within the process.

RIGHT

We are evolving now a system of ethics which has three conceptions in regard to right, conscience and duty which are different from much of our former ethical teaching: (1) we do not follow right, we create right, (2) there is no private conscience, (3) my duty is never to "others" but to the whole.

First, we do not follow right merely, we create right. It is often thought vaguely that our ideals are all there, shining and splendid, and we have only to apply them. But the truth is that we have to create our ideals. No ideal is worth while which does not grow from our actual life. Some people seem to keep their ideals all carefully packed away from dust and air, but arranged alphabetically so that they can get at them quickly in need. But we can never take out a past ideal for a present need. The ideal which is to be used for our life must come out from that very life itself. The only way our past ideals can help us is in moulding the life which produces the present ideal; we have no further use for them. But we do not discard them: we have built them into the present — we have used them up as the cocoon is used up in making the silk. It has been sometimes taught that given the same situation, the individual must repeat the same behavior. But the situation is never the same, the individual is never the same; such a conception has nothing to do with life. We cannot do our duty in the old sense, that is of following a crystallized ideal, because our duty is new at every moment.

Moreover, the knowledge of what is due the whole is revealed within the life of the whole. This is above everything else what a progressive ethics must teach — not faithfulness to duty merely, but faithfulness to the life which evolves duty. Indeed "following our duty" often means mental and moral atrophy. Man cannot live by tabus; that means stagnation. But as one tabu after another is disappearing, the call is upon us deliberately to build our own moral life. Our ethical sense will surely starve on predigested food. It is we by our acts who progressively construct the moral universe; to follow some preconceived body of law — that is not for responsible moral beings. In so far as we obey old standards without interpenetrating them with the actual world, we are abdicating our creative power.

Further, the group in its distributive aspect is bringing such new elements into the here and now that life is wholly changed, and the ethical commands therein involved are different, and therefore the task of the group is to discover the new formulation which these new elements demand. The moral law thus gathers to itself all the richness of science, of art, of all the fulness of our daily living.

The group consciousness of right thus developed becomes our daily imperative. No mandate from without has power over us. There are many forms of the fallacy that the governing and the governed can be two different bodies, and this one of conforming to standards which we have not created must be recognized as such before we can have any sound foundation for society. When the ought is not a mandate from without, it is no longer a prohibition but a self-expression. As the social consciousness develops, ought will be swallowed up in will. We are some time truly to see our life as positive, not negative, as made up of continuous willing, not of restraints and prohibition. Morality is not the refraining from doing certain things — it is a constructive force.

So in the education of our young people it is not enough to teach them their "duty," somehow there must be created for them to live in a world of high purpose to which their own psychic energies will instinctively respond. The craving for self-expression, self-realization, must see quite naturally for its field of operation the community. This is the secret of education: when the waters of our life are part of the sea of human endeavor, duty will be a difficult word for our young people to understand; it is a glorious consciousness we want, not a painstaking conscience. It is ourselves soaked with the highest, not a Puritanical straining to fulfil an external obligation, which will redeem the world.

Education therefore is not chiefly to teach children a mass of things which have been true up to the present moment; moreover it is not to teach them to learn about life as fast as it is made, not even to interpret life, but above and beyond everything, to create life for themselves. Hence education should be largely the training in making choices. The aim of all proper training is not rigid adherence to a crystallized right (since in ethics, economics or politics there is no crystallized right), but the power to make a new choice at every moment. And the greatest lesson of all is to know that every moment *is* new. "Man lives in the dawn forever. Life is beginning and nothing else but beginning. It begins ever-lastingly."

We must breed through the group process the kind of man who is not fossilized by habit, but whose eye is intent on the present situation, the present moment, present values, and can decide on the forms which will best express them in the actual world.

To sum up this point: morality is never static; it advances as life advances. You cannot hang your ideals up on pegs and take down no. 2 for certain emergencies and no. 4 for others. *The true test of our morality is not the rigidity with which we adhere to standard, but*

the loyalty we show to the life which constructs standards.
The test of our morality is whether we are living not to
follow but to create ideals, whether we are pouring our
life into our visions only to receive it back with its
miraculous enhancement for new uses.

Secondly, I have said that the conception of right as a
group product, as coming from the ceaseless interplay of
men, shows us that there is no such thing as an individual
conscience in the sense in which the term is often used.
As we are to obey no ideals dictated by others or the
past, it is equally important that we obey no ideal set
up by our unrelated self. To obey the moral law is to
obey the social ideal. The social ideal is born, grows
and shapes itself through the associated life. The individual cannot alone decide what is right or wrong.
We can have no true moral judgment except as we live
our life with others. It is said, "Every man is subject
only to his own conscience." But what is my conscience?
Has it not been produced by my time, my country, my
associates? To make a conscience by myself would be
as difficult as to try to make a language by myself.[1]

It is sometimes said, on the other hand, "The individual must yield his right to judge for himself; let the
majority judge." But the individual is not for a moment
to yield his right to judge for himself; he can judge
better for himself if he joins with others in evolving a
synthesized judgment. Our individual conscience is not
absorbed into a national conscience; our individual conscience must be incorporated in a national conscience as

---

[1] This does not, however, put us with those biologists who make conscience a "gregarious instinct" and — would seem to be willing to keep
it there. This is the insidious herd fallacy which crops up constantly in
every kind of place. We may to-day partake largely of the nature of
the herd, our conscience may be to some extent a herd conscience, but
such is not the end of man for it is not the true nature of man — man
does not find his expression in the herd.

one of its constituent members.[1] Those of us who are
not wholly in sympathy with the conscientious objectors do not think that they should yield to the majority.
When we say that their point of view is too particularistic, we do not mean that they should give up the dictates
of their own conscience to a collective conscience. But
we mean that they should ask themselves whether their
conscience is a freak, a purely personal, conscience, or a
properly evolved conscience. That is, have they tried,
not to saturate themselves with our collective ideals, but
to take their part in evolving collective standards by
freely giving and taking. Have they lived the life which
makes possible the fullest interplay of their own ideas
with all the forces of their time? Before they range
themselves against society they must ask themselves if
they have taken the opportunities offered them to help
form the ideas which they are opposing. I do not say
that there is no social value in heresy, I only ask the
conscientious objectors to ask themselves whether they
are claiming the "individual rights" we have long
outgrown.

What we want is a related conscience, a conscience
that is intimately related to the consciences of other
men and to all the spiritual environment of our time, to
all the progressive forces of our age. The particularistic
tendency has had its day in law, in politics, in international relations and as a guiding tendency in our daily
lives.

We have seen that a clearer conception to-day of the
unity of the social process shows us: first, that we are not
merely to follow but to create "right," secondly, that there
is no private conscience, and third, that my duty is never
to "others" but to the whole. We no longer make a dis-

[1] To a misunderstanding of this point are due some of the fallacies
of the political pluralists (see ch. XXXII).

tinction between selfishness and altruism.[1] An act done for our own benefit may be social and one done for another may not be. Some twenty or thirty years ago our "individual" system of ethics began to be widely condemned and we have been hearing a great deal of "social" ethics. But this so-called "social" ethics has meant only my duty to "others." There is now emerging an idea of ethics entirely different from the altruistic school, based not on the duty of isolated beings to one another, but on integrated individuals acting as a whole, evolving whole-ideas, working for whole-ideals. The new consciousness is of a whole.

PURPOSE

As right appears with that interrelating, germinating activity which we call the social process, so purpose also is generated by the same process. The goal of evolution most obviously must evolve itself. How self-contradictory is the idea that evolution is the world-process and yet that some other power has made the goal for it to reach. The truth is that the same process which creates all else creates the very purpose. That purpose is involved in the process, not prior to process, has far wider reaching consequences than can be taken up here. The whole philosophy of cause and effect must be rewritten. If the infinite task is the evolution of the whole, if our finite tasks are wholes of varying degrees of scope and perfection, the notion of causality must have an entirely different place in our system of thought.

The question is often asked, "What is the proposed unity of European nations after the war to be for?" This question implies that the alliance will be a mere method of accomplishing certain purposes, whereas it

[1] See p. 45.

is the union which is the important thing. With the union the purpose comes into being, and with its every step forward, the purpose changes. No one would say that the aims of the Allies to-day are the same as in 1914, or even as in April, 1917. As the alliance develops, the purpose steadily shapes itself.

Every teleological view will be given up when we see that purpose is not "preëxistent," but involved in the unifying act which is the life process. It is man's part to create purpose and to actualize it. From the point of view of man we are just in the dawn of self-consciousness, and his purpose is dimly revealing itself to him. The life-force wells up in us for expression — to direct it is the privilege of self-consciousness.[1]

LOYALTY

As this true purpose evolves itself, loyalty springs into being. Loyalty is awakened through and by the very process which creates the group. The same process which organizes the group energizes it. We cannot "will" to be loyal. Our task is not to "find" causes to awaken our loyalty, but to live our life fully and loyalty issues. A cause has no part in us or we in it if we have fortuitously to "find" it.

[1] This view of purpose is not necessarily antagonistic to the "interest" school of sociology, but we may perhaps look forward to a new and deeper analysis of self-interest. And the view here put forward is not incompatible with the "objective" theory of association (see ch. XXIX) nor with the teleological school of jurisprudence (see ch. XV), it merely emphasizes another point of view — a point of view which tends to synthesize the "subjective" and "objective" theories of law. But those jurists who say that a group is governed by its purpose and leave the matter there are making a thing-in-itself of the purpose; we are governed by the purpose, yes, but we are all the time evolving the purpose. Modern jurists wish a dynamic theory of law — only such a conception of purpose as is revealed by group psychology will give value to a teleological school of jurisprudence.

Thus we see that we do not love the Beloved Community because it is lovable — the same process which makes it lovable produces our love for it. Moreover it is not enough to love the Beloved Community, we must find out how to create it. It is not there for us to accept or reject — it exists only through us. Loyalty to a collective will which we have not created and of which we are, therefore, not an integral part, is slavery. We belong to our community just in so far as we are helping to make that community; then loyalty follows, then love follows. Loyalty means the consciousness of oneness, the full realization that we succeed or fail, live or die, are saved or damned together. The only unity or community is one we have made of ourselves, by ourselves, for ourselves.[1]

Thus the social process is one all-inclusive, Self-sufficing process. The vital impulse which is produced by all the reciprocally interacting influences of the group is also itself the generating and the vivifying power. Social unity is not a sterile conception but an active force. It is a double process — the activity which goes to make the unity and the activity which flows from the unity. There is no better example of centripetal and centrifugal force. All the forces which are stored up in the unity flow forth eternally in activity. We create the common will and feel the spiritual energy which flows into us from the purpose we have made, for the purpose which we seek.

[1] In a relation even of two I am not faithful to the other person but to my conception of the relation in the whole. Loyalty is always to the group idea not to the group-personnel. This must change our idea of patriotism.

VII

THE INDIVIDUAL

AS the collective idea and the collective will, right and purpose, are born within the all-sufficing social process, so here too the individual finds the wellspring of his life. The visible form in which this interplay of relations appears is society and the individual. A man is a point in the social process rather than a unit in that process, a point where forming forces meet straightway to disentangle themselves and stream forth again. In the language of the day man is at the same time a social factor and a social product.

People often talk of the social mind as if it were an abstract conception, as if only the individual were real, concrete. The two are equally real. Or rather the only reality is the relating of one to the other which creates both. Our sundering is as artificial and late an act as the sundering of consciousness into subject and object. The only reality is the interpenetrating of the two into experience. Late intellectualism abstracts for practical purposes the ego from the world, the individual from society.

But there is no way of separating individuals, they coalesce and coalesce, they are "confluent," to use the expression of James, who tells us that the chasm between men is an individualistic fiction, that we are surrounded by fringes, that these overlap and that by means of these I join with others. It is as in Norway when the colors of the sunset and the dawn are mingling, when to-day and to-morrow are at the point of breaking, or of uniting,

60

and one does not know to which one belongs, to the
yesterday which is fading or the coming hour — perhaps
this is something like the relation of one to another: to
the onlookers from another planet our colors might seem
to mingle.

The truth about the individual and society has been
already implied, but it may be justifiable to develop the
idea further because of the paramount importance for
all our future development of a clear understanding of
the individual.   Our nineteenth-century legal theory
(individual rights, contract, "a man can do what he
likes with his own," etc.) was based on the conception
of the separate individual.[1]   We can have no sound
legal doctrine, and hence no social or political progress,
until the fallacy of this idea is fully recognized.   The
new state must rest on a true conception of the individual.   Let us ask ourselves therefore for a further
definition of individuality than that already implied.

The individual is the unification of a multiplied variety
of reactions.   But the individual does not react to society.
The interplay constitutes both society on the one hand
and individuality on the other: individuality and society
are evolving together from this constant and complex
action and reaction.   Or, more accurately, the relation
of the individual to society is not action and reaction,
but infinite interactions by which both individual and
society are forever a-making: we cannot say if we would
be exact that the individual acts upon and is acted upon,
because that way of expressing it implies that he is a
definite, given, finished entity, and would keep him
apart merely as an agent of the acting and being acted
on.   We cannot put the individual on one side and
society on the other, we must understand the complete
interrelation of the two.   Each has no value, no exist-

[1] See ch. XV, " From Contract to Community."

ence without the other. The individual is created by the social process and is daily nourished by that process. There is no such thing as a self-made man. What we think we possess as individuals is what is stored up from society, is the subsoil of social life. We soak up and soak up and soak up our environment all the time.

Of what then does the individuality of a man consist? Of his relation to the whole, not (1) of his apartness nor (2) of his difference alone.

Of course the mistake which is often made in thinking of the individual is that of confusing the physical with the real individual. The physical individual is seen to be apart and therefore apartness is assumed of the psychic or real individual. We think of Edward Fitzgerald as a recluse, that he got his development by being alone, that he was largely outside the influences of society. But imagine Fitzgerald's life with his books. It undoubtedly did not suit his nature to mix freely with other people in bodily presence, but what a constant and vivid living with others his life really was. How closely he was in vital contact with the thoughts of men.

We must bear in mind that the social spirit itself may impose apartness on a man; the method of uniting with others is not always that of visible, tangible groups. The pioneer spirit is the creative spirit even if it seems to take men apart to fulfil its dictates. On the other hand the solitary man is not necessarily the man who lives alone; he may be one who lives constantly with others in all the complexity of modern city life, but who is so shut-up or so set upon his own ideas that he makes no real union with others.

Individuality is the capacity for union. The measure of individuality is the depth and breadth of true relation. I am an individual not as far as I am apart from, but as far as I am a part of other men. Evil is non-relation.

The source of our strength is the central supply. You may as well break a branch off the tree and expect it to live. Non-relation is death.

I have said that individuality consists neither of the separateness of one man from the other, nor of the differences of one man from the other. The second statement is challenged more often than the first. This comes from some confusion of ideas. My individuality is difference springing into view as relating itself with other differences. The act of relating is the creating act. It is vicious intellectualism to say, "Before you relate you must have things to relate, therefore the differences are more elemental: there are (1) differences which (2) unite, therefore uniting is secondary." The only fact, the only truth, is the creative activity which appears as the great complex we call humanity. The activity of creating is all. It is only by *being* this activity that we grasp it. To view it from the outside, to dissect it into its different elements, to lay these elements on the dissecting table as so many different individuals, is to kill the life and feed the fancy with dead images, empty, sterile concepts. But let us set about relating ourselves to our community in fruitful fashion, and we shall see that our individuality is bodying itself forth in stronger and stronger fashion, our difference shaping itself in exact conformity with the need of the work we do.

For we must remember when we say that the essence of individuality is the relating of self to other difference, that difference is not something static, something given, that it also is involved in the world of becoming. This is what experience teaches me — that society needs my difference, not as an absolute, but just so much difference as will relate me. Differences develop within the social process and are united through the social process. Difference which is not capable of relation is eccentricity. Eccentricity, caprice, put me outside, bring anarchy; true spontaneity, originality, belong not to chaos but to system. But spontaneity must be coördinated; irrelevancy produces nothing, is insanity. It is not my uniqueness which makes me of value to the whole but my power of relating. The nut and the screw form a perfect combination not because they are different, but because they exactly fit into each other and together can perform a function which neither could perform alone, or which neither could perform half of alone or any part of alone. It is not that the significance of the nut and screw is increased by their coming together, they have no significance at all unless they do come together. The fact that they have to be different to enter into any fruitful relation with each other is a matter of derivative importance — derived from the work they do.

Another illustration is that of the specialist. It is not a knowledge of his specialty which makes an expert of service to society, but his insight into the relation of his specialty to the whole. Thus it implies not less but more relation, because the entire value of that specialization is that it is part of something. Instead of isolating him and giving him a narrower life, it gives him at once a broader life because it binds him more irrevocably to the whole. But the whole works both ways: the specialist not only contributes to the whole, but all his relations to the whole are embodied in his own particular work.

Thus difference is only a part of the life process. To exaggerate this part led to the excessive and arrogant individualism of the nineteenth century. It behooves us children of the twentieth century to search diligently after the law of unity that we may effectively marshal and range under its dominating sway all the varying diversities of life.

Our definition of individuality must now be "finding my place in the whole": "my place" gives you the individual, "the whole" gives you society, but by connecting them, by saying "my place in the whole," we get a fruitful synthesis. I have tried hard to get away from any mechanical system and yet it is difficult to find words which do not seem to bind. I am now afraid of this expression — my place in the whole. It has a rigid, unyielding sound, as if I were a cog in a machine. But my place is not a definite portion of space and time. The people who believe in their "place" in this sense can always photograph their "places." But my place is a matter of infinite relation, and of infinitely changing relation, so that it can never be captured. It is neither the anarchy of particularism nor the rigidity of the German machine. To know my place is not to know my niche, not to know whether I am cog no. 3 or cog no. 4; it is to be alive at every instant at every finger tip to every contact and to be conscious of those contacts.

We see now that the individual both seeks the whole and is the whole.

First, the individual, biology tells us, is never complete, completeness spells death; social psychology is beginning to show us that man advances towards completeness not by further aggregations to himself, but by further and further relatings of self to other men. We are always reaching forth for union; most, perhaps all, our desires have this motive. The spirit craves totality, this is the motor of social progress; the process of getting it is not by adding more and more to ourselves, but by offering more and more of ourselves. Not appropriation but contribution is the law of growth. What our special contribution is, it is for us to discover. More and more to release the potentialities of the individual means the more and more progressive organization of society if at the same time we are learning how to coördinate all the variations. The individual in wishing for more wholeness does not ask for a chaotic mass, but for the orderly wholeness which we call unity. The test of our vitality is our power of synthesis, of life synthesis.

But although we say that the individual is never complete, it is also true that the individual is a being who, because his function is relating and his relatings are infinite, is in himself the whole of society. It is not that the whole is divided up into pieces; the individual is the whole at one point. This is the incarnation: it is the whole flowing into me, transfusing, suffusing me. The fulness, bigness of my life is not measured by the amount I do, nor the number of people I meet, but how far the whole is expressed through me. This is the reason why unifying gives me a sense of life and more unifying gives me a sense of more life — there is more of the whole and of me. My worth to society is not how valuable a part I am. I am not unique in the world because I am different from any one else, but because I am a whole seen from a special point of view.[1]

That the relation of each to the whole is dynamic and not static is perhaps the most profound truth which recent years have brought us.[2] We now see that when I give my share I give always far more than my share, such are the infinite complexities, the fulness and fruitfulness of the interrelatings. I contribute to society my mite, and then society contains not just that much more nourishment, but as much more as the loaves and

[1] This is the principle of the vote in a democracy (see ch. XXI). This must not, however, be confused with the old Hegelianism (see ch. XXIX on "Sovereignty").

[2] In art this is what impressionism has meant. In the era before impressionism art was in a static phase, that is, artists were working at fixed relations. The "balance" of modern artists does not suggest fixedness, but relation subject directly to the laws of the whole.

fishes which fed the multitude outnumbered the original seven and two. My contribution meets some particular need not because it can be measured off against that need, but because my contribution by means of all the cross currents of life always has so much more than itself to offer. When I withhold my contribution, therefore, I am withholding far more than my personal share. When I fail some one or some cause, I have not failed just that person, just that cause, but the whole world is thereby crippled. This thought gives an added solemnity to the sense of personal responsibility.

To sum up: individuality is a matter primarily neither of apartness nor of difference, but of each finding his own activity in the whole. In the many times a day that we think of ourselves it is not one time in a thousand that we think of our eccentricities, we are thinking indirectly of those qualities which join us to others: we think of the work we are doing with others and what is expected of us, the people we are going to play with when work is over and the part we are going to take in that play, the committee-meeting we are going to attend and what we are going to do there. Every distinct act of the ego is an affirmation of that amount of separateness which makes for perfect union. Every affirmation of the ego establishes my relation with all the rest of the universe. It is one and the same act which establishes my individuality and gives me my place in society. Thus an individual is one who is being created *by* society, whose daily breath is drawn *from* society, whose life is spent *for* society. When we recognize society as self-unfolding, self-unifying activity, we shall hold ourselves open to its influence, letting the Light stream into us, not from an outside source, but from the whole of which we are a living part. It is eternally due us that that whole should feed and nourish and sustain us at every moment, but it cannot do this unless at every moment we are creating it. This perfect interplay is Life. To speak of the "limitations of the individual" is blasphemy and suicide. The spirit of the whole is incarnate in every part. "For I am persuaded that neither death, nor life, nor angels, nor principalities, nor powers, nor things present, nor things to come, nor height, nor depth, nor any other creature, shall be able to separate" — the individual from society.

VIII

WHO IS THE FREE MAN?

THE idea of liberty long current was that the solitary man was the free man, that the man outside society possessed freedom but that in society he had to sacrifice as much of his liberty as interfered with the liberty of others. Rousseau's effort was to find a form of society in which all should be as free as "before." According to some of our contemporary thinkers liberty is what belongs to the individual or variation-giving-one. But this tells only half the tale. Freedom is the harmonious, unimpeded working of the law of one's own nature. The true nature of every man is found only in the whole. A man is ideally free only so far as he is interpermeated by every other human being; he gains his freedom through a perfect and complete relationship because thereby he achieves his whole nature.

Hence free-will is not caprice or whim or a partial wish or a momentary desire. On the contrary freedom means exactly the liberation from the tyranny of such particularist impulses. When the whole-will has supreme dominion in the heart of man, then there is freedom. The mandate of our real Self is our liberty. The essence of freedom is not irrelevant spontaneity but the fulness of relation. We do not curtail our liberty by joining with others; we find it and increase all our capacity for life through the interweaving of willings. It is only in a complex state of society that any large degree of freedom is possible, because nothing else can supply the many opportunities necessary to work out freedom. The social process is a completely Self-sufficing process. Free-will is one of its implications. I am free for two reasons: (1) I am not dominated by the whole because I *am* the whole; (2) I am not dominated by "others" because we have the genuine social process only when I do not control others or they me, but all intermingle to produce the collective thought and the collective will. I am free when I am functioning here in time and space as the creative will.

There is no extra-Will: that is the vital lesson for us to learn. There is no Will except as we act. Let us *be* the Will. Thereby do we become the Free-Will.

Perhaps the most superficial of all views is that free-will consists in choice when an alternative is presented. But freedom by our definition is obedience to the law of one's nature. My nature is of the whole: I am free, therefore, only when I choose that term in the alternative which the whole commands. I am not free when I am making choices, I am not free when my acts are not "determined," for in a sense they always are determined (freedom and determinism have not this kind of opposition). I am free when I am creating. I am determined *through* my will, not in spite of it.

Freedom then is the identifying of the individual will with the whole will — the supreme activity of life. Free the spirit of man and then we can trust the spirit of man, and is not the very essence of this freeing of the spirit of man the process of taking him from the self-I to the group-I? That we are free only through the social order, only as fast as we identify ourselves with the whole, implies practically that to gain our freedom we must take part in all the life around us: join groups, enter into many social relations, and begin to win freedom for ourselves. When we are the group in feeling, thought and will, we are free: it does what it wishes through us — that is our liberty. In a democracy the training of every child from the cradle — in nursery, school, at play — must be a training in group consciousness.

Then we shall have the spontaneous activity of freedom. Let us not be martyrs. Let us not give up bread and coal that the ends of the Great War may be won, with the feeling of a restricted life, but with the feeling that we have gained thereby a fuller life. Let us joyously do the work of the world because we are the world. Such is the *élan de vie*, the joy of high activity, which leaps forward with force, in freedom.

We have to begin to-day to live the life which will give us our freedom. Savants and plain men have affirmed the freedom of the will, but at the same time most of us, even while loudly claiming our freedom, have felt bound. While determinism has many theoretical adherents, it has many more practical ones; we have considered ourselves bound in thousands of ways — by tradition, by religion, by natural law, by inertia and ignorance, etc., etc. We have said God is free but man is not free. That we are not free has been the most deadening fallacy to which man has ever submitted. No outside power indeed can make us free. No document of our forefathers can "declare" us "independent." No one can ever give us freedom, but we can win it for ourselves.

It is often thought that when some restraint is taken away from us we are freer than before, but this is childish. Some women-suffragists talk of women as "enslaved" and advocate their emancipation by the method of giving them the vote. But the vote will not make women free. Freedom is always a thing to be attained. And we must remember too that freedom is not a static condition. As it is not something possessed "originally," and as it is not something which can be given to us, so

also it is not something won once for all.   It is in our
power to win our freedom, but it must be won anew at
every moment, literally every moment.   People think of
themselves as not free because they think of themselves
as obeying some external law, but the truth is *we* are
the law-makers.   My freedom is my share in creating,
my part in the creative responsibility.   The heart of our
freedom is the impelling power of the will of the whole.

Who then are free?   Those who *win* their freedom
through fellowship.

IX

THE NEW INDIVIDUALISM

THE new freedom is to be founded on the new individualism. Many people in their zeal for a "socialized" life are denouncing "individualism." But individualism is the latest social movement. We must guard against the danger of thinking that the individual is less important because the collective aspect of life has aroused our ardor and won our devotion. Collectivism is no short cut to do away with the necessity of individual achievement; it means the greatest burden possible on every man. The development of a truly social life takes place at the same time that the freedom and power and efficiency of its members develop. The individual on the other hand can never make his individuality effective until he is given collective scope for his activity. We sometimes hear it said that the strong man does not like combination, but in fact the stronger the man the more he sees coöperation with others as the fitting field for his strength.

But we must learn the method of a real coöperation. We cannot have any genuine collectivism until we have learned how to evolve the collective thought and the collective will. This can be done only by every one taking part. The fact that the state owns the means of production may be a good or a poor measure, but it is not necessarily collectivism or a true socialism. The wish for socialism is a longing for the ideal state, but it is embraced often by impatient people who want to take a short cut to the ideal state. That state must be grown — its branches will widen as its roots spread. The

73

socialization of property must not precede the socialization of the will. If it does, then the only difference
between socialism and our present order will be substituting one machine for another. We see more and
more collectivism coming: so far as it keeps pace with
the socialization of the will, it is good; so far as it does
not, it is purely mechanical. Some people's idea of
socialism is inventing a machine to grind out your duties
for you. But every man must do his work for himself.
Not socialization of property, but socialization of the
will is the true socialism.

The main aim in the reconstruction of society must
be to get all that every man has to give, to bring the
submerged millions into light and activity. Those of us
who are basing all our faith on the constructive vision
of a collective society are giving the fullest value to the
individual that has ever been given, are preaching individual value as the basis of democracy, individual affirmation as its process, and individual responsibility as its
motor force. True individualism has been the one thing
lacking either in motive or actuality in a so-called individualistic age, but then it has not been an individualistic
but a particularistic age. True individualism is this
moment piercing through the soil of our new understanding of the collective life.

X

WE have seen that the interpenetrating of psychic forces creates at the same time individuals and society, that, therefore, the individual is not a unit but a centre of forces (both centripetal and centrifugal), and consequently society is not a collection of units but a complex of radiating and converging, crossing and recrossing energies. In other words we are learning to think of society as a psychic process.

This conception must replace the old and wholly erroneous idea of society as a collection of units, and the later and only less misleading theory of society as an organism.[1]

The old individualism with all the political fallacies it produced — social contract of the seventeenth and eighteenth centuries, majority rule of the nineteenth, etc. — was based on the idea of developed individuals first existing and then coming together to form society. But the basis of society is not numbers: it is psychic power.

The organic theory of society has so much to recommend it to superficial thinking that we must examine it carefully to find its fatal defects. But let us first recognize its merits.

Most obviously, an organic whole has a spatial and temporal individuality of its own, and it is composed of parts each with its individuality yet which could not

---

[1] I speak of it as later because the biological analogy was different from the organism of mediæval doctrine.

exist apart from the whole. An organism means unity, each one his own place, every one dependent upon every one else.

Next, this unity, this interrelating of parts, is the essential characteristic. It is always in unstable equilibrium, always shifting, varying, and thereby changing the individual at every moment. But it is always produced and maintained by the individual himself. No external force brings it forth. The central life, the total life, of this self-developing, self-perpetuating being is involved in the process. Hence biologists do not expect to understand the body by a study of the separate cells as isolated units: it is the organic connection which unites the separate processes which they recognize as the fundamental fact.

This interrelating holds good of society when we view it externally. Society too can be understood only by the study of its flux of relations, of all the intricate reciprocities which go to make the unifying. Reciprocal ordering — subordinating, superordinating, coördinating — purposeful self-unifyings, best describe the social process. Led by James, who has shown us the individual as a self-unifying centre, we now find the same kind of activity going on in society, in the social mind. And this interrelating, this unity as unity, is what gives to society its authority and power.

Thus the term organism is valuable as a metaphor, but it has not strict psychological accuracy.

There is this world-wide difference between the self-interrelatings of society and of the bodily organism: the social bond is a psychic relation and we cannot express it in biological terms or in any terms of physical force. If we could, if "functional combination" could mean a psychological relation as well as a physiological, then the terms "functional" and "organic" might be ac-

cepted. But they denote a different universe from that
of thought. For psychical self-unitings knit infinitely
more closely and in a wholly different way. They are
freed from the limitations of time and space. Minds
can blend, yet in the blending preserve each its own
identity. They transfuse one another while being each
its own essential and unique self.

It follows that while the cell of the organism has only
one function, the individual may have manifold and
multiform functions: he enters with one function into
a certain group of people this morning and with another
function into another group this afternoon, because his
free soul can freely knit itself with a new group at any
moment.[1]

This self-detaching, self-attaching freedom of the individual saves us from the danger to democracy which
lurks in the organic theory. No man is forced to serve
as the running foot or the lifting hand. Each at any
moment can place himself where his nature calls. Certain continental sociologists are wholly unjustified in
building their hierarchy where one man or group of men
is the sensorium, others the hewers and carriers, etc. It
is exactly this despotic and hopeless system of caste from
which the true democracy frees man. He follows the
call of his spirit and relates himself where he belongs
to-day, and through this relating gains the increment of
power which knits him anew where he now belongs and
so continually as the wind of spirit blows.

Moreover in society every individual may be a complete expression of the whole in a way impossible for
the parts of a physical organism.[2] When each part is
itself potentially the whole, when the whole can live
completely in every member, then we have a true society,

[1] See ch. XXX, "Political Pluralism and Functionalism."
[2] See p. 66.

and we must view it as a rushing of life — onrush, out-
rush, inrush — as a mobile, elastic, incalculable, Protean
energy seeking fitting form for itself. This ideal society
is the divine goal towards which life is an infinite progress. Such conception of society must be visibly before
us to the exclusion of all other theories when we ask
ourselves later what the vote means in the true democracy.[1]

[1] See ch. XXI. I have been told that the distinction between the
organic and the psychic theory of society is merely academic. But no
one should frame amendments on the initiative and referendum without
this distinction; no one without it can judge wisely the various schemes
now being proposed for occupational representation — something every
one of us will have soon to do.

XI

THE SELF-AND-OTHERS ILLUSION

IT is now evident that self and others are merely different points of view of one and the same experience, two aspects of one thought. Neither of these partial aspects can hold us, we seek always that which includes self and others. To recognize the community principle in everything we do should be our aim, never to work with individuals as individuals. If I go to have a talk with a mother about her daughter, I cannot appeal to the mother, the daughter, or my own wishes, only to that higher creation which we three make when we come together. In that way only will spiritual power be generated. Every decision of the future is to be based not on my needs or yours, nor on a compromise between them or an addition of them, but on the recognition of the community between us. The community may be my household and I, my employees and I, but it is only the dictate of the whole which can be binding on the whole. This principle we can take as a searchlight to turn on all our life.

It is the lack of understanding of this principle which works much havoc among us. When we watch men in the lobbies at Washington working for their state and their town as against the interests of the United States, do we sometimes think, "These men have learnt loyalty and service to a small unit, but not yet to a large one ?" If this thought does come to us, we are probably doing those men more than justice. The man who tries to get something in the River and Harbor appropriation for his town, whether or not it needs it as much as other places, is pretty sure back in his own town to be working not for that but for his own pocket. It is not because America is too big for him to think of, that he might perhaps think of Ohio or Millfield, it is just because he cannot think of Ohio or Millfield. There he thinks of how this or the other local development, rise in land values etc., is going to benefit himself; when he is in Washington he thinks of what is going to benefit Millfield. But the man who works hardest and most truly for Millfield and Ohio will probably when he comes to Washington work most truly for the interests, not of Millfield and Ohio, but of the United States, because he has learned the first lesson of life — to think in wholes.

The expressions social and socially-minded, which should refer to a consciousness of the whole, are often confused with altruism. We read of "the socialized character of modern industry." There is a good deal of altruism in modern industry, but little that is socialized yet. The men who provide rest rooms, baths, lectures, and recreation facilities for their employees, do not by so doing prove themselves to be socially-minded; they are altruistically-minded, and this is involved in the old individualism.[1] Moreover, in our attempts at social legislation we have been appealing chiefly to the altruism of people: women and children ought not to be overworked, it is cruel not to have machinery safeguarded, etc. But our growing sense of unity is fast bringing us to a realization that all these things are for the good of ourselves too, for the entire community. And the war is rapidly opening our eyes to this human solidarity: we now see health, for instance, as a national asset.

All of us are being slowly, very slowly, purged of our

[1] It must be remembered, however, that these welfare arrangements are often accompanied by truly social motives, and experiments looking towards a more democratic organization of industries.

particularistic desires. The egotistic satisfaction of giving things away is going to be replaced by the joy of owning things together. As our lives become more and more intricately interwoven, more and more I come to suffer not merely when I am undergoing personal suffering, more and more I come to desire not only when I am feeling personal desires. This used to be considered a fantastic idea not to be grasped by the plain man, but every day the plain man is coming more and more to feel this, every day the "claims" of others are becoming My desires. "Justice" is being replaced by understanding. There are many people to-day who feel as keenly the fact of child labor as if these children were their own. I vote for prohibition, even although it does not in the least touch me, because it does touch very closely the Me of which I am now coming into realization.

The identification of self and others we see in the fact that we cannot keep ourselves "good" in an evil world any more than we can keep ourselves well in a world of disease. The method of moral hygiene as of physical hygiene is social coöperation. We do not walk into the Kingdom of Heaven one by one.

The exposition of the self-and-others fallacy has transformed the idea of self-interest. Our interests are inextricably interwoven. The question is not what is best for me or for you, but for all of us. My interests are not less important to the world than yours; your interests are not less important to the world than mine. If the "altruistic" man is not a humbug, that is, if he really thinks his affairs of less importance to the world than those of others, then there is certainly something the matter with his life. He must raise his life to a point where it is of as much value to the world as any one's else.

The self-and-others fallacy has led directly to a conception which has wrought much harm among us, namely, the identification of "others" with "society" which leads the self outside society and brings us to one of the most harmful of dualisms. The reason we are slow to understand the matter of the subordination of the individual to society is because we usually think of it as meaning the subordination of the individual to "others," whereas it does not at all, it means the subordination of the individual to the whole of which he himself is a part. Such subordination is an act of assertion; it is fraught with active power and force; it affirms and accomplishes. We are often told to "surrender our individuality." To *claim* our individuality is the one essential claim we have on the universe.

We give up self when we are too sluggish for the heroic life. For our self is after all the greatest bother we ever know, and the idea of giving it up is a comfortable thought for sluggish people, a narcotic for the difficulties of life. But it is a cowardly way out. The strong attitude is to face that torment, our self, to take it with all its implications, all its obligations, all its responsibilities, and be ourselves to the fullest degree possible.

I do not mean to imply, however, that unselfishness has become obsolete. With our new social ideal there is going to be a far greater demand on our capacity for sacrifice than ever before, but self-sacrifice now means for us self-fulfilment. We have now a vision of society where service is indeed our daily portion, but our conception of service has entirely changed. The other day it was stated that the old idea of democracy was a society in which every man had the right to pursue his own ends, while the new idea was based on the assumption that every man should serve his fellow-men. But I do not believe that man should "serve his fellow-men"; if we started on that task what awful prigs we should become. Moreover, as we see that the only efficient people are the servers, much of the connotation of humility has gone out of the word service! Moreover, if service is such a very desirable thing, then every one must have an equal opportunity for service.

We have had a wrong idea of individualism which has made those who had more strength, education, time, money, power, feel that they must do for those who had less. In the individualism we see coming, all our efforts will be bent to making it possible for every man to depend upon himself instead of depending upon others. So *noblesse oblige* is really egoistic. It is what I owe to myself to do to others. *Noblesse oblige* has had a splendid use in the world, but it is somewhat worn out now simply because we are rapidly getting away from the selfish point of view. I don't do things now because my position or my standing or my religion or *my* anything else demands it, nor because others need it, but because it is a whole-imperative, that is, a social imperative. We cannot transcend self by means of others, but only through the synthesis of self and others. Wholeness is an irresistible force compelling every member. The consciousness of this is the wellspring of our power.

An English writer says that we get leadership from the fact that men are capable of being moved to such service by the feeling of altruism; he attributes public spirit to love, pity, compassion and sensitiveness to suffering. This is no doubt largely true at the present moment, but public spirit will sometime mean, as it does to-day in many instances, the recognition that it is not merely that my city, my nation needs me, but that I need it as the larger sphere of a larger self-expression.

I remember some years ago a Boston girl just entering social work, fresh from college, with all the ardor and enthusiasm of youth and having been taught the ideals of service to others. She was talking to me about her future and said that she was sorry family circumstances obliged her to work in Boston instead of New York, there was so much more to reform in New York! She seemed really afraid that justice and morality had reached such a point with us that she might not be afforded sufficient scope for her zeal. It was amusing, but think of the irony of it: that girl had been taught such a view of life that her happiness, her outlet, her self-expression, depended actually on there being plenty of misery and wretchedness for her to change; there would be no scope for her in a harmonious, well-ordered world.

The self-and-others theory of society is then wrong. We have seen that the Perfect Society is the complete interrelating of an infinite number of selves knowing themselves as one Self. We see that we are dependent on the whole, while seeing that we are one with it in creating it. We are separate that we may belong, that we may greatly produce. Our separateness, our individual initiative, are the very factors which accomplish our true unity with men. We shall see in the chapter on "Political Pluralism" that "irreducible pluralism" and the self-unifying principle are not contradictory.

XII

MANY people are ready to accept the truth that association is the law of life. But in consequence of an acceptance of this theory with only a partial understanding of it, many people to-day are advocating the life of the crowd. The words society, crowd, and group are often used interchangeably for a number of people together. One writer says, "The real things are breathed forth from multitudes . . . the real forces of to-day are group forces." Or we read of "the gregarious or group life," or "man is social because he is suggestible," or, "man is social because he likes to be with a crowd." But we do not find group forces in multitudes: the crowd and the group represent entirely different modes of association. Crowd action is the outcome of agreement based on concurrence of emotion rather than of thought, or if on the latter, then on a concurrence produced by becoming aware of similarities, not by a slow and gradual creating of unity. It is a crowd emotion if we all shout "God save the King." Suggestibility, feeling, impulse — this is usually the order in the crowd mind.

I know a little boy of five who came home from school one day and said with much impressiveness, "Do you know whose birthday it is to-morrow?" "No," said his mother, "whose?" "Ab'm Lincoln's," was the reply. "Who is he?" said the mother. With a grave face and an awed voice the child replied, "He freed the slates!" and then added, "I don't know whether they were the big kind like mine or the little kind like Nancy's." But

85

his emotion was apparently as great, his sentiment as sincere, as if he had understood what Lincoln had done for his country. This is a good example of crowd suggestion because thought was in this case inhibited by contagious emotion.

Suggestion is the law of the crowd, interpenetration of the group. When we study a crowd we see how quickly B takes A's ideas and also C and D and E; when we study a group we see that the ideas of A often arouse in B exactly opposite ones. Moreover, the crowd often deadens thought because it wants immediate action, which means an unthinking unanimity not a genuine collective thought.[1] The group on the other hand stimulates thought. There are no "differences" in the crowd mind. Each person is swept away and does not stop to find out his own difference. In crowds we have unison, in groups harmony. We want the single voice but not the single note; that is the secret of the group. The enthusiasm and unanimity of a mass-meeting may warm an inexperienced heart, but the experienced know that this unanimity is largely superficial and is based on the spread of similar ideas, not the unifying of differences. A crowd does not distinguish between fervor and wisdom; a group usually does. We do not try to be eloquent when we appear before a board or a commission; we try merely to be convincing. Before a group it is self-control, restraint, discipline which we need, we don't "let ourselves go"; before a crowd I am sorry to say we usually do. Many of us nowadays resent being used as part of a crowd; the moment we hear eloquence we are on

[1] A good example of the crowd fallacy is the syndicalist theory that the vote should be taken in a meeting of strikers not by ballot but by acclamation or show of hands. The idea is that in an open meeting enthusiasm passes from one to another and that, therefore, you can thus get the collective will which you could not get by every man voting one by one.

the defensive. The essential evil of crowds is that they do not allow choice, and choice is necessary for progress. A crowd is an undifferentiated mass; a group is an articulated whole.

It is often difficult to determine whether a number of people met together are a crowd or a group (that is, a true society), yet it is a distinction necessary for us to make if we would understand their action. It is not in the least a question of numbers: it is obvious that according to our present definition a group is not a small number of people and a crowd a large number. If some-one cries "Fire," and you and I run to the window, then you and I are a crowd. The difference between a group and a crowd is not one of degree but of kind. I have seen it stated in a sociological treatise that in any de-liberative assembly there is a tendency for the wisest thought to prevail. This assumes that "any delibera-tive assembly" is more like a group than a crowd — a very pleasant thing to assume!

Some writers seem to think that the difference be-tween a crowd and a not-crowd is the difference between organized and unorganized, and the example is given of laborers unorganized as a crowd and of a trade-union as a not-crowd. But a trade-union can be and often is a crowd.

We have distinguished between the crowd and the group; it is also necessary to distinguish between the crowd and the mob. Often the crowd or mass is con-fused with the mob. The examples given of the mass or crowd mind are usually a lynching-party, the panic-stricken audience in a theatre fire, the mobs of the French Revolution. But all these are very different from a mass of people merely acting under the same suggestion, so dif-ferent that we need different names for them. We might for the moment call one a crowd and the other a mob.

An unfortunate stigma has often attached itself to the crowd mind because of this tendency to think of the crowd mind as always exhibiting itself in inferior ways. Mass enthusiasm, it is true, may lead to riots, but also it may lead to heroic deeds. People talk much of the panic of a crowd, but every soldier knows that men are brave, too, in a mass. Students have often studied what they called the mass mind when it was under the stress of great nervous strain and at a high pitch of excitement, and then have said the mass acts thus and so. It has been thought legitimate to draw conclusions concerning the nature of the mass mind from an hysterical mob. It has been assumed that a crowd was necessarily, as a crowd, in a condition of hysteria. It has often been taken for granted that a crowd *is* a pathological condition. And color has been given to this theory by the fact that we owe much of our knowledge of the laws of suggestion to pathologists.

But the laws of the mass can be studied in ordinary collections of people who are not abnormally excited, who are not subjects for pathologists. The laws of the mass as of the mob are, it is true, the laws of suggestion and imitation, but the mob is such an extreme case of the mass that it is necessary to make some distinction between them. Emotion in the crowd as in the mob is intensified by the consciousness that others are sharing it, but the mob is this crowd emotion carried to an extreme. As normal suggestibility is the law of the mass, so abnormal suggestibility is the law of the mob. In abnormal suggestibility the controlling act of the will is absent, but in normal suggestibility you have the will in control and using its power of choice over the material offered by suggestion. Moreover, it must be remembered that emotional disturbance is not always the cause of the condition of suggestibility: the will may lose its ascendancy from other causes than excitement; suggestibility often comes from exhaustion or habit.

The fact is we know little of this subject. Billy Sunday and the Salvation Army, political bosses and labor agitators, know how to handle crowds, but the rest of us can deal with individuals better than with the mass; we have taken courses in first-aid to the injured, but we have not yet learned what to do in a street riot or a financial panic.

Besides the group and the crowd and the mob, there is also the herd. The satisfaction of the gregarious instinct must not be confused with the emotion of the crowd or the true sense of oneness in the group. Some writers draw analogies from the relation of the individual to the herd to apply to the relation of man to society; such analogies lead to false patriotism and wars. The example of the wild ox temporarily separated from his herd and rushing back to the "comfort of its fellowship" has adorned many a different tale. The "comfort" of feeling ourselves in the herd has been given as the counterpart of spiritual communion, but are we seeking the "comfort" of fellowship or the creative agonies of fellowship? The latter we find not in herd life, but in group life.

Then besides the group, the crowd, the mob, the herd, there are numbers as mere numbers. When we are a lot of people with different purposes we are simply wearied, not stimulated. At a bazaar, for instance, far from feeling satisfaction in your fellow-creatures, you often loathe them. Here you are not swayed by one emotion, as in a crowd, nor unified by some intermingling of thought as in a group.

It must be understood that I do not wish to make any arbitrary dictum in regard to distinctions between the crowd and the herd, the crowd and mere numbers, etc.

I merely wish to point out that the subject has not yet received sufficient study. What is it we feel at the midnight mass of the Madeleine? It is not merely the one thought which animates all; it is largely the great mass of people who are feeling the one thought. But many considerations and unanswered questions leap to our mind just here. All this is an interesting field for the further study and close analysis of psychologists.

We must not, however, think from these distinctions that man as member of a group and man as member of a crowd, as one of a herd or of a mob or of a mere assemblage, is subject to entirely different laws which never mingle; there are all the various shadings and minglings of these which we see in such varied associations as business corporation, family, committee, political meeting, trade-union etc. Our herd traditions show in our group life; there is something of the crowd in all groups and there is something of the group in many crowds, as in a legislative assembly. Only further study will teach us to distinguish how much herd instinct and how much group conviction contribute to our ideas and feelings at any one time and what the tendencies are when these clash. Only further study will show us how to secure the advantages of the crowd without suffering from its disadvantages. We have all felt that there was much that was valuable in that emotional thrill which brings us into a vaster realm although not a coördinated realm; we have all rejoiced in the quickened heart-beat, the sense of brotherhood, the love of humanity, the renewed courage which have sometimes come to us when we were with many people. Perhaps the ideal group will combine the advantages of the mass and the group proper: will give us collective thought, the creative will and at the same time the inspiration for renewed effort and sustained self-discipline.

Crowd association has, however, received more study than group association because as a matter of fact there is at present so much more of the former than of the latter. But we need not only a psychology which looks at us as we are, but a psychology which points the way to that which we may become. What our advanced thinkers are now doing is to evolve this new psychology. Conscious evolution means giving less and less place to herd instinct and more to the group imperative. We are emerging from our gregarious condition and are now to enter on the rational way of living by scanning our relations to one another, instead of bluntly feeling them, and so adjusting them that unimpeded progress on this higher plane is secured.

And now that association is increasing so rapidly on every hand, it is necessary that we see to it that this shall be group association, not crowd association. In the business world our large enterprises are governed by boards, not by one man: one group (corporation) deals with another group (corporation). Hospitals, libraries, colleges, are governed by boards, trustees, faculties. We have committees of arbitration, boards of partial management (labor agreements) composed of representatives of employers and employed. Many forms of coöperation are being tried: some one must analyze the psychological process of the generation of coöperative activity. All this means a study of group psychology. In the political world there is a growing tendency to put the administrative part of government more and more into the hands of commissions. Moreover, we have not legislatures swayed by oratory and other forms of mass suggestion, but committee government. Of course legislative committees do not try to get the group idea, they are largely controlled by partisan and financial interests, but at any rate they are not governed wholly

by suggestion.   In the philanthropic world we no longer
deal with individuals: we form a committee or association to deal with individuals or with groups of individuals.   The number of associations of every kind for
every purpose increases daily.   Hence we must study
the group.

XIII

I HAVE said that the essence of the social process is the creating of ever new values through the interplay of all the forces of life. But I have also tried to show that these forces must be organized; from confusion nothing is born. The spiritual order grows up within us as fast as we make new correlations. Chaos, disorder, destruction, come everywhere from refusing the syntheses of life.

The task of coadaptation is unending, whether it means getting on with a difficult member of my family, playing the game at school or college, doing my part in my business, my city, or whether it means Germany and the Allies living together on the same planet.

Nietzsche thought that the man who showed the most force was the most virtuous. Now we say that all this brute energy is merely the given, that the life-process is the unifying of the given — he who shows the unifying power in greatest degree is the superman. Progress is not determined then by economic conditions, by physical conditions nor by biological factors solely, but more especially by our capacity for genuine coöperation.

This idea of progress clear-cuts some long-established notions. We see now the truth and the fallacy in the assertions (1) that social evolution depends upon individual progress with imitation by the crowd, (2) that evolution means struggle and the survival of the fittest.

For some years the generally accepted theory of the social process was that the individual invents, society spreads. We have already examined one half of this

theory; let us look at the other half — the idea that
the individual originates.

If a man comes forward with an idea, what do we
mean by saying that he is more "original" than his
fellows? So far as the quality of originality can be described, do we not mean that his capacity for saturation
is greater, his connection with the psychic reservoir
more direct, so that some group finds in him its most
complete interpreter? Or even if it is quite evident that
in a particular instance a particular individual has not
derived his idea from the group of which he is at the
moment a member, but has brought it to the group,
none of us believes that that idea arose spontaneously
in his mind independent of all previous association.
This individual has belonged to many other groups,
has discussed with many men, or even if he has lived
his life apart he has read newspapers and magazines,
books and letters, and has mingled his ideas with those
he has found there. Thus the "individual" idea he
brings to a group is not really an "individual" idea; it
is the result of the process of interpenetration, but by
bringing it to a new group and soaking it in that the
interpenetration becomes more complex. The group idea
he takes away is now his individual idea so far as any
new group is concerned, and in fact it becomes an active
agent in his progress and the progress of society only by
meeting a new group. Our life is more and more stagnant in proportion as we refuse the group life.

According to the old theory, the individual proposes,
society accepts or rejects; the individual is forever walk-
ing up to society to be embraced or rejected — it sounds
like some game but is hardly life.

There is an interesting theory current which is the
direct outcome of the fallacy that the individual originates and society imitates, namely, the great man theory.

While it seems absurd in this age to be combating the idea of special creation, yet it is something very like this that one comes up against sometimes in the discussion of this theory. The question is often asked, "Does the great man produce his environment or is he the product of his environment ?" Although for my purpose I may seem to emphasize the other side of things, not for a moment do I wish to belittle the inestimable value of genius. But the fact of course is that great men make their environment and are made by their environment. There wells up in the individual a fountain of power, but this fountain has risen underground and is richly fed by all the streams of the common life.[1]

I have spoken of fallacies in the individual invention theory and in the struggle theory. But I am using the word struggle as synonymous with strife, opposition, war; effort, striving, the ceaseless labor of adjustment will always be ours, but these two ideas represent opposite poles of existence. In the true theory of evolution struggle has indeed always been adaptation. For many years the "strongest" man has been to science the being with the greatest number of points of union, the "fittest" has been the one with the greatest power of coöperation. Darwin we all know believed that the cause of the advance of civilization was in the social habits of man. Our latest biologists tell us that "mutual aid" has from the first been a strong factor in evolution, that the animal species in which the practice of "mutual aid"[2] has attained the greatest development are invariably the

[1] It is unfortunate to be obliged to treat this important point with such brevity.

[2] The expressions "mutual aid" and "animal coöperation" have, however, a slightly misleading connotation; mutual adaptation, coördinated activities, come nearer the truth. It is confusing to take the words and phrases we use of men in the conscious stage and transfer them to the world of animals in the unconscious stage.

most numerous and the most prosperous. We no longer
think of the animal world as necessarily a world of strife;
in many of its forms we find not strife but coördinated
activities.

But to too many people struggle suggests conquest
and domination; it implies necessarily victors and van-
quished. Some sociologists call the dissimilar elements
of a group the struggle elements, and the similar elements the unifying elements. But this is a false distinction which will, as long as persisted in, continue the war
between classes and between nations. The test of our
progress is neither our likenesses nor our unlikenesses,
but what we are going to do with our unlikenesses.
Shall I fight whatever is different from me or find the
higher synthesis? The progress of society is measured
by its power to unite into a living, generating whole
its self-yielding differences.

Moreover, we think now of the survival of groups
rather than of individuals. For the survival of the group
the stronger members must not crush the weaker but
cherish them, because the spiritual and social strength
which will come from the latter course makes a stronger
group than the mere brute strength of a number of
"strong" individuals. That is, the strength of the group
does not depend on the greatest number of strong men,
but on the strength of the bond between them, that is,
on the amount of solidarity, on the best organization.

But it might be said, "You still evidently believe in
struggle, only you make the group instead of the individual the unit." No, the progress of man must consist in extending the group, in belonging to many groups,
in the relation of these groups. If we accept life as endless battle, then we shall always have the strong over-
coming the weak, either strong individuals conquering
the weak, or a strong group a weak group, or a strong

nation a weak nation. But synthesis is the principle of life, the method of social progress. Men have developed not through struggle but through learning how to live together.

Lately the struggle theory has been transferred from the physical to the intellectual world. Many writers who see society as a continuous conflict think its highest form is discussion. One of these says, "Not for a moment would I deny that fighting is better carried on by the pen than by the sword, but some sort of fighting will be necessary to the end of the world." No, as long as we think of discussion as a struggle, as an opportunity for "argument," there will be all the usual evil consequences of the struggle theory. But all this is superficial. If struggle is unavailing, it is unavailing all along the line. It is not intellectual struggle that marks the line of progress, but any signs of finding another method than struggle. Two neighbors quarrelling in words are little more developed than two men fighting a duel. We must learn to think of discussion not as a struggle but as experiment in coöperation. We must learn coöperative thinking, intellectual team-work. There is a secret here which is going to revolutionize the world.

Perhaps the most profound reason against struggle is that it always erects a thing-in-itself. If I "fight" Mr. X, that means that I think of Mr. X as incapable of change — that either he or I must prevail, must conquer. When I realize fully that there are no things-in-themselves, struggle simply fades away; then I know that Mr. X and I are two flowing streams of activity which must meet for larger ends than either could pursue alone.

Is Germany the last stronghold of the old theory of evolution, is she the last being in a modern world to assert herself as a thing-in-itself? President Wilson's

contribution to this war is that he refuses to look upon
Germany as a thing-in-itself.

The idea of adaptation to environment has been so
closely connected with the "struggle for existence" theory
that some people do not seem to realize that in giving up
the latter, the former still has force, although with a
somewhat different connotation. We now feel not only
that adaptation to environment is compatible with co-
operation, but that coöperation is the basis of adaptation to environment. But our true environment is
psychic, and as science teaches adaptation to the physical, so group psychology will teach the secret of membership in the psychic environment, will teach the branch
to know its vine, where its own inner sources of life are
revealed to it. Then we shall understand that environment is not a hard and rigid something external to us,
always working upon us, whose influence we cannot
escape. Not only have self and environment acted and
reacted upon each other, but the action and reaction
go on every moment; both self and environment are
always in the making. The individual who has been
affected by his environment acts on an environment
which has been affected by individuals. We shall need
an understanding of this for all our constructive work:
it is not that formative influences work on a dead mass of
inertia, but formative influences work on an environment
which has already responded to initiatives, and these
initiatives have been affected by the responses. We
cannot be practical politicians without fully understanding this.

Progress then must be through the group process.
Progress implies respect for the creative process not the
created thing; the created thing is forever and forever
being left behind us. The greatest blow to a hide-bound
conservatism would be the understanding that life is

creative at every moment. What the hard-shelled conservative always forgets is that what he really admires in the past is those very moments when men have strongly and rudely broken with tradition, burst bonds, and created something. True conservatism and true progressivism are not two opposites: conservatives dislike "change," yet they as well as progressives want to grow; progressives dislike to "stand pat," yet they as well as conservatives want to preserve what is good in the present. But conservatives often make the mistake of thinking they can go on living on their spiritual capital; progressives are often too prone not to fund their capital at all.

What we must get away from is "the hell of rigid things." There is a living life of the people. And it must flow directly through our government and our institutions, expressing itself anew at every moment. We are not fossils petrified in our social strata. *We are alive.* This is the first lesson for us to learn. That very word means change and change, growth and growth. To live gloriously is to change undauntedly — our ideals must evolve from day to day, and it is upon those who can fearlessly embrace the doctrine of "becoming" that the life of the future waits. All is growing; we must recognize this and free the way for the growth. We must unclose our spiritual sources, we must allow no mechanism to come between our spiritual sources and our life. The *élan vital* must have free play.

Democracy must be conceived as a process, not a goal. We do not want rigid institutions, however good. We need no "body of truth" of any kind, but the will to will, which means the power to make our own government, our own institutions, our own expanding truth. *We progress, not from one institution to another, but from a lesser to a greater will to will.*

We know now that there are no immutable goals —
there is only a way, a process, by which we shall, like
gods, create our own ends at any moment — crystallize
just enough to be of use and then flow on again. The
flow of life and we the flow: this is the truth. Life is
not a matter of desirable objects here and there; the
stream flows on and he who waits with his object is left
with a corpse. Man is equal to life at every moment,
but he must live for *life* and not for the *things* life has
produced.

Yet while it is true that life can never be formalized
or formulated, that life is movement, change, onward-
ness, this does not mean that we must give up the
abiding. The unchangeable and the unchanging are
both included in the idea of growth.[1] Stability is neither
rigidity nor sterility: it is the perpetual power of bringing forth.

Writers are always fixing dates for the dividing line
between the ancient and the modern world, or between
the mediæval and the modern world. Soon the beginning of modern times, of modern thought, will, I believe,
be dated at the moment when men began to look at a
plastic world, at a life constantly changing, at institutions as only temporary crystallizations of life forces, of
right as evolving, of men as becoming.

The real work of every man is then to build. The chal-
lenge is upon us. This is the task to which all valiant
souls must set themselves. We are to rise from one
mastery to another. We are to be no longer satisfied
with the pace of a merely fortuitous progress. We must
know now that we are coworkers with every process
of creation, that our function is as important as the
power which keeps the stars in their orbits. We are

---

[1] It is because of this profound truth that we must always respect
conservatism.

creators here and now. We are not in the anteroom
of our real life. This is real life.

We cannot, however, mould our lives each by himself;
but within every individual is the power of joining himself fundamentally and vitally to other lives, and out of
this vital union comes the creative power. Revelation,
if we want it to be continuous, must be through the community bond. No *individual* can change the disorder
and iniquity of this world. No chaotic *mass* of men and
women can do it. Conscious *group* creation is to be the
social and political force of the future. Our aim must
be to live consciously in more and more group relations
and to make each group a means of creating. It is the
group which will teach us that we are not puppets of
fate.

Then will men and women spend their time in trivial
or evil ways when they discover that they can make a
world to their liking? We are sometimes told that young
men and women working all day under the present very
trying industrial conditions live in our great cities a
round of gaiety at night. Go and look at them. It is
a depressing sight. A tragedy is a tragedy and has its
own nobility, but this farce of a city population enjoy-
ing itself at night is a pitiful spectacle. Go to clubs, go
to dances, go to theatres or moving-pictures, and the
mass of our young people look indifferent and more or
less bored — they have *not* found the joy of life. Play,
as useless idling, does not give us joy. Work, as drudg-
ery, does not give us joy. Only creating gives us joy.
When we see that we are absolute masters of our life,
that in every operation, however humble, we are working out the fundamental laws of being, then we shall
walk to our daily work as the soldiers march to the
Marseillaise.

We know what happened on that lonely island in a

distant sea when the young Prince came to the people
of the Kingdom of Cards, who had always lived by Rules,
and taught them to live by their Ichcha, their will.
Images became men and women, rules gave place to
wills, the caste of the Court cards was lost, a mechanism
changed into life. The inhabitants of the Kingdom of
Cards, who had never thought, who had never made a
decision, learned the royal power of choosing for themselves. Regulations were abandoned, and the startling
discovery was made that *they could walk in any direction
they chose.* This is what we need to learn — that we can
walk in any direction we choose. We are not a pack of
cards to be put here and there, to go always in rows,
to totter and fall when we are not propped up. We
must obey our Ichcha.

Already the change has begun. I have said that we
are beginning to recognize this power — there are many
indications that we are beginning to live this power.
We are no longer willing to leave human affairs to
"natural" control: we do not want war because it is
"natural" to fight; we do not want a haphazard population at the dictates of "nature." We no longer believe that sickness and poverty are sent by God; people
are being taught that they need not be sick, that it is
largely in their own hands, their own collective hands
(social hygiene etc.). Modern charity is not aimed at
relieving individual poverty, but at freeing the individual
from the particular enslavement which has produced his
poverty, in freeing society from the causes which produce poverty at all.[1]

Our once-honored blind forces are more and more
losing their mastery over us. We are at this moment,
however, in a difficult transition period. We are "freer"

[1] The claim of the individual to a larger share in government and to
a share in the control of industry will be taken up in later chapters.

than ever before; the trouble is we do not know what to
do with this freedom. It is easy to live the moral, the
"social," life when it consists in following a path carefully marked out for us, but the task given us to-day is
to revalue all the world values, to steer straight on and
on into the unknown — a gallant forth-faring indeed.
But conscious evolution, the endless process of a perfect
coördinating, demands vital people. War is the easy
way: we take to war because we have not enough vitality for the far more difficult job of agreeing. So also
that kind of religion which consists of contemplation
of other-worldliness is the easy way, and we take to that
when we have not enough vitality deliberately to direct
our life and construct our world. It takes more spiritual
energy to express the group spirit than the particularist
spirit. This is its glory as well as its difficulty. We
have to be higher order of beings to do it — we become
higher order of beings by doing it. And so the progress
goes on forever: it means life forever in the making, and
the creative responsibility of every man.

Conscious evolution is the key to that larger view of
democracy which we are embracing to-day. The key?
Every man sharing in the creative process *is* democracy;
this is our politics and our religion. People are always
inquiring into their relation to God. God is the moving
force of the world, the ever-continuing creating where
men are the co-creators. "*Chaque homme fait dieu, un
peu, avec sa vie,*" as one of the most illumined of the
younger French poets says.[1] Man and God are corre-
lates of that mighty movement which is Humanity self-
creating. God is the perpetual Call to our self-fulfilling.
We, by sharing in the life-process which binds all to-

[1] "Ce que Nait" is the title of a volume of poems by Arcos, and that
which is being born through all the activity of our common life is God.
It is of the "naissance" and "croissance" of God that Arcos loves to sing.

gether in an active, working unity are all the time sharing in the making of the Universe. This thought calls forth everything heroic that is in us; every power of which we are capable must be gathered to this glorious destiny. This is the True Democracy.[1]

---

[1] I have said that we gain creative power through the group. Those who feel enthralled by material conditions, and to whom it seems an irony to be told that they are "creators," will demand something more specific. Concrete methods of group organization are given in Part III.

XIV

OUR rate of progress, then, and the degree in which we actualize the perfect democracy, depend upon our understanding that man has the power of creating, and that he gets this power through his capacity to join with others to form a real whole, a living group. Let us see, therefore, what signs are visible to-day of the group principle at work.

First, our whole idea of education is rapidly changing. The chief aim of education now is to fit the child into the life of the community; we do not think of his "individual" development except as contributing to that. Or it would be nearer the truth to say that we recognize that his individual development is essentially just that. The method of accomplishing this is chiefly through (1) the introduction of group class-room work in the place of individual recitations, (2) the addition of vocational subjects to the curriculum and the establishment of vocational schools, and (3) the organizing of vocational guidance departments and placement bureaus in connection with the public schools.

In many of the large cities of the United States the public schools have a vocational guidance department, and it is not considered that the schools have done their duty by the child until they have helped him to choose his life occupation, have trained him in some degree for it, and have actually found him a job, that is, fitted him into the community. It is becoming gradually accepted that this is a function of the state, and several of our

105

states are considering the appropriation of funds for the carrying on of such departments.[1]

The further idea of education as a continuous process, that it stops neither at 14 nor 21 nor 60, that a man should be related to his community not only through services rendered and benefits received but by a steady process of preparation for his social and civic life, will be discussed later.[2]

The chief object of medical social service is to put people into harmonious and fruitful relation, not only because illness has temporarily withdrawn certain people from the community, but because it is often some lack of adaptation which has caused the illness.

Our different immigration theories show clearly the growth of the community idea. First came the idea of amalgamation: our primary duty to all people coming to America was to assimilate them as quickly and as thoroughly as possible. Then people reacted against the melting-pot theory and said, "No, we want all the Italians have to offer, all the Syrians can give us; the richness of these different civilizations must not be engulfed in ours." So separate colonies were advocated, separate organizations were encouraged. Many articles were written and speeches made to spread this thought. But now a third idea is emerging — the community idea. We do not want Swedes and Poles to be lost in an undifferentiated whole, but equally we do not want all the evils of the separatist method; we are trying to get an articulated whole. We want all these different peoples to be part of a true community — giving all they have to give and receiving equally. Only by a mutual permeation of ideals shall we enrich their lives and they ours.

[1] It is interesting to notice that Miss Lathrop's whole conception of the Children's Bureau is that it is to fit children into the life of the community.　　　　[2] See Appendix.

Again our present treatment of crime shows the community principle in two ways: (1) the idea of community responsibility for crime is spreading rapidly; (2) we are fast outgrowing the idea of punishing criminals merely, our object is to fit them into society.

First, the growing idea of community responsibility for crime. We read in an account of the new penology that "Crime in the last analysis is not to be overcome after arrest but before," that crime will be abolished by a change of environment and that "environment is transformed by child labor laws and the protection of children, by housing laws and improved sanitation, by the prevention of tuberculosis and other diseases, by health-giving recreational facilities, by security of employment, by insurance against the fatalities of industry and the financial burdens of death and disease, by suitable vocational training, by all that adds to the content of human life and gives us higher and keener motives to self-control, strenuous exertion and thrift." We of course do not exonerate the individual from responsibility, but it must be shared by the whole society in which he lives.

Secondly, the old idea of justice was punishment, a relic of personal revenge; this punishment took the form of confinement, of keeping the man outside society. The new idea is exactly the opposite: it is to join him to society by finding out just what part he is best fitted to play in society and training him for it. A former Commissioner of Corrections in New York told me that a number of people, including several judges, were looking forward to the time very soon being ripe for making the "punishment" of a crime the doing some piece of social service in order to fit the criminal into the social order. One man who had shown in his crime marked organizing ability had been sent to oversee the reclaim-

ing of some large tracts of abandoned farm land, and
this had worked so well that a number of judges wished
to try similar experiments.

Thus criminals are coming to be shown that their
crime has not been against individuals but against society, that it has divorced them from their community
and that the object of their imprisonment is that they
may learn how to unite themselves to their community.
The colony system means that they must learn to live
in a community *by* living in a community. This is the
object of Mr. William George's "Social Sanitarium,"
where the men are to live in a graded series of farm
villages, govern themselves, support themselves and also
their families as far as possible, and pass from "village"
to "village" on their way towards the society from which
their crime has separated them.

This same principle, to make the life while under
punishment a preparation for community life, underlay
the work of Mr. Osborne at Sing Sing. Through his
Mutual Welfare League he tried to develop a feeling of
responsibility to the community, a feeling first of all
that there was a community within the prison. All the
men knew gang loyalty; it was Mr. Osborne's aim to
build upon this. He thought they could not feel responsibility to a community outside when they left unless they
learnt community consciousness inside. He did not provide recreation for them solely for the sake of recreation;
he did not allow them self-government because of any
abstract idea of the justice of self-government; he tried
to bring the men of Sing Sing to a realization of a community, to a sense of responsibility to a community.
The two men who escaped from Sing Sing in 1916 and
voluntarily returned had learned this lesson.[1]

[1] The new farm industrial system which is to replace Sing Sing is
founded largely on the community idea.

Both these principles — community responsibility for crime and the necessity of fitting the offender into the community life — underlie the work of the juvenile court. The probation officer's duty is not exhausted by knitting the child again into worthy relations; he must try to see that community life shall touch children on all sides in a helpful not a harmful way.

A future task for the juvenile court is to organize groups back of the child as part of the system of probation. All our experience is showing us the value of using the group incentive. The approval or blame of our fellow-men is an urgent factor in our lives; a man can stand any sort of condemnation better than that of his club. It was the idea of community punishment which was such an interesting part of the "Little Commonwealth" which Mr. Homer Lane established near Detroit for boys and girls on probation. If a boy did not work he was not punished for it, he did not even go without food, but the whole commonwealth had to pay for it out of their earnings. The whole moral pressure of the community was thus brought to bear upon that boy to do his share of the work — an incentive which Mr. Lane found more powerful than any punishment.

A colonel of the American army says that fewer offenses are committed in our army than in the Continental armies, not because human nature is different in America but because our methods of army discipline are different: the custom in our army is to punish a company for the offense of an individual; the company, therefore, looks after its own members.

The procedure of our courts also shows signs of change in the direction of the recognition of the group principle. Until recently we have had in our courts two lawyers, each upholding his side: this means a real struggle, there is no effort at unifying, one or the other must win; the judge is a sort of umpire. But the Reconciliation Court of Cleveland (and some other western cities) marks a long step in advance. This does away with lawyers each arguing one side; the judge deals directly with the disputants, trying to make them see that a harmonizing of their differences is possible. In our municipal courts, to be sure, the principal function of the judge has long been not to punish but to take those measures which will place the individual again in his group, but this applies only to criminal cases, whereas the Reconciliation Court of Cleveland, following the practice of the conciliation courts of certain continental countries,[1] deals with civil cases. The part of the judge in our juvenile courts is too well known to need mention.

In a jury I suppose we have always had an example of the group idea in practical life. Here there is no question of counting up similar ideas — there must be one idea and the effort is to seek that.

In our legislatures and legislative committees we get little integrated thought because of their party organization; even among members of the same party on a committee there are many causes at work to prevent the genuine interplay we should have. The governors' commissions, on the other hand, hear both sides, call in many experts and try to arrive at some composite judgment.

Nowhere has our social atomism been more apparent than in our lack of city-planning: (1) we have had many beautiful single buildings, but no plan for the whole city; (2) and more important, we could not get any general plan for our cities accepted because the individual

[1] France, Norway, Switzerland. In Norway it is said that more than three-quarters of the cases which come before the conciliation courts are settled without law suits.

property owner (this was called individualism!) must be protected against the community.   City-planning includes not only plans for a beautiful city but for all its daily needs — streets, traffic regulations, housing, schools, industry, transportation, recreational facilities; we cannot secure these things while property owners are being protected in their "rights."   The angry protest which goes up from real estate owners when it is proposed to regulate the height of buildings we have heard in all our cities.   The struggle for enough light and air in tenements has been fought step by step.   The "right" claimed was the right of every man to do what he liked with his own property.   Now we are beginning to recognize the error of this, and to see that it is not a state of individualism but of anarchy that our new building laws are trying to do away with.   No real estate owner is to be allowed to do that with his own property which will not fit into a general plan for the beauty and efficiency of the city.   The key-note of the new city-planning is adaptation, adaptation of means to end and of part to part.   This does not stifle individual initiative, but directs it.

And the interesting point for us here is that the real estate men themselves are now beginning to see that particularistic building has actually hurt real estate interests.   The "Report of the Advisory Council of the Real Estate Interests of New York City" admits that "light, air and access, the chief factors in fixing rentable values, had been impaired by high buildings and by the proximity of inappropriate or nuisance buildings and uses."   It is impossible to talk ten minutes with real estate men to-day without noticing how entirely changed their attitude has been in the last ten or twenty years. Moralists used to tell us that the only path of progress was to make people willing to give up their own interests for the sake of others. But this is not what our real estate men are doing. They are coming to see that their interests are in the long run coincident with the interests of all the other members of the city.

The growing recognition of the group principle in the business world is particularly interesting to us. The present development of business methods shows us that the old argument about coöperation and competition is not fruitful. Coöperation and competition are being taken up into a larger synthesis. We are just entering on an era of collective living. "Cut-throat" competition is beginning to go out of fashion. What the world needs to-day is a coöperative mind. The business world is never again to be directed by individual intelligences, but by intelligences interacting and ceaselessly influencing one another. Every mental act of the big business man is entirely different from the mental acts of the man of the last century managing his own competitive business. There is of course competition between our large firms, but the coöperation between them is coming to occupy a larger and larger place relatively. We see this in the arrangement between most of our large printers in Boston not to outbid one another, in those trades which join to establish apprentice schools, in the coöperative credit system, worked out so carefully in some of the western cities as almost to eliminate bad debts, in the regular conferences between the business managers of the large department stores, in our new Employment Managers' associations in Boston and elsewhere, in the whole spirit of our progressive Chambers of Commerce. When our large stores "compete" to give the highest class goods and best quality service, and meet in conference to make this "competition" effective, then competition itself becomes a kind of coöperation! There are now between thirty and forty associations in this country organized on the open-price plan. The Leather Belting Exchange, an excellent example of "coöperative competition," was organized in 1915. Some of its avowed objects are: standardization of grades of leather, promotion of use of leather belting by scientific investigation of its possible uses, uniform contract system, uniform system of cost accounting, daily charts of sales, monthly statistical reports, collection and distribution of information relative to cost of raw material and to methods and cost of manufacturing and distribution.[1] How vastly different a spirit from that which used to animate the business world!

Modern business, therefore, needs above all men who can unite, not merely men who can unite without friction, but who can turn their union to account. The successful business man of to-day is the man of trained coöperative intelligence. The world as well as the psychologist places a higher value on the man who can take part in collective thinking and concerted action, and has higher positions to offer him in the business and political field. The secretary of a Commission investigates a subject, is clever in mastering details, in drawing conclusions and in presenting them, perhaps far cleverer in these respects than any member of the Commission. But the chairman of the Commission must have another and higher power — the power of uniting these conclusions with the conclusions of others, the power of using this material to evolve with others plans for action. This means a more developed individual and brings a higher price in the open market.

Another illustration of the group principle in the business world is that a corporation is obliged by law to act in joint meeting, that is, it cannot get the vote of

[1] "Experiences in Coöperative Competition," by W. V. Spaulding.

its members by letter and then act according to the majority.

But more important than any of the illustrations yet given is the application of the group principle to the relations of capital and labor. People are at last beginning to see that industrial organization must be based on the community idea. If we do not want to be dominated by the special interests of the capital-power, it is equally evident that we do not want to be dominated by the special interests of the labor-power. The interests of capital and labor must be united.[1]

Even collective bargaining is only a milestone on the way to the full application of the group principle. It recognizes the union, it recognizes that some adjustment between the interests of capital and labor is possible, but it is still "bargaining," still an adjustment between two warring bodies, it still rests on the two pillars of concession and compromise. We see now the false psychology underlying compromise and concession. Their practical futility has long been evident: whenever any difference is "settled" by concession, that difference pops up again in some other form. Nothing will ever truly settle differences but synthesis. No wonder the syndicalists label the "compromises" made between "antagonistic interests" as insincere. In a way all compromise is insincere, and real harmony can be obtained only by an integration of "antagonistic" interests which can take place only when we understand the method. The error of the syndicalists is in thinking that compromise is the only method; their fundamental error is in thinking that different interests are necessarily "antagonistic" interests.

Compromise is accepted not only as inevitable and

[1] The great value of Robert Valentine's work consisted in his recognition of this fact.

as entirely proper, but as the most significant fact of
human association, by those economists who belong to
that school of "group sociologists" which sees present
society as made up of warring groups, ideal society as
made up of groups in equilibrium.   Not only, I believe, is
conflict and compromise not the true social process, but
also it is not, even at present, the most significant, although usually the largest, part of the social process.
The integrating of ideas which comes partly from direct
interpenetration, and partly from that indirect interpenetration which is the consequence of the overlapping
membership of groups, I see going on very largely in
the groups to which I belong, and is surely an interesting sign-post to future methods of association.

The weakness of Arbitration and Conciliation Boards,
with their "impartial" member, is that they tend to mere
compromise even when they are not openly negotiations between two warring parties.[1] It is probable from
what we see on all sides that the more "concessions"
we make, the less "peace" we shall get. Compulsory
Arbitration in New Zealand has not succeeded as well
as was hoped just because it has not found the community between capital and labor.

The latest development of collective bargaining, the
Trade Agreement,[2] with more or less permanent boards
of representatives from employers and workers, brings
us nearer true community than we have yet found in
industrial relations.   The history of these Agreements
in England and America is fruitful study.   One of the
best known in America is Mr. Justice Brandeis' protocol

[1] I am speaking in general. It is true that the history of cases settled
by arbitration reveals many in which the "umpire" has insisted that
negotiations continue until the real coincident interest of both sides
should be discovered.

[2] It has long been known in England and America but recently it
has been spreading rapidly.

scheme in 1910 for the garment industries of New York, which provided for an industrial court composed of employers and employed to which all disagreements should be brought, and for six years this prevented strikes in the needle trades of New York.[1]

One of the most interesting of the Trade Agreements to be found in the Bulletins of the National Labor Department, and one which can be studied over a long term of years, is that between the Stove Founders' National Defence Association (employers) and the Iron Moulders' Union of North America. It is not only that the permanent organ of "conference" (employers and employees represented) has brought peace to the stove industry after forty years of disastrous strikes and lockouts, but that question after question has been decided not by the side which the market rendered strongest at the moment seizing its advantage, but by a real harmonizing of interest. A good illustration is the treatment of the question of who should pay for the bad castings: that was not decided at once as a matter of superior strength or of compromise, but after many months a basis of mutual advantage was found.

For some years Trade Agreements have been coming to include more and more points; not wages and hours alone, but many questions of shop management, discipline etc. are now included. Moreover it has been seen over and over again that the knowledge gained through joint conference is the knowledge needed for joint control: the workmen ought to know the cost of production and of transportation, the relative value of different processes of production, the state of the market, the conditions governing the production and marketing of the competing product etc.; the employer must know

[1] Recently abandoned.

the real conditions of labor and the laborer's point of view.

The fundamental weakness of collective bargaining is that while it provides machinery for adjustment of grievances, while it looks forward to all the conceivable emergencies which may arise to cause disagreement between labor and capital, and seeks methods to meet these, it does not give labor a direct share in industrial control. In the collective *bargain* wages and the conditions of employment are usually determined by the relative *bargaining* strength of the workers and employers of the industrial group. Not bargaining in any form, not negotiation, is the key to industrial peace and prosperity; the collective contract must in time go the way of the individual contract. Community is the key-word for all relations of the new state. Labor unions have long been seeking their "rights," have looked on the differences between capital and labor as a fight, and have sought an advantageous position from which to carry on the fight: this attitude has influenced their whole internal organization. They quite as much as capital must recognize that this attitude must be given up. If we want harmony between labor and capital, we must make labor and capital into one group: we must have an integration of interests and motives, of standards and ideals of justice.

It is a mistake to think that social progress is to depend upon anything happening to the working people: some say that they are to be given more material goods and all will be well; some think they are to be given more "education" and the world will be saved. It is equally a mistake to think that what we need is the conversion to "unselfishness" of the capitalist class. Those who advocate profit-sharing are not helping us. The quarrel between capital and labor can never be settled on material grounds. The crux of that quarrel is not profits and wages — it is the joint control of industry.

There has been an increasing tendency of recent years for employers to take their employees into their councils. This ranges from mere "advisory" boards, which are consulted chiefly concerning grievances, through the joint committees for safety, health, standardization, wages etc., to real share in the management.[1] But even in the lowest form of this new kind of coöperation we may notice two points: the advisory boards are usually representative bodies elected by the employees, and they are consulted as a whole, not individually. The flaw in these advisory boards is not so much, as is often thought, because the management still keeps all the power in its own hands, as that the company officials do not sit with these boards in joint consultation. There is, however, much variety of method. In some shops advisory committees meet with the company officials. Some companies put many more important questions concerning conditions of employment before these bodies than other companies would think practical. A few employers have even given up the right to discharge — dismissal must be decided by fellow-employees.

Usually the management keeps the final power in its own hands. This is not so, however, in the case of Wm. Filene Son's Co., Boston, which has gone further than any other plant in co-management. Here the employees have the right by a two-thirds vote to change, initiate, or amend any rule that affects the discipline or working conditions of the employees of the store, and such vote becomes at once operative even against the veto of

[1] The three firms which have carried co-management furthest are the Printz-Biederman Co. of Cleveland, the Wm. Filene's Sons Co. of Boston and the U. S. Cartridge Co. of Lowell. See Report of Committee on Vocational Guidance, Fourth Annual Convention of National Association of Corporation Schools, by Henry C. Metcalf.

the management. Further, out of eleven members of the board of directors, four are representatives of the employees.[1]

The great advantage of company officials and workers acting together on boards or committees (workshop committees, discipline boards, advisory councils, boards of directors, etc.) is the same as that of the regular joint conferences of the Trade Agreement: employers and employed can thus learn to function together and prepare the way for joint control. Workshop committees should be encouraged, not so much because they remove grievances etc., as because in the joint workshop committee, managers and workers are learning to act together. Industrial democracy is a process, a growth. The joint control of industry may be established by some fiat, but it will not be the genuine thing until the *process* of joint control is learned. To be sure, the workshop committees which are independent of the management are often considered the best for the workers because they can thus keep themselves free to maintain and fight for their own particular interests, but this is exactly, I think, what should be avoided.

The labor question is — Is the war between capital and labor to be terminated by fight and conquest or by learning how to function together? I face fully the fact that many supporters of labor believe in what they call the "frank" recognition that the interests of capital and labor are "antagonistic." I believe that the end of the wars of nations and of the war between labor and capital will come in exactly the same way: by making

[1] We have a number of minor instances of the recognition of the group principle in industry. An interesting example is the shop piece-work in the Cadbury works, where the wages are calculated on the output of a whole work-room, and thus every one in the room has to suffer for the laziness of one. (See "Experiments in Industrial Organization," by Edward Cadbury.)

the nations into one group, by making capital and labor into one group. Then we shall learn to distinguish between true and apparent interests, or rather, between long-run and immediate interests; then we shall give up the notion of "antagonisms," which belong to a static world, and see only difference — that is, that which is capable of integration. This is not an idealistic treatment of the labor problem. Increase of wages and reduction in cost of production were once considered an irreconciliable antagonism — now their concurrence is a matter of common experience. If the hope of that concurrence had been abandoned as visionary or idealistic, we should be sadly off to-day. Many people are now making a distinction, however, between production and distribution in this respect: in the former the interests of capital and labor are the same, it is said, but not in the latter. When that reorganization of the business world, which it is no longer utopian to think of, is further actualized, then in distribution too we shall be able to see the coincident interests of labor and capital.

As the most hopeful sign in the present treatment of industrial questions is the recognition that man with his fundamental instincts and needs is the very centre and heart of the labor problem, so the most hopeful sign that we shall fully utilize the constructive powers which will be released by this psychological approach to industrial problems, is the gradually increasing share of the workman in the actual control of industry.

The recognition of community rather than of individuals or class, the very marked getting away from the attitude of pitting labor interests against the interests of capital, is the most striking thing from our point of view about the famous report formulated by a sub-committee of the British Labor Party in the autumn of 1917. In every one of the four "Pillars" of the new social order this stands out as the most dominant feature. In explaining the first, The Universal Enforcement of the National Minimum, it is explicitly stated that this is not to protect individuals or a class, but to "safeguard" the "community" against the "insidious degradation of the standard of life." The second, The Democratic Control of Industry, proposes national ownership and administration of the railways, canals and mines and "other main industries . . . as opportunity offers," with "a steadily increasing participation of the organized workers in the management," the extension of municipal enterprise to housing and town planning, public libraries, music and recreation, and the fixing of prices. This "Pillar," too, we are told, is not a class measure, but is "to safeguard the interests of the community as a whole."

Under the heading, "Revolution in National Finance," the third "Pillar," it is again definitely stated and moreover convincingly shown that this is not "in the interests of wage-earners alone." Under "The Surplus Wealth for the Common Good," the fourth "Pillar," it is stated that the surplus wealth shall be used for what "the community day by day needs for the perpetual improvement and increase of its various enterprises," "for scientific investigation and original research in every branch of knowledge," and for "the promotion of music, literature and fine arts." "It is in the proposal for this appropriation of every surplus for the common good — in the vision of its resolute use for the building up of the community as a whole . . . that the Labor Party . . . most distinctively marks itself off from the older political parties." [1]

[1] I have not spoken of the coöperative buying and selling movement because by the name alone it is obvious how well it illustrates my point, and also because it is so well known to every one.

Another evidence of the spreading of the community idea is the wide acceptance of the right of the community to value created by the community.

XV

FROM CONTRACT TO COMMUNITY

BUT perhaps nowhere in our national life is the growing recognition of the group or community principle so fundamental for us as in our modern theory of law. Mr. Roscoe Pound has opened a new future for America by his exposition of modern law, an exposition which penetrates and illumines every department of our thought. Let us speak briefly of this modern theory of law. It is: (1) that law is the outcome of our community life, (2) that it must serve, not individuals, but the community.

Mr. Pound, in a series of articles on "The Scope and Purpose of Sociological Jurisprudence" in the Harvard Law Review (1910–1912), points out that it was an epoch-making moment when attention began to be turned from the nature of law to its purpose. The old conception of law was that "new situations are to be met always by deductions from old principles." The new school (headed by Jhering) believe that "law is a product of conscious and increasingly determinate human will." "Legal doctrines and legal interests do not work themselves out blindly, but have been fashioned by human wants to meet human needs." Before Jhering the theory of law had been individualistic; Jhering's is a social theory of law. "The eighteenth century conceived of law as something which the individual invoked against society; . . . Jhering taught that it was something created by society through which the individual found a means of securing his interests, so far as society recognized them." And Jhering called his a jurisprudence of

122

realities; he wanted legal precepts worked out and tested by results. For instance, if a rule of commercial law were in question, the search should be for the rule which best accords with and gives effect to sound business practice.[1]

So, Mr. Pound tells us, the idea of justice as the maximum of individual self-assertion, which began to appear at the end of the sixteenth century and reached its highest development in the nineteenth century, began to give way towards the end of the nineteenth century to the new idea of the end of law. Modern jurists have come to consider the working of law more than its abstract content; they lay stress upon the social purposes which law subserves rather than upon sanction.[2]

Mr. Pound then shows us that Gierke's theory of association "became as strong an attack upon the individualistic jurisprudence of the nineteenth century upon one side as Jhering's theory of interests was upon another." The "real personality" of the group is plainly expounded by Gierke, that it is not a legal fiction, that is that the law does not create it but merely recognizes that which already exists, that this "real person" is more than an aggregation of individuals, that there is a group will which is something real apart from the wills of the associated individuals.

Thus German jurists recognize the principle of "community." The theory of Vereinbarung, as expounded by Jellinek,[3] is also a recognition of the fact that one will can be formed from several. The present tendency to work out the law of association through the study of the group is marked and significant.

[1] Col. Law Rev. 8, 610.

[2] Pound, Outlines of Lectures on Jurisprudence, p. 20. The influence of sociology on law has here been very marked. For further discussion of a teleological jurisprudence, see ch. XXIX.

[3] Duguit, L'Etat, Le Droit Objectif et La Loi Positive, 398–409, from Jellinek, System der subjektiren öffentlichen Rechte, 193.

The chief consequence of this growing tendency in modern juristic thinking is seen in the change in attitude towards contract. The fundamental question of relation, of association, is — Can you make one idea grow where two grew before? *This* is the law of fruitful increase. The gradual progress away from contract in legal theory is just the gradual recognition of this principle. You can have a contractual relation between two wills or you can have those two wills uniting to form one will. Contract never creates one will. It is the latter process which is shown in the development of corporation law.[1] The laws regulating partnership are based on contractual relations between the individual members. The laws regulating corporations are based on the theory that a corporation is something quite different from the individuals who constitute it or the sum of those individuals, that a new entity has been created. I am writing at this moment (February, 1918) in a room with the thermometer at 42, but the law would not uphold me in going and getting my share, as a stock holder, of the coal now in the New York, New Haven and Hartford sheds! But to many the personality of the corporation is a fiction: they do not consider the corporation a self-created entity but a state-created entity. To others, following Gierke, the corporation is merely a state-*recognized* entity, it has the inherent power to create itself. The increasing acceptance of this latter theory has made it possible to hold liable groups which have not been legally incorporated but which exercise powers analogous to those of corporations. This has been the principle of some of the English decisions making trade-unions responsible, as notably in the Taff-Vale case.

[1] The whole legal history of associations and the development of association law throws much light on the growth of the community idea.

The paradox of contract is that while it seems to be based on relation, it is in reality based on the individual. Contract is a particularist conception. Mr. Pound speaks of the significance of the "parallel movement away from liberty of contract and yet at the same time towards the full recognition of association." It is the legal theory of association based on our growing understanding of group psychology which will finally banish contract. When Duguit, the eminent French jurist, tells us that contract is diminishing, it is because he sees a time when all juridical manifestations will come from unilateral acts.[1] We see contract diminishing because we believe in a different mode of association: as fast as association becomes a "community" relation, as fast as individuals are recognized as community-units, just so fast does contract fade away. Jellinek points out that legal theory is coming to recognize that violation of community is quite different from the violation of contract.

From status to contract we do not now consider the history of liberty but of particularism — the development of law through giving a larger and larger share to the particular will. The present progress of law is from contract to community. Our particularistic law is giving way to a legal theory based on a sound theory of interrelationship. Our common law has considered men as separate individuals, not as members of one another. These separate individuals were to be "free" to fight out their differences as best they could, it being overlooked that freedom for one might not mean freedom for the other, as in the case of employer and employed. "Individual rights" in practice usually involve some difference

---

[1] Also, I recognize, because his "*droit objectif*" based on social solidarity tends to sweep away contract. It is interesting to notice that contract is being attacked from more than one point of view. The bearing of all this on politics will be seen later, especially in ch. XXIX, "Political Pluralism and Sovereignty."

of opinion as to who is the individual! Mr. Olney said of the Adair case: "It is archaic, it is a long step into the past, to conceive of and deal with the relations between the employer in such industries and the employee as if the parties were individuals." [1]

The principles of individual rights and contract which have long dominated our courts [2] are giving way now to sounder doctrine. The old idea was that a man could do what he liked with his own; this is not the modern notion of law. We find a judge recently saying: "The entire scheme of prohibition as embodied in the Constitution and laws of Kansas might fail, if the right of each citizen to manufacture intoxicating liquors for his own use or as a beverage were recognized. Such a right does not inhere in citizenship." [3] Our future law is to serve neither classes nor individuals, but the community. The lawyer is to bring his accumulation of knowledge not to his clients merely, but to enrich and interpret and adjust our whole social life.

We have many signs to-day of the growing recognition of community as the basis of law. The following are taken from an article by Mr. Pound: [4]

The increasing tendency of law to impose limitations on the use of property, limitations designed to prevent the anti-social use of property. This has already been noticed in our new building laws.

The limitations now imposed on freedom of contract. This is shown in the statutes regulating the hours and

[1] Quoted by Roscoe Pound in Col. Law Rev. 8, 616.

[2] Statutes limiting the hours of labor were held unconstitutional, railway corporations were held not to be required to furnish discharged employees with a cause for dismissal, etc.

[3] Harlan, J., in Mugler v. Kansas, 123 U. S. 623. Taken from Roscoe Pound, Liberty of Contract, Yale Law Journal, 18, 468.

[4] The End of Law as Developed in Legal Rules and Doctrines, Harv. Law Rev. 27, 195–234.

conditions of labor, in the law of insurance,[1] in the judicial decisions which have established that the duties of public service corporations are not contractual, flowing from agreement, but quasi-contractual, flowing from the calling in which the public servant is engaged.

Limitations on the part of creditor or injured party to exact satisfaction. This is illustrated by the homestead exemptions which prevail in many states, and such exemptions as tools to artisans, libraries to professional men, and animals and implements to farmers.

Imposition of liability without fault, as illustrated in workmen's compensation and employers' liability.[2]

Water rights are now interpreted with limitations on the owners. The idea is becoming accepted that running water is an asset of society which is not capable of private appropriation or ownership except under regulations that protect the general interest. This tendency is changing the whole water law of the western states.

Insistence on interest of society in dependent members of household. With respect to children it is not the individual interest of the parents, but the interest of society which is regarded.

Thus modern law is being based more and more upon a recognition of the community principle.

When we sometimes hear a lawyer talk of such measures as old age pensions as a matter of "social expediency," we know that he has not yet caught the com-

[1] "Statutes . . . have taken many features of the subject out of the domain of agreement and the tendency of judicial decision has been in effect to attach rights and liabilities to the relation of insurer and insured and thus to remove insurance from the category of contract."

[2] The old idea of "contributory negligence" is seen in the following decision: "We must remember that the injury complained of is due to the negligence of a fellow workman, for which the master is responsible neither in law nor morals." Durkin v. Coal Co. 171, Pa. St. 193, 205. Quoted by Roscoe Pound in Yale Law Journal, 18, 467.

munity idea in law. Modern law considers individuals not as isolated beings, but in their relation to the life of the whole community. Thus in shortening the hours of work the courts can no longer say this is an "unwarrantable interference" with individual liberty; they have to consider the health of the individual in its relation to his family and his work, also the use he will make of his leisure, the need he has for time to perform his duties as citizen, etc. etc. Mr. Pound points out with great clearness that relation is taking the place of contract in modern law. Workmen's compensation arises from the theory of reciprocal rights and duties and liabilities which flow from a relation. This he tells us was the common law conception until deflected by contract; now we are going back to it and we do not ask the strict terms of the contract, but what the relation demands.

Perhaps social psychology can give two warnings to this new tendency of law. First this relation must not be a personal relation. I have spoken several times of our modern legal system as based on relation, but this must not be confused with the relation of the Middle Ages. Then the fundamental truth of relation, that life is a web of relationships, was felt intuitively, but it was worked out on its personal side. The feudal age lived in the idea of relation, but the heart of the feudal system was personal service. It was like loyalty to the party chief: right or wrong, the vassal followed his lord to the battlefield and died with him there. Because it was worked out on its personal side it had many imperfections, and the inevitable reaction swung far away. Now the pendulum is returning to relation as the truth of life, but it is to be impersonal. Employers and employed must study the ideal relation and try to actualize that. We seek always the law of true community.

Secondly, the relation itself must always be in relation. But these warnings are not necessary for our progressive judges. It is interesting to read the decisions of our common-law judges with this in view: to see how often the search is for the law of the actual conditions and what obligations those actual conditions create, not for a personal relation with some abstract conception of a static relation. It is of a *relation in relation* that judges must, and often to-day do, consider: not landlord and tenant as landlord and tenant, not master and servant as master and servant, but of that relation in relation to other relations, or, we might say, to society. This growing conception of a dynamic relation in itself means a new theory of law.[1]

Thus our law to-day is giving up its deductions from juristic conceptions, from the "body of rules" upon which trial procedure has so largely rested, and is beginning to study the condition given with the aim of reaching the law of that condition. Mr. Pound says distinctly that law is to be no longer based on first principles, but on "the conditions it is to govern." And we are told that "Mr. Justice Holmes has been unswerving in his resistance to any doctrinaire interpretation," that his decisions follow the actual conditions of life even often against his own bias of thought.[2] The great value of Mr. Justice Brandeis' brief in the Oregon case concerning the constitutionality of limiting the hours of women in industry, was his insistence upon social facts. And Mr. Felix Frankfurter made an address before the

---

[1] This is the "new natural law" of which Mr. Pound speaks as "the revival of the idealist interpretation which is the enduring possession of philosophical jurisprudence." Formerly, we are told, "equity imposed moral limitations. The law to-day is beginning to impose social limitations." Harv. Law Rev. 27, 227.

[2] "The Constitutional Opinions of Justice Holmes," by Felix Frankfurter, Harv. Law Rev. 29, 683–702.

American Bar Association in August, 1915, the burden of which was that "law must follow life." His plea for a "creative" system of law in the place of the crystallized system of the past which we are trying with hopeless failure to apply to present conditions points the way with force and convincingness to a New Society based on the evolving not the static principle of life.

As our theory of the state no longer includes the idea of contractual obligation, we begin to see the interdependence of state and law, that neither is prior to the other. The same process which evolves the state evolves the law. Law flows from our life, therefore it cannot be above it. The source of the binding power of law is not in the consent of the community, but in the fact that it has been produced by the community. This gives us a new conception of law. Some writers talk of social justice as if a definite idea of it existed, and that all we have to do to regenerate society is to direct our efforts towards the realization of this ideal. But the ideal of social justice is itself a collective and a progressive development, that is, it is produced through our associated life and it is produced anew from day to day. We do not want a "perfect" law to regulate the hours of women in industry; we want that kind of life which will make us, all of us, grow the best ideas about the hours of women in industry, about women in industry, about women, about industry.

We cannot assume that we possess a body of achieved ideas stamped in some mysterious way with the authority of reason and justice, but even were it true, the reason and justice of the past must give way to the reason and justice of the present. You cannot bottle up wisdom — it won't keep — but through our associated life it may be distilled afresh at every instant. We are coming now to see indeed that law is a social imperative in the strict psychological sense, that is, that it gets its authority through the power of group life. Wundt says, The development of law is a process of the psychology of peoples, therefore law will forever be a process of becoming.[1] Our obedience to law then must not be obedience to past law, but obedience to that law which we with all the experience of the past at our command, with all the vision of the future which the past has taught us, with all the intelligence which vivid living in the present has developed in us, are able to make for our generation, for our country, for the world. We are told that one of the most salient points in modern juristic thinking is its faith in the efficacy of effort, its belief that law has been and may be made consciously.

When we look upon law as a thing we think of it as a finished thing; the moment we look upon it as a process we think of it always in evolution. Our law must take account of our social and economic conditions, and it must do it again to-morrow and again day after to-morrow. We do not want a new legal system with every sunrise, but we do want a method by which our law shall be capable of assimilating from day to day what it needs to act upon that life from which it has drawn its existence and to which it must minister. The vital fluid of the community, its life's blood, must pass so continuously from the common will to the law and from the law to the common will that a perfect circulation will be established. We do not "discover" legal principles which it then behooves us to burn candles before forever, but legal principles are the outcome of our daily life. Our law therefore cannot be based on "fixed" principles: our law must be intrinsic in the social process.

There has been a distinction made between legal prin-

[1] Quoted by Roscoe Pound in Harv. Law Rev. 25, 505.

ciples and the application of these principles: legal principles partook of the nature of the absolute, and to our
high-priests, the lawyers, fell the privilege of applying
them. But this is an artificial distinction. If our methods could be such that the energy of lawyers, which now
often goes in making the concrete instance and the legal
principle in some way (by fiction, or twisting, or "interpreting") fit each other, could help evolve day by day
a crescent law which is the outcome of our life as it is to
be applied to our life, an enormous amount of energy
would be saved for the development of our American
people. It is static law and our reverence for legal
abstractions which has produced "privilege." It is dynamic law, as much as anything else, which will bring us
the new social order.

To sum up: Law should not be a "body" of knowledge; it should be revitalized anew at every moment.
Our judges cannot administer law by knowing law
alone. They have to be so closely in touch with a living,
growing society, so at one with the conceptions that are
being evolved by that society that their interpretations
will be the method by which our so-called "body of law"
shall indeed be alive and grow in correspondence with
the growth of society. This is what gives to our American supreme courts their large powers, and makes us
choose for judges not only men who understand law
and who can be trusted for accurate interpretation, but
men who have a large comprehension of our country's
needs, wide conceptions of social justice, and who have
creative minds — who can make legal interpretation contribute to the structure of our government.[1] The modern

---

[1] It has been proposed that we should have trained business men on
the benches of our supreme courts as well as lawyers. I should think it
would be better for our lawyers to be so conversant with social facts that
this need not be necessary.

lawyer must see, amidst all the complexity of the twentieth-century world, where we are tending, what our true purpose is, and the part law can take in making manifest that purpose. The modern lawyer must create a new system of service. A living law we demand to-day — this is always the law of the given condition, never a "rule."

Part II
THE TRADITIONAL DEMOCRACY

XVI

DEMOCRACY NOT "LIBERTY" AND "EQUALITY": OUR POLITICAL DUALISM

THE purpose of this book is to indicate certain changes which must be made in our political methods in order that the group principle, the most fruitful principle of association we have yet found, shall have free play in our political life. In Part III we shall devote ourselves specifically to that purpose. Here let us examine some of our past notions of democracy and then trace the growth of true democracy in America.

Democracy has meant to many "natural" rights, "liberty" and "equality." The acceptance of the group principle defines for us in truer fashion those watchwords of the past. If my true self is the group-self, then my only rights are those which membership in a group gives me. The old idea of natural rights postulated the particularist individual; we know now that no such person exists. The group and the individual come into existence simultaneously: with this group-man appear group-rights. Thus man can have no rights apart from society or independent of society or against society. Particularist rights are ruled out as everything particularist is ruled out. When we accept fully the principle of rights involved in the group theory of association, it will change the decisions of our courts, our state constitutions, and all the concrete machinery of government. The truth of the whole matter is that our only concern with "rights" is not to protect them but to create them. Our efforts are to be bent not upon guarding the rights

137

which Heaven has showered upon us, but in creating all
the rights we shall ever have.[1]

As an understanding of the group process abolishes
"individual rights," so it gives us a true definition of
liberty. We have seen that the free man is he who actu-
alizes the will of the whole. I have no liberty except as
an essential member of a group. The particularist idea
of liberty was either negative, depending on the removal
of barriers, or it was quantitative, something which I
had left over after the state had restrained me in every
way it thought necessary. But liberty is not measured
by the number of restraints we do not have, but by the
number of spontaneous activities we do have. Law and
liberty are not like the two halves of this page, mutually
exclusive — one is involved in the other. One does not
decrease as the other increases. Liberty and law go
hand in hand and increase together in the larger synthesis of life we are here trying to make.

We see that to obey the group which we have helped
to make and of which we are an integral part is to be
free because we are then obeying ourself. Ideally the
state is such a group, actually it is not, but it depends
upon us to make it more and more so. The state must
be no external authority which restrains and regulates
me, but it must be myself acting as the state in every
smallest detail of life. Expression, not restraint, is always
the motive of the ideal state.

There has been long a kind of balance theory preva-
lent: everything that seems to have to do with the one
is put on one side, everything that has to do with the
many, on the other, and one side is called individuality
and freedom, and the other, society, constraint, authority. Then the balancing begins: how much shall

[1] See ch. XXIX for the theory of "objective rights" now held by many
as the basis of the new state.

we give up on one side and how much on the other to
keep the beautiful equilibrium of our daily life? How
artificial such balancing sounds! We are beginning to
know now that our freedom depends not on the weakness
but on the strength of our government, our government
being the expression of a united people. We are freer
under our present sanitary laws than without them; we
are freer under compulsory education than without it.
A highly organized state does not mean restriction of
the individual but his greater liberty. The individual
is restricted in an unorganized state. A greater degree
of social organization means a more complex, a richer,
broader life, means more opportunity for individual
effort and individual choice and individual initiative.
The test of our liberty is not the number of limitations
put upon the powers of the state. The state is not an
extra-will. If we are the state we welcome Our liberty.

But liberty on the popular tongue has always been
coupled with equality, and this expression too needs
revaluation. The group process shows us that we are
equal from two points of view: first, I am equal to
every one else as one of the necessary members of the
group; secondly, each of these essential parts is the tap
from an infinite supply — in every man lives an infinite
possibility. But we must remember that there are no
mechanical, no quantitative equalities. Democracy in
fact insists on what are usually thought of as inequali-
ties. Of course I am not "as good as you" — it would
be a pretty poor world if I were, that is if you were no
better than I am. Democracy without humility is in-
conceivable. The hope of democracy is in its inequali-
ties. The only real equality I can ever have is to fill my
place in the whole at the same time that every other
man is filling his place in the whole.

Much of our present class hatred comes from a dis-

torted view of equality. This doctrine means to many
that I have as much "right" to things as any one else,
and therefore if I see any one having more things than
I have, it is proper to feel resentment against that person or class. Much legislation, therefore, is directed to
lopping off here and there. But such legislation is a
negative and therefore non-constructive interpretation
of equality. The trouble with much of our reform is
that it is based on the very errors which have brought
about the evils it is fighting. The trade-unionists say
that the courts give special privileges to employers and
that they do not have equal rights. But this is just the
complaint of the employers: that the unionists are doing
them out of their time-honored equal rights.[1]

Our distorted ideas of rights and liberty and equality
have been mixed up with our false conception of the
state, with the monstrous fallacy of man *vs.* the state.
But as we now see that the individual and society are
different aspects of the same process, so we see that the
citizen and the state are one, that their interests are
identical, that their aims are identical, that they are
absolutely bound up together. Our old political dualism
is now disappearing. The state does not exist for the
individual or the individual for the state: we do not
exalt the state and subordinate the individual or, on the
other hand, apotheosize the individual and give him
the state as his "servant." *The state is not the servant of
the people.* The state must *be* the people before it can
reach a high degree of effective accomplishment. The
state is one of the collective aspects of the individual;

---

[1] This is a hoary quarrel. From the beginning of our government it
was seen that the equal rights doctrine was a sword which could cut
both ways. Both Federalists and Republicans believed in equal rights:
the Federalists, therefore, wanted to protect individuals with a strong
government; the Republicans wanted a weak government so that individuals could be let alone in the exercise of their equal rights.

the individual is from one point of view the distributive aspect of the state. The non-existence of self-sufficing individuals gives us the whole of our new theory of democracy. Those who govern and those who are governed are merely two aspects of the common will. When we have a state truly representative of our collective citizenship, then the fear of the state will disappear because the antithesis between the individual and the state will have disappeared.

To sum up: our present idea of the state is that it is not something outside ourselves, that it must flow out from ourselves and control our social life. But it must "control" our life by expressing it. The state is always the great Yes, not the great No. Liberty and restraint are not opposed, because ideally the expression of the social will in restraint *is* our freedom. The state has a higher function than either restraining individuals or protecting individuals. It is to have a great forward policy which shall follow the collective will of the people, a collective will which embodied through our state, in our life, shall be the basis of a progress yet undreamed of. When we can give up the notion of individual rights, we shall have taken the longest step forward in our political development. When we can give up the idea of national rights — but it is too soon to talk of that yet.

XVII

IF many people have defined democracy as liberty and equal rights, others have defined it as "the ascendancy of numbers," as "majority rule." Both these definitions are particularistic. Democracy means the will of the whole, but the will of the whole is not necessarily represented by the majority, nor by a two-thirds or three-quarters vote, nor even by a unanimous vote; majority rule is democratic when it is approaching not a unanimous but an integrated will. We have seen that the adding of similarities does not produce the social consciousness; in the same way the adding of similar votes does not give us the political will. We have seen that society is not an aggregation of units, of men considered one by one; therefore we understand that the will of the state is not discovered by counting.[1] This means a new conception of politics: it means that the organization of men in small, local groups must be the next form which democracy takes. Here the need and will of every man and woman can appear and mingle with the needs and wills of all to produce an all-will. Thus will be abolished the reign of numbers.

A crude view of democracy says that when the working-people realize their power they can have what they want, since, their numbers being so great, they can out-vote other classes. But the reason the working-people have not already learned something so very obvious is

---

[1] This view of democracy was well satirized by some one, I think Lord Morley, who said, "I do not care who does the voting as long as I do the counting."

because it is not true — *we are never to be ruled by numbers alone.*

Moreover, a fatal defect in majority rule is that by its very nature it abolishes itself. Majority rule must inevitably become minority rule: the majority is too big to handle itself; it organizes itself into committees — Committee of Fifty, Fifteen, Three — which in their turn resolve themselves into a committee of one, and behold — the full-fledged era of bosses is at hand, with the "consent of the governed" simply because the governed are physically helpless to govern themselves. Many men want majority rule so that they can be this committee of one; some of our most worthy citizens are incipient Greek tyrants longing to give us of their best — tyranny.

Many working-men are clamoring for majority rule in industry, yet we know how often in their own organizations the rule of the many becomes the rule of the few. If "industrial democracy" is to mean majority rule, let us be warned by our experience of it in politics — it will rend whoever dallies with it.

Yet it will be objected, "But what other means under the sun is there of finding the common will except by counting votes?" We see already here and there signs of a new method. In many committees, boards and commissions we see now a reluctance to take action until all agree; there is a feeling that somehow, if we keep at it long enough, we can unify our ideas and our wills, and there is also a feeling that such unification of will has value, that our work will be vastly more effective in consequence. How different from our old methods when we were bent merely upon getting enough on our side to carry the meeting with us. Some one has said, "We count heads to save breaking them." We are beginning to see now that majority rule is only a clumsy

makeshift until we shall devise ways of getting at the
genuine collective thought. We have to assume that we
have this while we try to approximate it. We are not
to circumvent the majority, but to aim steadily at getting the majority will nearer and nearer to a true collective will.

This may sound absurdly unlike the world as mainly
constituted. Is this the way diplomats meet? Is this
the way competing industrial interests adjust their differences? Not yet, but it must be. And what will help
us more than anything else is just to get rid of the idea
that we ever meet to get votes. The corruption in city
councils, state legislatures, Congress, is largely the outcome of the idea that the getting of votes is the object
of our meeting. The present barter in votes would not
take place if the unimportance of votes was once clearly
seen.

Even now so far as a majority has power it is not by
the brute force of numbers; it is because there has been
a certain amount of unifying; it has real power directly
in proportion to the amount of unifying. The composi-
tion of a political majority depends at present partly on
inheritance and environment (which includes sentiment
and prejudice), partly on the mass-induced idea (the
spread of thought and feeling throughout a community
by suggestion), and partly on some degree of integration
of the different ideas and the different forces of that
particular society. Its power is in proportion to the
amount of this integration. When we use the expression "artificial majority" we mean chiefly one which
shows little integration, and we have all seen how quickly
such majorities tend to melt away when the artificial
stimulus of especially magnetic leadership or of an especially catchy and jingoistic idea is withdrawn. Moreover a majority meaning a preponderance of votes can

easily be controlled by a party or an "interest"; majorities which represent unities are not so easily managed. Group organization is, above everything else perhaps, to prevent the manipulation of helpless majorities.

But "helpless majority" may sound amusing to those who are telling us of the tyranny of majorities. From one point of view indeed majority rule tends to become majority tyranny, so we do not want a majority in either case, either as a tyrant or as an inert mass. But those who talk of the tyranny of majorities are usually those who are advocating the "rights of minorities." If it is necessary to expose the majority fallacy, it is equally necessary to show that the present worship of minorities in certain quarters is also unsound. There is no inherent virtue in a minority. If as a matter of fact we cannot act forcefully without a certain amount of complacency, then perhaps it is a good thing for those in a minority to flatter themselves that of twenty people nine are more apt to be right than eleven. It may be one of those false assumptions more useful than a true one, and in our pragmatic age we shall not deny its value. Still sour grapes hang sometimes just as high and no higher than the majority, and it seems possible to find a working assumption that will work even better than this. In fact the assumption that the minority is always right is just as much an error as the assumption that the majority is always right. The right is not with the majority or minority because of preponderance of numbers or because of lack of preponderance of numbers.

But many people tell us seriously that this is not a question of opinion at all, but of fact: all the great reforms of the past, they say, whose victories are now our common heritage, were inaugurated by an intelligent and devoted few. You can indeed point to many causes led by a faithful minority triumphing in the end over a numerical and inert majority, but this minority was usually a majority of those who thought on the subject at all.

But all talk of majority and minority is futile. It is evident that we must not consider majority versus minority, but only the methods by which unity is attained. Our fetich of majorities has held us back, but most of the plans for stopping the control of majorities look to all kinds of bolstering up of minorities. This keeps majorities and minorities apart, whereas they have both one and only use for us — their contribution to the all-will. Because such integration must always be the ideal in a democracy, we cannot be much interested in those methods for giving the minority more power on election day. The integration must begin further back in our life than this.

I know a woman of small school education, but large native intelligence, who spends her time between her family and the daily laundry work she does to support that family, who, when she goes to her Mothers' Club at the "School Centre" penetrates all the superficialities she may find there, and makes every other woman go home with higher standards for her home, her children and herself. The education of children, the opportunities of employment for girls and boys, sanitation, housing, and all the many questions which touch one's everyday life are considered in a homely way on those Thursday afternoons. Sometime these women will vote on these questions, but a true intermingling of majority and minority will have taken place before election day.

Moreover, while representation of the minority, as proportional representation,[1] is always an interesting experiment, just because it is a method of representa-

[1] Proportional representation is interesting to the view put forward in this book because it is a method to bring out all the differences.

tion and not a mode of association the party can circumvent it. We are told that minority representation tried in the lower house of the Illinois legislature has been completely subverted to their own ends by the politicians. And also that in Belgium, where proportional representation has been introduced, this system has become a tool in the hands of the dominant party. No electoral or merely representative method can save us.

Representation is not the main fact of political life; the main concern of politics is *modes of association*. We do not want the rule of the many or the few; we must find that method of political procedure by which majority and minority ideas may be so closely interwoven that we are truly ruled by the will of the whole. We shall have democracy only when we learn to produce this will through group organization — when young men are no longer lectured to on democracy, but when they are made into the stuff of democracy.

XVIII

DEMOCRACY NOT THE CROWD: OUR POPULAR DELUSION

WHEN we define democracy as the "rule of the whole," this is usually understood as the rule of all, and unless we fully understand the meaning of "all," we run the danger of falling a victim to the crowd fallacy. The reaction to our long years of particularism, of "individual rights" and "liberty," which led to special privilege and all the evils in its train, has brought many to the worship of the crowd. Walt Whitman sang of men "en masse." Many of our recent essayists and poets and novelists idealize the crowd. Miss Jane Harrison in her delightful volume, "Alpha and Omega," says, "Human life is lived to the full only in and through the herd." There is an interesting group of young poets in France [1] who call themselves Unanimistes because they believe in the union of all, that an "Altogetherness" is the supreme fact of life. Mr. Ernest Poole in "The Harbor" glorifies the crowd, and the New York "*Tribune*" said of this book, "'The Harbor' is the first really notable novel produced by the New Democracy," thus identifying the new democracy with the crowd. Another writer, looking at our present social

---

[1] Arcos, Romains and Vildrac are the chief of these. Romains, who has written "La Vie Unanime," is the most interesting for our present purpose, for his togetherness is so plainly that of the herd:

    . . . "quelle joie
        De fondre dans ton corps [la ville] immense
        où l'on a chaud!"

Here is our old friend, the wild ox, in the mask of the most civilized (perhaps) portion of our most civilized (perhaps) nation. Again

        "Nous sommes indistincts: chacun de nous est mort;
        Et la vie unanime est notre sépulture."

and political organization and finding it based largely on class and therefore unsound, also leaps to the conclusion that our salvation rests not on this individual or that, this class or that, this body of people or that, but on all together, on "this mass-life, seething, tumultuous, without compass or guide or will or plan."

This school is doing good service in leading us from the few or the many to the all, in preaching that the race contains within itself the power of its own advancement; but this power which the race contains within itself is not got through its being a crowd, "without guide or will or plan," but just because it contains the potentialities of guide, will, plan, all within itself, through its capability of being a true society, that is, through its capability of adopting group methods. It is in the group that we get that complex interpenetration which means both modification and adjustment and at the same time coöperation and fulfilment. The group process, not the crowd or the herd, is the social process. Out of the intermingling, interacting activities of men and women surge up the forces of life: powers are born which we had not dreamed of, ideas take shape and grow, forces are generated which act and react on each other. This is the dialectic of life. But this upspringing of power from our hidden sources is not the latent power of the mass but of the group. It is useless to preach "togetherness" until we have devised ways of making our together ness fruitful, until we have thought out the methods of a genuine, integrated togetherness. Anything else is indeed "blubbering sentimentality," as Bismarck defined democracy.

But there are two sets of people who are victims of the crowd fallacy: those who apotheosize the crowd and those who denounce the crowd; both ignore the group. The latter fear the crowd because they see in the crowd

the annihilation of the individual. They are opposed
to what they call collective action because they say that
this is herd action and does not allow for individual
initiative. We are told, "Man loses his identity in a
crowd," "The crowd obliterates the individual mind."
Quite true, but these writers do not see that the crowd
is not the only form of association, that man may belong to a group rather than to a crowd, and that a group
fulfils, not wipes out his individuality. The collective
action of the group not only allows but consists of individual initiative, of an individual initiative that has
learned how to be part of a collective initiative.

Collective thought, moreover, is often called collective mediocrity. But the collective thought evolved by
the group is not collective mediocrity. On the contrary
there is always a tendency for the group idea to express
the largest degree of psychic force there is in a group,
ideally it would always do so. Herein lies the difference
between the group idea and the mass idea. When we
hear it stated as a commonplace of human affairs that
combined action is less intelligent than individual action,
we must point out that it all depends upon whether it is
a crowd combination or a group combination. The insidious error that democracy means the "average" is
at the root of much of our current thought.

The confusion of democratic rule and mass rule, the
identification of the people with the crowd, has led many
people to denounce democracy. One writer, thinking
the collective man and the crowd man the same, condemns democracy because of his condemnation of the
crowd man. Another speaks of "the crowd-mind or
the state," and therefore abandons the state. All
these writers think that the more democracy, the more
complete the control of the crowd. Our faith in democracy means a profound belief that this need not be

true. Moreover this idea that the crowd man must necessarily be the unit of democracy has led many to oppose universal suffrage because they have seen it as a particularist suffrage, giving equal value, they say, to the enlightened and the unenlightened. True democracy frees us from such particularist point of view. It is the group man, not the crowd man, who must be the unit of democracy.

The philosophy of the all is supposed, by its advocates, to be opposed to the philosophy of the individual, but it is interesting to notice that the crowd theory and the particularistic theory rest on the same fallacy, namely, looking on individuals one by one: the crowd doctrine is an attempt to unite mechanically the isolated individuals we have so ardently believed in. This is the danger of the crowd. The crowd idea of sovereignty is thoroughly atomistic. This is sometimes called an era of crowds, sometimes an era of individuals: such apparent opposition of judgment need not confuse us, the crowd spirit and the particularistic spirit are the same; that spirit will continue to corrupt politics and disrupt society until we replace it by the group spirit.

The crowd theory, like the particularist doctrine, has been strengthened by the upholders of the imitation theory of society. Many of our political as well as our sociological writers have seen life as some exceptional individual suggesting and the crowd following without reasoning, without effort of mind or will. Even Bagehot, who did so much to set us in the right way of thinking, overemphasizes the part of imitation. What he says of the "imitative part of our natures" is indeed true, but by not mentioning the creative part of our natures more explicitly, he keeps himself in the crowd school.

It is true that at present the people are to a large extent a mass led by those who suggest. The suggestion

and imitation of sociology are the leading and following
of politics — the leadership of the boss and the following
of the mass. The successful politician is one who understands crowds and how to dominate them. He appeals
to the emotions, he relies on repetition, he invents catch
phrases. The crowd follows. As long as the corner-
stone of our political philosophy is the theory that the
individual originates and society accepts, of course any
man who can get the people to "accept" will do so.
This is the fallacy at the foundation of our political
structure. When we have a genuine democracy, we
shall not have the defective political machinery of the
present, but some method by which people will be able
not to accept or reject but to create group or whole ideas,
to produce a genuine collective will. Because we have
invented some governmental machinery by which clever
politicians can rule with the entirely artificial "assent"
of their constituencies, does not mean that we know anything about democracy.

It is the ignoring of the group which is retarding our
political development. A recent writer on political
science says that a study of the interaction between
individual and crowd is the basis of politics, and that
"the will of nations or states is the sum of individual
wills fashioned in accordance with crowd psychology."
In so far as this is true it is to be steadily opposed. Many
writers imply that we must either believe in homogeneity, similarity, uniformity (the herd, the crowd), or lose
the advantages of fellowship in order to discover and
assert our own particularistic ideals. But our alterna-
tives are not the individual and the crowd: the choice
is not between particularism with all its separatist tendencies, and the crowd with its levelling, its mediocrity,
its sameness, perhaps even its hysteria; there is the
neglected group. Democracy will not succeed until

assemblages of people are governed consciously and deliberately by group laws. We read, "No idea can conquer until a crowd has inscribed it on its banner." I
should say, "No idea can finally conquer which has not
been created by those people who inscribe it on their
banner." The triumph of ideas will never come by
crowds. Union, not hypnotism, is the law of development. There can be no real spiritual unity in the mass
life, only in the group life.

Whether the people of America shall be a crowd, under
the laws of suggestion and imitation, or follow the laws
of the group, is the underlying problem of to-day.

The promise for the future is that there now is in
associations of men an increasing tendency for the laws
of the group rather than the laws of the crowd to govern.
Our most essential duty to the future is to see that that
tendency prevail. As we increase the conscious functioning of the group we shall inevitably have less and
less of the unconscious response, chauvinists will lose
their job, and party bosses will have to change their
tactics. People as a matter of fact are not as suggestible as formerly. Men are reading more widely and they
are following less blindly what they read.

This largely increased reading, due to reduction in
price, spread of railroads, rural delivery, and lessening
hours of industry, is often spoken of as making men more
alike in their views. Tarde spoke of the "public," which
he defined as the people sitting at home reading newspapers, as a mental collectivity because of this supposed
tendency. Christensen confirms this when he says that
the people reading the newspapers are "a scattered
crowd." The usually accepted opinion is that the daily
press is making us more and more into crowds, but that
is not my experience. A man with his daily paper may
be obeying the group law or the crowd law as he unites

his own thoughts with the thoughts of others or as he is merely amenable to suggestion from others, and it seems to me we see a good deal of the former process. The newspaper brings home to us vividly what others are feeling and thinking. It offers many suggestions; we see less and less tendency to "swallow these whole," the colloquial counterpart of the technical "imitation." These suggestions are freely criticized, readers do a good deal of thinking and the results are fairly rational. The reader more and more I believe is selecting, is unifying difference. The result of all this is that men's minds are becoming more plastic, that they are deciding less by prejudice and hypnotism and more by judgment. And it must be remembered that a man is not necessarily a more developed person because he rejects his newspaper's theories than if he accepts them; the developed man is the group man and the group man neither accepts nor rejects, but joins his own thought with that of all he reads to make new thought. The group man is never sterile, he always brings forth.[1]

Democracy can never mean the domination of the crowd. The helter-skelter strivings of an endless number of social atoms can never give us a fair and ordered world. It may be true that we have lived under the domination either of individuals or of crowds up to the present time, but now is the moment when this must be deliberately challenged. The party boss must go, the

[1] Other results of the increased reading of newspapers and magazines are that large questions are driving out trivial interests (I find this very marked in the country), and the enormous amount of publicity now given everything finds a channel to the public through the press. The reports of commissions, like the Industrial Relations Commission, the surveys, like the Pittsburgh Survey, the reports of foundations, like the Russell Sage, the reports of the rapidly increasing bureaus of research, like the New York Municipal Bureau, all find their way to us through the columns of our daily or weekly or monthly. Therefore we have more material on which to found individual thinking.

wise men chosen by the reform associations must go, the crowd must be abandoned. The idea of the All has gripped us — but the idea has not been made workable, we have yet to find the way. We have said, "The people must rule." We now ask, "How are they to rule?" It is the technique of democracy which we are seeking. We shall find it in group organization.

XIX

DEMOCRACY is the rule of an interacting, inter-permeating whole. The present advocates of democracy have, therefore, little kinship with those ardent writers of the past who when they said they believed in the people were thinking of working-men only. A man said to me once, "I am very democratic, I thoroughly enjoy a good talk with a working-man." What in the world has that to do with democracy? Democracy is faith in humanity, not faith in "poor" people or "ignorant" people, but faith in every living soul. Democracy does not enthrone the working-man, it has nothing to do with sympathy for the "lower classes"; the champions of democracy are not looking down to raise any one up, they recognize that all men must face each other squarely with the knowledge that the give-and-take between them is to be equal.

The enthusiasts of democracy to-day are those who have caught sight of a great spiritual unity which is supported by the most vital trend in philosophical thought and by the latest biologists and social psychologists. It is, above all, what we have learnt of the psychical processes of association which makes us believe in democracy. Democracy is every one building the single life, not my life and others, not the individual and the state, but my life bound up with others, the individual which *is* the state, the state which *is* the individual. "When a man's eye shall be single" — do we quite know yet what that means? Democracy is the fullest possible acceptance of the single life.

Thus democracy, although often considered a centrifugal tendency, is rather a centripetal force. Democracy is not a spreading out: it is not the extension of the suffrage — its merely external aspect — it is a drawing together; it is the imperative call for the lacking parts of self. It is the finding of the one will to which the will of every single man and woman must contribute. We want women to vote not that the suffrage may be extended to women but that women may be included in the suffrage: we want what they may have to add to the whole. Democracy is an infinitely including spirit. We have an instinct for democracy because we have an instinct for wholeness; we get wholeness only through reciprocal relations, through infinitely expanding reciprocal relations. Democracy is really neither extending nor including merely, but creating wholes.

This is the primitive urge of all life. This is the true nature of man. Democracy must find a form of government that is suited to the nature of man and which will express that nature in its manifold relations. Or rather democracy is the self-creating process of life appearing as the true nature of man, and through the activity of man projecting itself into the visible world in fitting form so that its essential oneness will declare itself. Democracy then is not an end, we must be weaving all the time the web of democracy.

The idea of democracy as representing the all-will gives us a new idea of aristocracy. We believe in the few but not as opposed to the many, only as included in all. This makes a tremendous change in political thought. We believe in the influence of the good and the wise, but they must exert their influence within the social process; it must be by action and reaction, it must be by a subtle permeation, it must be through the sporting instinct to take back the ball which one has thrown. The wise can never help us by standing on one side and trying to get their wisdom across to the unwise. The unwise can never help us (what has often been considered the most they could do for the world) by a passive willingness for the wise to impose their wisdom upon them. We need the intermingling of all in the social process. We need our imperfections as well as our perfections. So we offer what we have — our unwisdom, our imperfections — on the altar of the social process, and it is only by this social process that the wonderful transmutation can take place which makes of them the very stuff of which the Perfect Society is to be made. Imperfection meets imperfection, or imperfection meets perfection; it is the *process* which purifies, not the "influence" of the perfect on the imperfect. This is what faith in democracy means. Moreover, there is the ignorance of the ignorant and the ignorance of the wise; there is the wisdom of the wise and the wisdom of the ignorant. Both kinds of ignorance have to be overcome, one as much as the other; both kinds of wisdom have to prevail, one as much as the other.

In short, there is not a static world for the wise to influence. This truth is the blow to the old aristocracy. But we need the wise within this living, moving whole, this never-ceasing action and interaction, and this truth is the basis of our new conception of aristocracy. Democracy is not opposed to aristocracy — it includes aristocracy.

As biology shows us nature evolving by the power within itself, so social psychology shows us society evolving by the power of its own inner forces, of *all* its inner forces. There is no passive material within it to be guided by a few. There is no dead material in a true democracy.

When people see the confusion of our present life, its

formlessness and planlessness, the servile following of
the crowd, the ignorance of the average man, his satisfaction in his ignorance, the insignificance of the collective life, its blindness and its hopelessness, they say
they do not believe in democracy. But this is not democracy. The so-called evils of democracy — favoritism,
bribery, graft, bossism — are the evils of our lack of
democracy, of our party system and of the abuses which
that system has brought into our representative government. It is not democracy which is "on trial," as is so
often said, but it is we ourselves who are on trial. We
have been constantly trying to see what democracy
meant from the point of view of institutions, we have
never yet tried to see what it meant from the point of
view of men.

If life could be made mechanical, our method would be
correct, but as mechanics is creature and life its super-
abounding creator, such method is wholly wrong. When
people say that the cure for the evils of democracy is
more democracy, they usually mean that while we have
some "popular" institutions, we have not enough, and
that when we get enough "popular" institutions, our
inadequacies will be met. But no form is going to fulfil
our needs. This is important to remember just now,
with all the agitation for "democratic control." You
cannot establish democratic control by legislation: it
is not democratic control to allow the people to assent
to or refuse a war decided on by diplomats; there is only
one way to get democratic control — by people learning
how to evolve collective ideas. The essence of democracy is not in institutions, is not even in "brotherhood";
it is in that organizing of men which makes most sure,
most perfect, the bringing forth of the common idea.
Democracy has one task only — to free the creative spirit
of man. This is done through group organization. We

are sometimes told that democracy is an attitude and must grow up in the hearts of men. But this is not enough. Democracy is a method, a scientific technique of evolving the will of the people. For this reason the study of group psychology is a necessary preliminary to the study of democracy. Neither party bosses nor unscrupulous capitalists are our undoing, but our own lack of knowing how to do things together.

The startling truth that the war is bringing home to many of us is that unity must be something more than a sentiment, it must be an actual system of organization. We are now beginning to see that if you want the fruits of unity, you must *have* unity, a real unity, a coöperative collectivism. Unity is neither a sentiment nor an intellectual conception, it is a psychological process produced by actual psychic interaction.

How shall we gain a practical understanding of this essential unity of man? By practising it with the first person we meet; by approaching every man with the consciousness of the complexity of his needs, of the vastness of his powers. Much is written of the power of history and tradition in giving unity to a community or nation. This has been overemphasized. If this were the only way of getting unity, there would be little hope for the future in America, where we have to make a unity of people with widely differing traditions, and little hope for the future in Europe where peace is unthinkable unless the past can be forgotten and new ties made on the basis of mutual understanding and mutual obligation. To have democracy we must live it day by day. Democracy is the actual commingling of men in order that each shall have continuous access to the needs and the wants of others. Democracy is not a form of government; the democratic soul is born within the group and then it develops its own forms.

Democracy then is a great spiritual force evolving itself from men, utilizing each, completing his incompleteness by weaving together all in the many-membered community life which is the true Theophany. The world to-day is growing more spiritual, and I say this not in spite of the Great War, but because of all this war has shown us of the inner forces bursting forth in fuller and fuller expression. The Great War has been the Great Call to humanity and humanity is answering. It is breaking down the ramparts to free the way for the entrance of a larger spirit which is to fill every single being by interflowing between them all. France, England, America — how the beacon lights flash from one to the other — the program of the British Labor Party, the speeches of our American President, the news of the indomitable courage of France — these are like the fires in Europe on St. John's Eve, which flash their signals from hill-top to hill-top. Even the school children of France and America write letters to each other. American men and women are working for the reconstruction of France as they would work for the reconstruction of their own homes — and all this because we are all sharing the same hope. A new faith is in our hearts. The Great War is the herald of another world for men. The coming of democracy is the spiritual rebirth. We have been told that our physical birth and life are not all, that we are to be born again of water and the spirit. Not indeed of *water* and spirit, but of *blood* and spirit, are the warring children of men, a groaning, growing humanity, coming to the Great Rebirth.

XX

THE two problems of democracy to-day are: (1) how to make the individual politically effective, and (2) how to give practical force to social policies. Both of these mean that the individual is at last recognized in political life. The history of democracy has been the history of the steady growth towards individualism. The hope of democracy rests on the individual. It is all one whether we say that democracy is the development of the social consciousness, or that democracy is the development of individualism; until we have become in some degree socially conscious we shall not realize the value of the individual. It is not insignificant that a marked increase in the appreciation of social values has gone hand in hand with a growing recognition of the individual.

From the Middle Ages the appreciation of the individual has steadily grown. The Reformation in the sixteenth century was an individualistic movement. The apotheosis of the individual, however, soon led us astray, involving as it did an entirely erroneous notion of the relation of the individual to society, and gave us the false political philosophy of the seventeenth and eighteenth centuries. Men thought of individuals as separate and then had to invent fictions to join them, hence the social contract fiction. The social contract theory was based on the idea of the state as an aggregate of units; it therefore followed that the rights of those units must be maintained. Thus individual rights became a kind of contractual rights. And during the nineteenth century, fostered by Bentham's ideas of individual happiness, by the *laissez-faire* of the Manchester school and the new industrial order, by Herbert Spencer's interpretations of the recent additions to biological knowledge, by Mill, etc., the doctrine of "individual rights" became more firmly entrenched. Government interference was strenuously resisted, "individual" freedom was the goal of our desire, "individual" competition and the survival of the fittest the accredited method of progress. The title of Herbert Spencer's book, "The Man versus the State," implies the whole of this false political philosophy built on an unrelated individual.

But during the latter part of the nineteenth century there began to grow up, largely at first through the influence of T. H. Green, influenced in his turn by Kant and Hegel, an entirely different theory of the state. The state was now not to be subordinate to the individual, but it was to be the fulfilment of the individual. Man was to get his rights and his liberty from membership in society. Green had at once a large influence on the political thought of England and America, and gradually, with other influences, upon practical politics. The growing recognition of the right and duty of the state to foster the life of its members, so clearly and unequivocally expressed in the social legislation of Lloyd George, we see as early as the Education Act of 1870, the Factory Act of 1878 (which systematized and extended previous Factory Acts), and the various mines and collieries acts from 1872.

I do not mean to imply that the growing activity of the state was due entirely or mainly to the change of theory in regard to the individual and the state; when the disastrous results of *laissez-faire* were seen, then people demanded state regulation of industry. Theory and practice have acted and reacted on each other. Some one must trace for us, step by step, the interaction of theory

and practice in regard to the individual and his relation
to society, from the Middle Ages down to the present day.[1]

What has been the trend of our development in America? Particularism was at its zenith when our government was founded. Our growth has been away from
particularism and towards a true individualism.[2]

It is usual to say that the framers of our constitution
were individualists and gave to our government an individualistic turn. We must examine this. They did safeguard and protect the individual in his life and property,
they did make the bills of rights an authoritative part
of our constitutions, they did make it possible for individuals to aggrandize themselves at the expense of society, their ideal of justice was indeed of individual not
of social justice. And yet all this was negative. The
individual was given no large positive function. The
individual was feared and suspected. Our early constitutions showed no faith in men: the Massachusetts
constitution expressly stated that it was not a government of men. The law of the land was embodied in
written documents with great difficulty of amendment
just because the people were not trusted. As we look at
the crudities of the Declaration of Independence, as we
examine our aristocratic state constitutions, as we study
our restricted federal constitution, as we read the bor-
rowed philosophy of our early statesmen, we see very
little indication of modern democracy with its splendid
faith in man, but a tendency towards aristocracy and a
lack of real individualism on every side.

To be sure it was at the same time true that the government was given no positive power. Every one was

---

[1] Also the development of the relation of individualistic theories to
the rise and decline of the doctrines regarding the national state.

[2] I do not wish, however, to minimize the truly democratic nature of
our local institutions.

thoroughly frightened of governments which were founded on status and resulted in arbitrary authority. The executive power was feared, therefore it was so equipped as to be unequal to its task; the legislative power was feared, so the courts were given power over the legislatures, were allowed to declare their acts valid or invalid; the national government was feared, therefore Congress was given only certain powers. Power was not granted because no man and no institution was trusted. The will to act could not be a motive force in 1789, because no embodiment of the will was trusted; the framers of our constitutions could not conceive of a kind of will which could be trusted. Fear, not faith, suspicion not trust, were the foundation of our early government. The government had, therefore, no large formative function, it did not look upon itself as a large social power. As the individual was to be protected, the government was to protect. All our thinking in the latter part of the eighteenth century was rooted in the idea of a weak government; this has been thought to show our individualism.[1]

But our government as imagined by its founders did not work.[2] Our system of checks and balances gave no

[1] While it is true that there were undemocratic elements in the mental equipment and psychological bent of our forefathers, and it is these which I have emphasized because from them came our immediate development, it is equally true that there were also sound democratic elements to which we can trace our present ideas of democracy. Such tracing even in briefest form there is not space for here.

[2] It became at once evident that a government whose chief function was to see that individual rights, property rights, state rights, were not invaded, was hardly adequate to unite our colonies with all their separatist instincts, or to meet the needs of a rapidly developing continent. Our national government at once adopted a constructive policy. Guided by Hamilton it assumed constructive powers authority for which could be found in the constitution only by a most liberal construction of its terms. When Jefferson, an antinationalist, acquired Louisiana in 1803, it seemed plain that no such restricted national government as was at first conceived could possibly work.

real power to any department. Above all there was no way of fixing responsibility. A condition of chaos was the result. Such complicated machinery was almost unworkable; there was no way of getting anything done under our official system. Moreover, the individual was not satisfied with his function of being protected, he wanted an actual share in the government. Therefore an extra-official system was adopted, the party organization. The two chief reasons for this adoption were: (1) to give the individual some share in government, (2) to give the government a chance to carry out definite policies, to provide some kind of a unifying power.

What effect has party organization had on the individual and on government? The domination of the party gives no real opportunity to the individual: originality is crushed; the aim of all party organization is to turn out a well-running voting machine. The party is not interested in men but in voters — an entirely different matter. Party organization created artificial majorities, but gave to the individual little power in or connection with government. The basic weakness of party organization is that the individual gets his significance only through majorities. Any method which looks to the fulfilment of the individual through the domination of majorities is necessarily not only partial but false. The present demand that the nation shall have the full power of the individual is the heaviest blow that party organization has ever received.

Now consider, on the other hand, what party organization has done for the government. The powers of government moved steadily to political bosses and business corporations. Boss-rule, party domination and combinations of capital filled in the gaps in the system of government we inaugurated in the eighteenth century. The marriage of business and politics, while it has been the chief factor in entrenching the party system, was the outcome of that system, or rather it was the outcome of the various unworkabilities of our official government. The expansion of big business, with its control of politics, evasion of law, was inevitable; we simply had no machinery adequate to our need, namely, the development of a vast, untouched continent. The urge of that development was an overwhelming force which swept irresistibly on, carrying everything before it, swallowing up legal disability, creating for itself extra-legal methods. We have now, therefore, a system of party organization and political practice which subverts all our theories. Theoretically the people have the power, but really the government is the primaries, the conventions, the caucuses. Officials hold from the party. Party politics became corrupt because party government was irresponsible government. The insidious power of the machine is due to its irresponsibility.

The evils of our big business have not come because Americans are prone to cheat, because they want to get the better of their fellows, because their greed is inordinate, their ambition domineering. Individuals have not been to blame, but our whole system. It is the system which must be changed. Our constitutions and laws made possible the development of big business; our courts were not "bought" by big business, but legal decision and business practice were formed by the same inheritance and tradition. The reformation of neither will accomplish the results we wish, but the nation-wide acceptance, through all classes and all interests, of a different point of view.

The next step was the wave of reform that swept over the country. The motive was excellent; the method poor. The method was poor because the same method was adopted which these reform movements were organized to fight, one based on pure crowd philosophy. It was a curious case of astigmatism. The trouble was that the reformers did not see accurately what they were fighting; they were fighting essentially the non-recognition of the individual, but they did not see this, so they went on basing all their own work on the non-appreciation of men. Their essential weakness was the weakness of the party machine—all their efforts were turned to the voter not the man. Their triumphs were always the triumphs of the polls. Their methods were principally three: change in the forms of government (charters, etc.), the nomination of "good" men to office, and exhortation to induce "the people" to elect them.

The idea of "good" men in office was the fetich of many reform associations. They thought that their job was to find three or four "good" men and then once a year to hypnotize the electorate to "do their duty" and put these men into office, and then all would go well if before another year three or four more good men could be found. What a futile and childish idea which leaves out of account the whole body of citizenship! It is only through this main body of citizenship that we can have a decent government and a sound social life. That is, in other words, it is only by a genuine appreciation of the individual, of every single individual, that there can be any reform movement with strength and constructive power. The wide-spread fallacy that good officials make a good city is one which lies at the root of much of our thinking and insidiously works to ruin our best plans, our most serious efforts. This extraordinary belief in officials, this faith in the panacea of a change of charters, must go. If our present mechanical government is to turn into a living, breathing, pulsing life, it must be composed of an entire citizenship educated and responsible.

This the reform associations now recognize, in some cases partially, in some cases fully. The good government association of to-day has a truer idea of its function. The campaign for the election of city officials is used as a means of educating the mass of citizens: besides the investigation and publication of facts, there is often a clear showing of the aims of government and an enlightening discussion of method. Such associations have always considered the interests of the city as a whole; they have not appealed, like the party organizations, to local sentiment.

I have spoken of the relation of the reform movement of the last of the nineteenth century to the body of citizenship. What was its relation to government? The same spirit applied to government meant patching, mending, restraining, but it did not mean constructive work, it had not a formative effect on our institutions. Against any institution that has to be guarded every moment lest it do evil, there is a strong a priori argument that it should not exist. This until recently has not been sufficiently taken into account. Now, however, in the beginning of the twentieth century, we see many evidences that the old era of restraint is over and the constructive period of reform begun. We see it, for instance, in our Bureaus of Municipal Research; we see it in the more progressive sections of our state constitutional conventions. But the chief error of the nineteenth-century reformers was not that they were reactionary, nor that they were timid, nor that they were insincere, nor that they were hedgers. They were wanting in neither sincerity nor courage. Their error was simply that they did not appreciate the value of the individual. Individualism instead of being something we are getting away from, is something we are just catching sight of.

And if our institutions were founded on a false political philosophy which taught "individual rights," distorted ideas of liberty and equality, and thought of man versus the state, if our political development was influenced by a false social psychology which saw the people as a crowd and gave them first to the party bosses and next to the social reformers, our whole material development was dominated by a false economic philosophy which saw the greatest good of all obtained by each following his own good in his own way. This did not mean the development of individuals but the crushing of individuals — of all but a few. The Manchester school of economics, which was bound to flourish extensively under American conditions, combined with a narrow legal point of view, which for a hundred years interpreted our constitutions in accordance with an antiquated philosophy and a false psychology, to make particularism the dominant note in American life.

The central point of our particularism was the idea of being let alone. First, the *individual* was to be let alone, the pioneer on his reclaimed land or the pioneer of industry. But when men saw that their gains would be greater by some sort of combination, then the *trusts* were to be let alone — freedom of contract was called liberty! Our courts, completely saturated with this philosophy, let the trusts alone. The interpretations of our courts, our corrupt party organization, our institutions and our social philosophy, hastened and entrenched the monopolistic age. Natural rights meant property rights. The power of single men or single corporations at the end of the nineteenth century marked the height of our particularism, of our subordination of the state to single members. They were like *pâté de foie gras* made by the enlargement of the goose's liver. It is usual to disregard the goose. The result of our false individualism has been non-conservation of our national resources, ex-

ploitation of labor, and political corruption. We see
the direct outcome in our slums, our unregulated industries, our "industrial unrest," etc.

But egotism, materialism, anarchy are not true individualism. To-day, however, we have many evidences
of the steadily increasing appreciation of the individual
and a true understanding of his place in society, his relation to the state. Chief among these are: (1) the movement towards industrial democracy, (2) the woman
movement, (3) the increase of direct government, and
(4) the introduction of social programs into party
platforms. These are parallel developments from the
same root. What we have awakened to now is the importance of every single man.

The first, the trend towards industrial democracy, will,
in its relation to the new state, be considered later. The
second, the woman movement, belongs to the past rather
than to the present. Its culmination has overrun the century mark and makes what is really a nineteenth-century
movement seem as if it belonged to the twentieth. It
belongs to the past because it is merely the end of the
movement for the extension of the suffrage. Our suffrage
rested originally in many states on property distinctions;
in New Hampshire there was a religious and property
qualification, — only Protestant tax-payers could vote.
Gradually it became manhood suffrage, then the immi-
grants were admitted, later the negroes, then Colorado
opened its suffrage to women, and now in thirteen states
women have the full suffrage. The essence of the woman
movement is not that women as women should have the
vote, but that women as individuals should have the
vote. There is a fundamental distinction here.

The third and fourth indications of the growth of
democracy, or the increase of individualism (I speak of
these always as synonymous) — the tendency towards

more and more direct government and the introduction
of social programs into party platforms — will be considered in the next chapter together with a third tendency
in American politics which is bound up with these two:
I refer to the increase of administrative responsibility.

The theory of government based on individual rights
no longer has a place in modern political theory; it no
longer guides us entirely in legislation but has yielded
largely to a truer practice; yet it still occupies a large
place in current thought, in the speeches of our practical
politicians, in our institutions of government, and in
America in our law court decisions. This being so it is
important for us to look for the reasons. First, there
are of course always many people who trail along behind. Secondly, partly through the influence of Green
and Bosanquet, the idea of contract has been slowly
fading away, and many people have been frightened at
its disappearance because Hegelianism, even in the modi-
fied form in which it appears in English theory, *seems* to
enthrone the state and override the individual.[1] Third,
the large influence which Tarde, Le Bon, and their followers have had upon us with their suggestion and imitation theories of society — theories based on a pure
particularism. The development of social and political
organization has been greatly retarded by this school
of sociology. Fourth, our economic development is still
associated in the minds of many with the theories of individual rights.

A more penetrating analysis of society during recent
years, however, has uncovered the true conception of individualism hidden from the first within the "individualistic" movement. All through history we see the feeling

[1] These English writers to whom our debt is so large are not responsible for this, but their misinterpreters.

out for the individual; there are all the false trails
followed and there are the real steps taken.   The false
trails led to the individual rights of politics, the *laissez-faire* of economics and our whole false particularism.
The real steps have culminated in our ideas of to-day.
To substitute for the fictitious democracy of equal rights
and "consent of the governed," the living democracy of
a united, responsible people is the task of the twentieth
century.   We seek now the method.

XXI

WE have outgrown our political system. We must face this frankly. We had, first, government by law,[1] second, government by parties and big business, and all the time some sort of fiction of the "consent of the governed" which we said meant democracy. But we have never had government by the people. The third step is to be the development of machinery by which the fundamental ideas of the people can be got at and embodied; further, by which we can grow fundamental ideas; further still, by which we can prepare the soil in which fundamental ideas can grow. Direct government will we hope lead to this step, but it cannot alone do this. How then shall it be supplemented ? Let us look at the movement for direct government with two others closely connected with it — the concentration of administrative responsibility and the increase of social legislation — three movements which are making an enormous change in American political life. Then let us see if we can discover what idea it is necessary to add to those involved in these three movements, in other words what new principle is needed in modern politics.

We are at present trying to secure (1) a more efficient government, and (2) a real not a nominal control of government by the people. The tendency to transfer power to the American citizenship, and the tendency towards efficient government by the employment of experts and

---

[1] With the executive and legislative limited in their powers, the decisions of the courts gradually came, especially as they developed constructive powers, to be a body of law which guided the American people.

174

the concentration of administrative authority, are working side by side in American political life to-day. These two tendencies are not opposed, and if the main thesis of this book has been proved, it is understood by this time why they are not opposed. Democracy I have said is not antithetical to aristocracy, but includes aristocracy. And it does not include it accidentally, as it were, but aristocracy is a necessary part of democracy. Therefore administrative responsibility and expert service are as necessary a part of genuine democracy as popular control is a necessary accompaniment of administrative responsibility. They are parallel in importance. Some writers seem to think that because we are giving so much power to our executives, we must safeguard our "liberty" by giving at the same time ultimate authority to the people. While this is of course so in a way, I believe a truer way of looking at the matter is to see centralized responsibility and popular control, not one dependent on the other, but both as part of the same thing — our new democracy.

Both our city and our state governments are being reorganized. We have long felt that city government should be concentrated in the hands of a few experts. The old idea that any honest citizen was fit for most public offices is rapidly disappearing. Over three hundred cities have adopted the commission form of government, and there is a growing movement for the city-manager plan. But at the same time we must have a participant electorate. We can see three stages in our thinking: (1) our early American democracy thought that public offices could be filled by the average citizen; (2) our reform associations thought that the salvation of our cities depended on expert officials; (3) present thinking sees the necessity of combining expert service and an active electorate.[1]

[1] For ways of doing this see Part III.

The increasing number of states which are holding, or are considering holding, constitutional conventions for the reconstruction of state governments shows the wide-spread dissatisfaction with our state machinery. The principal object of nearly all of these conventions is increased efficiency through concentration of responsibility. In our fear of abuse of power there has been no one to use power; we must change this if we are to have administrative efficiency. Most of the schemes for a reconstruction of state governments are based on (1) concentration of executive leadership in the hands of the governor, and (2) direct responsibility to the electorate. The former implies appointment of administrative officials by the governor, an executive budget, and readjustment in the relation of executive and legislative so that the governor can introduce and defend bills. The latter necessitates the ability of the electorate to criticize work done and plans proposed.

Therefore the tendency towards an effective responsibility through the increased power of our executive does not mean that less is required of citizens, but more. To the initiative, referendum and recall is to be added the general control by the people themselves of our state policies. Executive leadership may reduce the power of legislatures, but it will increase the power of the electorate both directly and indirectly: indirectly by weakening party organization, and directly by giving the people more and more control. It has been suggested, for instance, that in any dispute between governor and legislature the people might be called on to decide, either directly by passing on the proposed legislation itself, or by a new election. At any rate ultimate control must somehow be with the people. That this was not sufficiently provided for in the New York constitution submitted to the voters of New York a few years ago was one of the reasons for its rejection. What frightened the men of New York was undoubtedly the increased power of the state administrative without any corresponding increase in democratic control. To increase at the same time democratic control and administrative responsibility, while not an easy thing to do, is the task of our new constitutions.

With regard to direct government, we are at present making two mistakes: first, in thinking that we can get any benefit from it if it is operated from within the party organization;[1] secondly, in thinking that it is merely to record, that it is based on counting, on the preponderance of votes.

The question staring us in the face in American politics to-day is — What possible good can direct government do us if party organization remains in control? The movement for direct primaries, popular choice of United States senators, presidential primaries, initiative and referendum, the recall etc., will bear little fruit unless something is done at the same time to break the power of the party. Many people tell us that our present party system, with its method of caucuses, conventions, bosses etc., has failed, and they are now looking to the direct primary as their hope, but the direct primary in itself will not free us from the tyranny of party rule. Look at this much-lauded direct primary and see what it is actually giving us: the political machines have known from the beginning how to circumvent it, it often merely increases the power of the boss, and at its best it is accomplishing no integrating of the American people — the real task of democracy. No development of party machinery or reform of party machinery is going to give us the will of the people, only a new method.

[1] We used to think frequent elections democratic. Now we know that they mean simply an increase of party influence and a decrease of official responsibility.

Moreover, merely giving more power to the people does not automatically reduce the hold of the party; some positive measures must be taken if direct government is not to fail exactly as representative government has failed. The faith in direct government as a sure panacea is almost pathetic when we remember how in the past one stronghold after another has been captured by the party. Much has been written by advocates of direct government to show that it will destroy the arbitrary power of the party, destroy its relation to big business, etc., but we see little evidence of this. We all know, and we can see every year if we watch the history of referendum votes, that the party organization is quite able to use "direct government" for its own ends. Direct government worked by the machine will be subject to much the same abuses as representative government. And direct and representative government cannot be synthesized by executive leadership alone. All that is said in favor of the former may be true, but it can never be made operative unless we are able to find some way of breaking the power of the machine. Direct government can be beneficial to American politics only if accompanied by the organization of voters in non-partisan groups for the production of common ideas and a collective purpose. Of itself direct government can never become the responsible government of a people.

I have said that direct government will never succeed if operated from within the party organization, nor if it is considered, as it usually is, merely a method by which the people can accept or reject what is proposed to them. Let us now look at the second point. We have seen that party organization does not allow group methods, that the party is a crowd: suggestion by the boss, imitation by the mass, is the rule. But direct government also may and probably will be crowd government if it is merely a means of counting. As far as direct government can be given the technique of a genuine democracy, it is an advance step in political method, but the trouble is that many of its supporters do not see this necessity; they have given it their adherence because of their belief in majority rule, in their belief that to count one and one and one is to get at the will of the people. But for each to count as one means crowd rule — of course the party captures us. Yet even if it did not, we do not want direct government if we are to fall from party domination into the tyranny of numbers. That every man was to count as one was the contribution of the old psychology to politics; the new psychology goes deeper and further, — it teaches that each is to be the whole at one point. This changes our entire conception of politics. Voting at the polls is not to be the expression of one man after another. My vote should not be my freak will any more than it should be my adherence to party, but my individual expression of the common will. The particularist vote does not represent the individual will because the evolution of the individual will is bound up in a larger evolution. Therefore, *my duty as a citizen is not exhausted by what I bring to the state; my test as a citizen is how fully the whole can be expressed in or through me.*

The vote in itself does not give us democracy — we have yet to learn democracy's method. We still think too much of the solidarity of the vote; what we need is solidarity of purpose, solidarity of will. To make my vote a genuine part of the expression of the collective will is the first purpose of politics; it is only through group organization that the individual learns this lesson, that he learns to be an effective political member. People often ask, "Why is democracy so unprogressive?" It is just because we have not democracy in this sense. As long as the vote is that of isolated individuals, the tendency will be for us to have an unprogressive vote. This state of things can be remedied, first, by a different system of education, secondly, by giving men opportunities to exercise that fundamental intermingling with others which is democracy. To the consideration of how this can be accomplished Part III is mainly directed.

But I am making no proposal for some hard and fast method by which every vote shall register the will of a definite, fixed number of men rather than of one man. I am talking of a new method of living *by* which the individual shall learn to be part of social wholes, *through* which he shall express social wholes. The individual not the group must be the basis of organization. But the individual is created by many groups, his vote cannot express his relation to one group; it must ideally, I have said, express the whole from his point of view, actually it must express as much of the whole as the variety of his group life makes possible.[1]

When shall we begin to understand what the ballot-box means in our political life? *It creates nothing* — it merely registers what is already created. If direct government is to be more than ballot-box democracy it must learn not to record what is on the surface, but to dig down underneath the surface. No "democracy" which is based on a preponderance of votes can ever succeed. The essence of democracy is an educated and responsible citizenship evolving common ideas and *willing* its own social life. The dynamic thought is the thought which represents the most complete synthesis. In art the influence of a school does not depend upon the number of its adherents, but upon the extent to which that school represents a synthesis of thought. This is exactly so in

[1] See ch. XXX, "Political Pluralism and Functionalism."

politics. Direct government must create. It can do this through group organization. We are at the cross-roads now: shall we give the initiative and referendum to a crowd or to an interpenetrating group?

To sum up: the corruption of politics is due largely to the conception of the people as a crowd. To change this idea is, I believe, the first step in the reform of our political life. Unless this is done before we make sweeping changes in the mechanism of government, such changes will not mean progress. If the people are a crowd capable of nothing but imitation, what is the use of all the direct government we are trying to bring about, how can a "crowd" be considered capable of political decisions? Direct government gives to every one the right to express his opinion. The question is whether that opinion is to be his particularist opinion or the imitation of the crowd or the creation of the group. The party has dominated us in the past chiefly because we have truly believed the people to be a crowd. When we understand the law of association as the law of psychic interplay, then indeed shall we be on the way towards the New Democracy.

Direct government will not succeed if it is operated through the party organization; it will not succeed even if separated from party control if it means the crowd in another guise. To be successful direct government must be controlled by some method not yet brought into practical politics. When we have an organized electorate, we shall begin to see the advantages of direct government.

At the beginning of this chapter three closely related movements in American politics were mentioned. The third must now be considered — the introduction of social programs into party platforms.

We have had three policies in legislation: (1) the

let-alone policy,[1] (2) the regulation policy, and now (3) the constructive policy is just appearing.

In order to get away from the consequences of *laissez-faire*, we adopted, at the end of the nineteenth century, an almost equally pernicious one, the regulation theory. The error at the bottom of the "regulation" idea of government is that people may be allowed to do as they please (*laissez-faire*) until they have built up special rules and privileges for themselves, and then they shall be "regulated." The regulation theory of government is that we are to give every opportunity for efficiency to come to the top in order that we shall get the benefit of that efficiency, but at the same time our governmental machinery is to be such that efficiency is to be shorn of its power before it can do any harm — a sort of automatic blow-off. Gauge your boiler (society) at what it will stand without bursting, then when our ablest people get to that point the blow-off will make society safe.

But the most salient thing about present American politics is that we are giving up both our let-alone and our regulation policies in favor of a constructive policy. There has been a steady and comprehensible growth of democracy from this point of view, that is, of the idea of the function of government being not merely to protect, to adjust, to restrain, and all the negative rest of it, but that the function of government should be to build, to construct the life of its people. We think now that a constructive social policy is more democratic than the protection of men in their individual rights and property. In 1800 the opposite idea prevailed, and Jefferson, not Hamilton, was considered the Democrat. We must reinterpret or restate the fundamental principles of democracy.

[1] *Laissez-faire* was popular when there were great numbers of individual producers. When the large-scale business system made wage-earners of these, there was the beginning of the break-down of *laissez-faire*.

But why do we consider our present constructive social policies more democratic? Are they necessarily so? Has not paternalistic Germany constructive social policies for her people? Social legislation in England and America means an increase of democracy because it is a movement which is in England and America bound up with other democratic movements.[1] In America we see at the same time the trend towards (1) an increase of administrative responsibility, (2) an increase of direct control by the people, (3) an increase of social legislation. Not one of these is independent of the other two. They have acted and reacted on one another. Men have not first been given a more direct share in government and then used their increased power to adopt social policies. The two have gone on side by side. Moreover, the adoption of social policies has increased the powers of government and, therefore, it has more and more come to be seen that popular control of government is necessary. At the same time the making of campaign issues out of social policies has at once in itself made all the people more important in politics. Or it is equally true to say that giving the people a closer share in government means that our daily lives pass more naturally into the area of politics. Hence we see, from whichever point we begin, that these three movements are bound together.

Thus in America there is growing recognition of the fact that social policies are not policies invented for the good of the people, but policies created by the people. The regulation theory was based on the same fallacy as the let-alone theory, namely, that government is something external to the structural life of the people. Government cannot leave us alone, it cannot regulate us, it can only express us. The scope of politics should be our whole social life. Our present idea of an omnipres-

---

[1] Besides the more obvious one of "universal suffrage."

ent, ever-active, articulate citizenship building up its own
life within the frame of politics is the most fruitful idea
of modern times.

Moreover, social legislation is an indication of the
growth of democracy, the increase of individualism,
because it is legislation for the individual. We have
had legislation to protect home industries, we have encouraged agriculture, we have helped the railroads by
concessions and land grants, but we have not until
recently had legislation for the individual. Social legislation means legislation for the individual man: health
laws, shorter hours of work, workmen's compensation,
old age pensions, minimum wage, prevention of industrial
accidents, prohibition of child labor, etc. Over and over
again our social legislation is pointed to as a reaction
against individualism. On the contrary it shows an
increase of genuine individualism. The *individual* has
never been so appreciated as in the awakening *social*
world of to-day.

This is not a contradiction of what is said in chapter
XV, that law according to its most progressive exponents
is to serve not individuals, but the community; that
modern law thinks of men not as separate individuals,
but in their relation to one another. Modern law synthesizes the idea of individual and community through
its view of the social individual as the community-unit.
Law used to be for the particularist individual; now it
serves the community, but the community-unit is the
social individual.

In our most recent books we see the expression
" the new individualism." The meaning of this phrase,
although never used by him, is clearly implied in the
writings of Mr. Roscoe Pound. He says " As a social
institution the interests with which law is concerned are
social interests, but the chiefest of these social interests

is one in the full human life of the individual." Here is expressed the essential meaning of the new individualism —that it is a synthesis of individual and society. That the social individual, the community-unit, is becoming " the individual " for law is the most promising sign for the future of political method. When Mr. Pound says that the line between public law and private law in jurisprudence is nothing more than a convenient mode of expression, he shows us the old controversy in regard to the state and the individual simply fading away.

Social legislation, direct government, concentration of administrative responsibility, are then indications of the growth of democracy? Yes, but only indications. They can mean an actual increase of democracy only if they are accompanied by the development of those methods which shall make every man and his daily needs the basis and the substance of politics.

XXII

NEIGHBORHOOD NEEDS THE BASIS OF POLITICS

POLITICS are changing in character: shall the change be without plan or method, or is this the guiding moment?

We are at a critical hour in our history. We have long thought of politics as entirely outside our daily life manipulated by those set apart for the purpose. The methods by which the party platform is constructed are not those which put into it the real issues before the public; the tendency is to put in what will elect candidates or to cover up the real issues by generalities. But just so long as we separate politics and our daily life, just so long shall we have all our present evils. Politics can no longer be an extra-activity of the American people, they must be a means of satisfying our actual wants.

We are now beginning to recognize more and more clearly that the work we do, the conditions of that work, the houses in which we live, the water we drink, the food we eat, the opportunities for bringing up our children, that in fact the whole area of our daily life should constitute politics. There is no line where the life of the home ends and the life of the city begins. There is no wall between my private life and my public life. A man I know tells me that he "wouldn't touch politics with a ten-foot pole," but how can he help touching politics? He may not like the party game, but politics shape the life he leads from hour to hour. When this is once understood no question in history will seem more astonishing than the one so often reiterated in these days, "Should woman be given a place in politics?" Woman *is* in politics; no power under the sun can put her out.

Politics then must satisfy the needs of the people. What are the needs of the people? Nobody knows. We know the supposed needs of certain classes, of certain "interests"; these can never be woven into the needs of the people. Further back we must go, down into the ˙actual life from which all these needs spring, down into the daily, hourly living with all its innumerable cross currents, with all its longings and heart-burnings, with its envies and jealousies perhaps, with its unsatisfied desires, its embryonic aspirations, and its power, manifest or latent, for endeavor and accomplishment. The needs of the people are not now articulate: they loom out of the darkness, vague, big, portentously big, but dumb because of the separation of men. To open up this hinterland of our life the cross currents now burrowing under ground must come to the surface and be openly acknowledged.

We work, we spend most of our waking hours working for some one of whose life we know nothing, who knows nothing of us; we pay rent to a landlord whom we never see or see only once a month, and yet our home is our most precious possession; we have a doctor who is with us in the crucial moments of birth and death, but whom we ordinarily do not meet; we buy our food, our clothes, our fuel, of automatons for the selling of food, clothes and fuel. We know all these people in their occupational capacity, not as men like ourselves with hearts like ours, desires like ours, hopes like ours. And this isolation from those who minister to our lives, to whose lives we minister, does not bring us any nearer to our neighbors in their isolation. For every two or three of us think our-

selves a little better than every other two or three, and
this becomes a dead wall of separation, of misunderstanding, of antagonism. How can we do away with
this artificial separation which is the dry-rot of our life?
First we must realize that each has something to give.
Every man comes to us with a golden gift in his heart.
Do we dare, therefore, avoid any man? If I stay by
myself on my little self-made pedestal, I narrow myself
down to my own personal equation of error. If I go to
all my neighbors, my own life increases in multiple measure. The aim of each of us should be to live in the lives
of all. Those fringes which connect my life with the life
of every other human being in the world are the inlets
by which the central forces flow into me. I am a worse
lawyer, a worse teacher, a worse doctor if I do not know
these wider contacts. Let us seek then those bonds
which unite us with every other life. Then do we find
reality, only in union, never in isolation.

But it must be a significant union, never a mere coming together. How we waste immeasurable force in
much of our social life in a mere tossing of the ball, on
the merest externality and travesty of a common life
which we do not penetrate for the secret at its heart. The
quest of life and the meaning of life is reality. We may
flit on the surface as gnats in the sunlight, but in each
of us, however overlaid, is the hunger and thirst for
realness, for substance. We must plunge down to find
our treasure. The core of a worthy associated life is the
call of reality to reality, the calling and answering and
the bringing it forth from the depths forever more and
more. To go to meet our fellows is to go out and let
the winds of Heaven blow upon us — we throw ourselves
open to every breath and current which spring from
this meeting of life's vital forces.

Some of us are looking for the remedy for our fatal

isolation in a worthy and purposeful neighborhood life.
Our proposal is that people should organize themselves
into neighborhood groups to express their daily life, to
bring to the surface the needs, desires and aspirations of
that life, that these needs should become the substance
of politics, and that these neighborhood groups should
become the recognized political unit.

Let us consider some of the advantages of the neighborhood group. First, it makes possible the association
of neighbors, which means fuller acquaintance and a
more real understanding. The task of creation from
elektrons up is putting self in relation. Is man the only
one who refuses this task? I do not know my next-door
neighbor! One of the most unfortunate circumstances
of our large towns is that we expect concerted action
from people who are strangers to one another. So mere
acquaintance is the first essential. This will lead inevitably to friendly feeling. The story is told of some American official who begged not to be introduced to a political
enemy, for he said he could not hate any one with whom
he became acquainted. We certainly do feel more kindly
to the people we actually see. It is what has been called
"the pungent sense of effective reality." Neighborhood
organization will substitute confidence for suspicion — a
great gain.

Moreover, neighborhood organization gives opportunity for constant and regular intercourse. We are
indeed far more interested in humanity than ever before.
Look at what we are studying: social psychology, social
economics, social medicine and hygiene, social ethics
etc. But people must socialize their lives by practice,
not by study. Until we begin to acquire the habit of a
social life no theory of a social life will do us any good.
It is a mistake to think that such abstractions as unity,
brotherhood etc. are as self-evident to our wills as to

our intellect. I learn my duty to my friends not by
reading essays on friendship, but by living my life with
my friends and learning by experience the obligations
friendship demands. Just so must I learn my relation
to society by coming into contact with a wide range of
experiences, of people, by cultivating and deepening
my sympathy and whole understanding of life.

When we have come together and got acquainted with
one another, then we shall have an opportunity for
learning the rules of the game — the game of association which is the game of life. Certain organizations
have sprung up since 1914 with the avowed object of
fighting war with love. If only we knew how to love!
I am ready to say to you this minute, "I love my neighbors." But all that I mean by it is that I have a vague
feeling of kindliness towards them. I have no idea
how to do the actual deed. I shall offend against the
law of love within an hour. The love of our fellow-men
to be effective must be the love evolved from some actual
group relation. We talk of fellowship; we, puny separa-
tists bristling with a thousand unharmonized traits, with
our assertive particularist consciousness, think that all
we have to do is to *decide* on fellowship as a delightful
idea. But fellowship will be the slowest thing on earth
to create. An eager longing for it may help, but it can
come into being as a genuine part of our life only through
a deep understanding of what it really means.

Yet association is the impulse at the core of our being.
The whole social process is that of association, individual
with individual, group with group. Progress from one
point of view is a continuously widening of the area of
association. Our modern civilization has simply overlaid and falsified this primary instinct of life. But this
is rapidly changing. The most striking characteristic
of the present day is that people are doing more things

together: they are coming together as never before in labor organizations, in coöperative societies, in consumers' leagues, in associations of employers and employed, in municipal movements, for national purposes, etc. etc. We have the Men's City Club, the Women's City Club; professional societies are multiplying over night. The explanation sometimes given for this present tendency towards union is that we are beginning to see the material advantages of coöperation, but the root of the thing is far from utilitarian advantage. Our happiness, our sense of living at all, is directly dependent on our joining with others. We are lost, exiled, imprisoned until we feel the joy of union.

I believe that the realization of oneness which will come to us with a fuller sense of democracy, with a deeper sense of our common life, is going to be the substitute for what men now get in war. Some psychologists tell us that fighting is one of the fundamental instincts, and that if we do not have war we shall have all the dangers of thwarted instinct. But the lure of war is neither the instinct of hate nor the love of fighting; it is the joining of one with another in a common purpose. "And the heart of a people beat with one desire." Many men have gone joyfully to war because it gave them fellowship. I said to some one that I thought the reason war was still popular in spite of all its horrors was because of our lack of imagination, we simply could not realize war. "No," said the man I spoke to, "I know war, I know its horrors, and the reason that in spite of it all men like war is because there we are doing something all together. That is its exhilaration and why we can't give it up. We come home and each leads his separate life and it seems tame and uninteresting merely on that account, the deadly separateness of our ordinary life."

When we want a substitute for war, therefore, we need not seek for a substitute for fighting or for hating; we must find some way of making ourselves feel at one with some portion of our fellow-creatures. If the essential characteristic of war is doing things together, let us begin to do things together in peace. Yet not an artificial doing things together, we could so easily fall into that, but an entire reorganization of life so that the doing things together shall be the natural way — the way we shall all want to do things.

But mere association is not enough. We need more than the "collective life," the mere "getting-together," so much talked of in these days; our getting together must be made effective, must exercise our minds and wills as well as our emotions, must serve the great ends of a great life. Neighborhood organization gives all an opportunity to learn the technique of association.

A further advantage of neighborhood organization is that as a member of a neighborhood group we get a fuller and more varied life than as a member of any other kind of a group we can find, no matter how big our city or how complex or comprehensive its interests. This statement sounds paradoxical — it will seem to many like saying that the smaller is greater than the larger. Let us examine this statement therefore and see if perhaps in this case the smaller is not greater than the larger. Why is the neighborhood group better for us than the selected group? Why are provincial people more interesting than cosmopolitan, that is, if provincial people have taken advantage of *their* opportunities? Because cosmopolitan people are all alike — that has been the aim of their existence and they have accomplished it. The man who knows the "best" society of Petrograd, Paris, London and New York, and that only, is a narrow man because the ideals and standards of the "best" society of London, Paris and New York are the same. He knows life across but not down — it is a horizontal civilization instead of a vertical one, with all the lack of depth and height of everything horizontal. This man has always been among the same kind of people, his life has not been enlarged and enriched by the friction of ideas and ideals which comes from the meeting of people of different opportunities and different tastes and different standards. But this is just what we may have in a neighborhood group — different education, different interests, different standards. Think of the doctor, the man who runs the factory, the organist and choir leader, the grocer, the minister, the watch-maker, the school-teacher, all living within a few blocks of one another.

On the other hand consider how different it is when we *choose* the constituents of our group — then we choose those who are the same as ourselves in some particular. We have the authors' club, the social workers' club, the artists' club, the actors' society, the business men's club, the business women's club, the teachers' club etc.[1] The satisfaction and contentment that comes with same-ness indicates a meagre personality. I go to the medical association to meet doctors, I go to my neighborhood club to meet men. It is just because my next door neighbor has never been to college that he is good for me. The stenographer may come to see that her life is really richer from getting the factory girl's point of view.

In a neighborhood group you have the stimulus and the bracing effect of many different experiences and ideals. And in this infinite variety which touches you on every side, you have a life which enriches and en-

[1] This movement to form societies based on our occupations is of course, although usually unconscious, part of the whole syndicalist move-ment, and as such has real advantages which will be taken up later.

larges and fecundates; this is the true soil of human
development — just because you have here a natural
and not an artificial group, the members find all that is
necessary in order to grow into that whole which is true
community living.

Many young men and women think as they come to
the teeming cities that there they are to find the fuller
life they have longed for, but often the larger our world
the narrower we become, for we cannot face the vague
largeness, and so we join a clique of people as nearly
like ourselves as we can find.

In so far, therefore, as neighborhoods are the result
of some selective process, they are not so good for our
purpose. The Italian colony or the Syrian colony
does not give us the best material for group organization,
neither does any occupational segregation like the stock-
yard district of Chicago. (This is an argument against
the industrial colonies which are spreading.) In a more
or less mixed neighborhood, people of different nationali-
ties or different classes come together easily and naturally
on the ground of many common interests: the school,
recreational opportunities, the placing of their children
in industry, hygiene, housing etc. Race and class prejudices are broken down by working together for intimate objects.

Whenever I speak of neighborhood organization to
my friends, those who disagree with me at once become
violent on the subject. I have never understood why it
inflames them more easily than other topics. They
immediately take it for granted that I am proposing to
shut them up tight in their neighborhoods and seal
them hermetically; they assume that I mean to substitute the neighborhood for every other contact. They
tell me of the pettiness of neighborhood life, and I have
to listen to stories of neighborhood iniquities ranging

from small gossip to determined boycotting. Intolerance and narrowness thrive in the neighborhood group they say; in the wider group they do not. But I am not proposing to substitute the neighborhood group for others, yet even so I should like to say a word for the neighborhood.

We may like some selected group better than the company of our neighbors, but such a group is no "broader" necessarily, because it draws from all over the city, than a local one. You can have narrow interests as well as narrow spaces. Neighbors may, it is true, discuss the comings and goings of the family down the street, but I have heard people who are not neighbors discuss equally trivial subjects. But supposing that non-neighborhood groups are less petty in the sense of less personal in their conversation, they are often also less real, and this is an important point. If I dress in my best clothes and go to another part of the city and take all my best class of conversation with me, I don't know that it does me any good if I am the same person who in my every-day clothes goes in next door and talks slander. What I mean is that the only place in the world where we can change ourselves is on that level where we are real. And what is forgotten by my friends who think neighborhood life trivial is that (according to their own argument) it is the same people who talk gossip in their neighborhoods who are impersonal and noble in another part of the city.

Moreover, if we are happier away from our neighborhood it would be well for us to analyze the cause — there may be a worthy reason, there may not. Is it perhaps that one does not get as much consideration there as one thinks one's due? Have we perhaps, led by our vanity, been drawn to those groups where we get the most consideration? My neighbors may not think much

of me because I paint pictures, knowing that my back
yard is dirty, but my artist friends who like my color
do not know or care about my back yard. My neighbors
may feel no admiring awe of my scientific researches
knowing that I am not the first in the house of a neighbor in trouble.

You may reply, "But this is not my case. I am one
of the most esteemed people in my neighborhood and
one of the lowest in the City Club, but I prefer the
latter just because of that: there is room for me to aspire
there, but where I am leading what is there for me to
grow toward, how can I expand in such an atmosphere?"
But I should say that this also might be a case of vanity:
possibly these people prefer the City Club because they
do not like to think they have found their place in life
in what they consider an inferior group; it flatters them
more to think that they belong to a superior group even
if they occupy the lowest place there. But the final
word to be said is I think that this kind of seeking implies always the attitude of getting, almost as bad as the
attitude of conferring. It is extremely salutary to take
our place in a neighborhood group.

Then, too, that does not always do us most good which
we enjoy most, as we are not always progressing most
when thrills go up and down our spine. We may have a
selected group feeling "good," but that is not going to
make us good. That very homogeneity which we nestle
down into and in which we find all the comfort of a down
pillow, does not provide the differences in which alone
we can grow. We must know the finer enjoyment of
recognized diversity.

It must be noted, however, that while it is not proposed that the neighborhood association be substituted
for other forms of association — trade-union, church
societies, fraternal societies, local improvement leagues,

coöperative societies, men's clubs, women's clubs etc. —
yet the hope is that it shall not be one more association
merely, but that it shall be the means of coördinating
and translating into community values other local groups.
The neighborhood association might become a very mechanical affair if we were all to go there every evening
and go nowhere else.   It must not with its professed
attempt to give a richer life cut off the variety and spontaneity we now have.

But the trouble now is that we have so much unrelated variety, so much unutilized spontaneity.   The
small merchant of a neighborhood meets with the other
small dealers for business purposes, he goes to church
on Sundays, he gets his social intercourse at his lodge
or club, but where and when does he consider any possible integration of these into channels for community
life?   At his political rally, to be sure, he meets his neighbors irrespective of business or church or social lines,
but there he comes under party domination.   A free,
full community life lived within the sustaining and nour-
ishing power of the community bond, lived for community ends, is almost unknown now.   This will not
come by substituting the neighborhood group for other
groups, not even by using it as a clearing-house, but by
using it as a medium for interpretation and unofficial
integration.

There should be as much spontaneous association as
the vitality of the neighborhood makes possible, but
other groups may perhaps find their significance and
coördination through the neighborhood association.   If
a men's or women's club is of no use to the community
it should not exist; if it is of use, it must find out of what
use, how related to all other organizations, how through
and with them related to the whole community.   The
lawyers' club, the teachers' club, the trade association

or the union — these can have little influence on their community until they discover their relation to the community through and in one another. I have seen many examples of this. If the neighborhood group is to be the political unit, it must learn how to gather up into significant community expression these more partial expressions of individual wants.

It is sometimes said that the force of the neighborhood bond is lessening now-a-days with the ease of communication, but this is true only for the wealthy. The poor cannot afford constantly to be paying the ten-cent carfare necessary to leave and return to their homes, nor the more well-to-do of the suburbs the twenty or twenty-five cents it costs them to go to the city and back. The fluctuating population of neighborhoods may be an argument against getting all we should like out of the neighborhood bond, but at the same time it makes it all the more necessary that some organization should be ready at hand to assimilate the new-comers and give them an opportunity of sharing in civic life as an integral, responsible part of that life. Moreover a neighborhood has common traditions and memories which persist and influence even although the personnel changes.

To sum up: whether we want the exhilaration of a fuller life or whether we want to find the unities which will make for peace and order, for justice and for righteousness, it would be wise to turn back to the neighborhood group and there begin the a b c of a constructive brotherhood of man. We must recognize that too much congeniality makes for narrowness, and that the harmonizing, not the ignoring, of our differences leads us to the truth. Neighborhood organization gives us the best opportunity we have yet discovered of finding the unity underneath all our differences, the real bond between them — of living the consciously creative life.

We can never reform American politics from above, by reform associations, by charters and schemes of government. Our political forms will have no vitality unless our political life is so organized that it shall be based primarily and fundamentally on spontaneous association. "Government is a social contact," was found in the examination papers of a student in a near-by college. He was nearer the truth than he knew. Political progress must be˙ by local communities. Our municipal life will be just as strong as the strength of its parts. We shall never know how to be one of a nation until we are one of a neighborhood. And what better training for world organization can each man receive than for neighbors to live together not as detached individuals but as a true community, for no League of Nations will be successful which regards France and Germany, England and Russia as separatist units of a world-union.

Those who are working for particular reforms to be accomplished immediately will not be interested in neighborhood organization; only those will be interested who think that it is far more important for us to find the right method of attacking all our problems than to solve any one. We who believe in neighborhood organization believe that the neighborhood group is a more significant unit to identify ourselves with than any we have hitherto known in cities. People have been getting together in churches, in fraternal societies, in political parties, in industrial and commercial associations, but now in addition to these partial groups communities are to get together as communities.

The neighborhood organization movement is not waiting for ideal institutions, or perfect men, but is finding whatever creative forces there are within a community and taking these and building the future with them. The neighborhood organization movement is a protest against both utopias on the one hand and a mechanicalized humanity on the other. It consists of the process of building always with the best we have, and its chief problem is to discover the methods by which the best we have can be brought to the surface. Neighborhood organization gives us a method which will revolutionize politics.

XXIII

AN INTEGRATED NEIGHBORHOOD

HOW can an active and fruitful neighborhood life be brought into existence and fostered and nurtured? How can we unclose the sources within our own midst from which to draw our inspiration? And then how can the vision which we learn to see together be actualized? How can neighborhoods learn to satisfy their own needs through their own initiative? In other words how can the force generated by our neighborhood life become part of our whole civic and national life? How can an integrated neighborhood responsibility become a civic and national responsibility?

There is no such thing as a neighborhood in its true sense, something more, that is, than the physical contiguity of people, until you have a neighborhood consciousness. Rows of houses, rows of streets, do not make a neighborhood. The place bond must give way to a consciousness of real union. This neighborhood consciousness can be evolved in five ways:

1. By regular meetings of neighbors for the consideration of neighborhood and civic problems, not merely sporadic and occasional meetings for specific objects.

2. By a genuine discussion at these regular meetings.

3. By learning together — through lectures, classes, clubs; by sharing one another's experience through social intercourse; by learning forms of community art expression; in short by leading an actual community life.

4. By taking more and more responsibility for the life of the neighborhood.

5. By establishing some regular connection between the neighborhood and city, state and national governments.

The most deliberate and conscious movement for neighborhood organization is the Community Centre movement. This is a movement to mobilize community forces and to get these forces expressed in our social and political life. Each community, it is becoming recognized, has its own desires, its own gifts, its own inherent powers to bring to the life of the whole city. But these inner forces most be freed and utilized for public ends. The Community Centre movement is a movement to release the potential values of neighborhood life, to find a channel for them to flow in, to help people find and organize their own resources. It is to provide a means for the self-realization of neighborhoods. In considering, therefore, the various methods of neighborhood integration, it must be remembered that many of these methods are being already actualized in Community Centres, School Centres, Neighborhood Associations — there are many names for the many forms in which this vital need is finding expression.

Schoolhouses are being opened all over the country for neighborhood use. In the larger cities, indeed, where school buildings have auditoriums, gymnasiums, cooking-rooms, sewing-rooms etc., the School Centre is for many reasons the best form of community organization. In some cities, as in Chicago, the field-houses in the parks are used as community centres, in addition to the school-houses. In many smaller towns or villages, where field-houses are unknown and the schoolhouses unsuitable (although often we find valuable if not showy results in the little red schoolhouse at the cross-roads or in a Kansas cyclone cellar underneath the district school), "community buildings" are being built. Their name is significant. They have a reading room, library, rest room, club rooms and usually a small hall with stage for dramatic and musical entertainments.

And beyond this conscious effort to organize neighborhoods, or rather to help neighborhoods to organize themselves, much spontaneous initiative in both rural and urban communities, springing from the daily needs of the people, is finding neighborhood organization to be the result of concerted effort. Mothers want to learn more of the care of their homes, men want to discuss local improvements, young men and women want recreation, there is a hunger for a wider social intercourse or for some form of community art-expression, music or drama. Yet whichever of these motives leads us to the schoolhouse or the community building, the result is always the same — a closer forging of the neighborhood bond. Whoever takes the initiative in organizing the Community Centre — a parents' association, a men's civic club, a mothers' club, a committee of citizens, the city council, the board of education — the result is always the same, a closer forging of the community bond.

The Community Centre movement has made rapid progress in the last ten years. All over the country new Centres are springing up constantly. That the impulse for their organization is almost as varied as there are different towns and cities is evidence of their real need. I have had letters in regard to the organization of Centres from as widely different sources as the city council of a western city, girls teaching in rural schools, the mayor of a small city, and young working men in a big city. Indeed Centres have become so much the fashion that one man came to me and said, "We want a School Centre in our district — will you help us to get one — what is a School Centre?"

In the year 1915–16, 463 cities reported over 59,000

occasions in public school buildings after 6 P.M. in addition to evening school work.[1]

But School or Community Centres do not exist merely for the satisfaction of neighborhood needs, for the creating of a community bond, for the expression of that bond in communal action, — they also give the training necessary to bring that activity to its highest fulfilment. We all need not merely opportunities to exercise democracy, but opportunity for a training in democracy. We are not going to take any kind of citizen for the new state, we intend to grow our own citizens. Through group activities, through classes and lectures, through university extension, through actual practice in self government by the management of their own Centres and the varied activities therein, all, young and old, may prepare themselves for the new citizenship of the new democracy.[2]

Let us now consider the five ways given above for producing an integrated and responsible neighborhood. First, the regular meetings of neighbors in civic clubs. In Boston we have, in connection with the School Centres, the so-called "East Boston Town-Meeting," the "Charlestown Commonwealth," etc. At such meetings neighborhood needs can be discussed, and the men and women of those neighborhoods, while getting to know one another and their local conditions, can be training themselves to function with government and as government. The first advantage of such meetings is their regularity.

I am urging *regular* meetings of small groups of neighbors as a new method in politics. Neighbors now often

---

[1] Since April, 1917, with the rapidly extending use of the schoolhouse as a centre for war services, these numbers have probably greatly increased.

[2] See Appendix, The Training for the New Democracy.

meet for one object or two or three, and then when these are accomplished think that they need not meet again until there is another definite end to be gained. But in the meantime there should be the slow building up of the neighborhood consciousness. A mass-meeting will never do this. But this neighborhood consciousness is far more important than to get a municipal bath-house for a certain district. If the bath-house is considered the chief thing, and no effort made to get the neighborhood group together again until something else, a playground for instance, is wanted, this time perhaps not enough cohesion and concentration of purpose can be obtained to secure the playground. The question in neighborhood organization is — Is our object to get a new playground or to create methods by which playgrounds will become part of the neighborhood consciousness, methods which will above all educate for further concerted effort? If neighborhood organization is one among many methods of getting things, then it is not of great value; if, however, it is going to bring about a different mental life, if it will give us an open mind, a flexible mind, a coöperative mind, then it is the greatest movement of our time. For our object is not to get certain things, or to have certain things; our object is to evolve the kind of life, the way of thinking, within which these specific things will naturally have place. We shall make no real progress until we can do this.

Bernard Shaw has said of family life that it is often cut off equally from the blessings of society and the blessings of solitude. We must see that our neighborhood associations are so organized that we do get the advantages of society.

The second way of creating an integrated neighborhood is by learning and practising a genuine discussion, that is, a discussion which shall evolve a true collective purpose and bring the group will of the neighborhood to bear directly on city problems. When I speak of discussion I mean always the kind of discussion which is called out by a genuine group. The group idea, not the crowd idea, is to come from discussion. What is the remedy for a "ruthless majority"? What is the remedy for an "arrogant minority"? Group discussion. Group discussion will diminish suggestion as a social force and give place to interpermeation.

When we advocate discussion as a political method, we are not advocating the extension of a method already in use. There is little discussion to-day. Talk to air our grievances or as a steam-valve for the hot-headed, the avowed intention sometimes in the organization of so-called "discussion" societies, is not discussion. People often speak of "self-expression" as if it were a letting off of steam, as if there were something inside us that must be let out before it explodes. But this is not the use to which we must put the powers of self-expression; we must release these powers not to be wasted through a safety valve, but to be used constructively for the good of society. To change the metaphor, we must not make a petty effort to stem a stream which cannot and should not be stemmed but helped to direct itself.

Do we have discussion in debating societies? Never. Their influence is pernicious and they should be abolished in colleges, schools, settlements, Young Men's Christian Associations, or wherever found. In these societies the men as a rule take either side of the question allotted to them, but even if they choose their side the process of the debate is the same. The object is always to win, it is never to discover the truth. This is excellent training for our present party politics. It is wretched preparation for the kind of politics we wish to see in America, because there is no attempt to think together. Some one to whom I said this replied, "But each side has to think together." Not in the least: they simply pool their information and their arguments, they don't think together. They don't even think; that artificial mental process of maintaining a thesis which is not yours by conviction is not thinking. In debating you are always trying to find the ideas and facts which will support your side; you do not look dispassionately at all ideas and all facts, and try to make out just where the truth lies. You do not try to see what ideas of your opponent will enrich your own point of view; you are bound to reject without examination his views, his ideas, almost I might say his facts. In a discussion you can be flexible, you can try experiments, you can grow as the group grows, but in a debate all this is impossible.

One of the great advantages of the forum movement is that here we are beginning to have discussion.[1]

Let us analyze briefly the advantages of discussion. Genuine discussion is truth-seeking. First, then, it presses every man to think clearly and appreciatively and discriminatingly in order to take his part worthily. What we need above everything else is clear thinking. This need has been covered over by the demand for "honest" men, but hardly any one would say to-day, "Give the management of your city over to a group of the most honest men you can find." A group of honest men — what a disconcerting picture the phrase calls up! We want efficient men, thinking men, as well as honest men. Take care of your thinking and your morals will take care of themselves — is a present which would have benefited certain reform campaigns.

The first advantage of discussion then is that it tends to make us think and to seek accurate information in

[1] That it is also in many instances leading the way to real community organization makes it one of the most valuable movements of our time.

order to be able to think and to think clearly. I belong
to a civic conference lunch club which meets once a
month to discuss civic questions. On one occasion the
program committee discovered a few days before the
luncheon that on the question to be considered (a certain bill before the legislature), we were all of the same
opinion, and so the discussion did not seem likely to be
very lively. But it happened that our secretary knew
some one who was on the other side, and this woman
was therefore invited to be our guest and present her
point of view to us. She accepted with pleasure as she
said she felt strongly on the matter. On the morning
of the day of our meeting, however, she telephoned that
she could not come, as she had just read the bill, thinking it would be wise to do so before she publicly opposed
it, and she found she agreed with it heartily!

Moreover, no one question can be adequately discussed without an understanding of many more. Reme-
dies for abuses are seldom direct because every abuse is
bound up with our whole political and economic system.
And if discussion induces thinking by the preparation
necessary, it certainly stimulates thinking by the opposition we meet.

But the great advantage of discussion is that thereby
we overcome misunderstanding and conquer prejudice.
An Englishman who visited America last winter said
that he had seen in an American newspaper this advice,
"Get acquainted with your neighbor, you might like
him," and was much struck with the difference between
the American and the English way of looking at the
matter. The Englishman, he said, does not get acquainted with his neighbor for fear he might like him!
I sometimes feel that we refuse to get acquainted with
the arguments of our opponents for fear we might sym-
pathize with them.

Genuine discussion, however, will always and should always bring out difference, but at the same time it teaches us what to do with difference. The formative process which takes place in discussion is that unceasing reciprocal adjustment which brings out and gives form to truth.

The whole conception of discussion is now changing. Discussion is to be the sharpest, most effective political tool of the future. The value of the town-meeting is not in the fact that every one goes, but in what every one does when he gets there. And discussion will overcome much indifference, much complacency. We must remember that most people are not for or against anything; the first object of getting people together is to make them respond somehow, to overcome inertia. To disagree, as well as to agree, with people brings you closer to them. I always feel intimate with my enemies. It is not opposition but indifference which separates men.

Another advantage of discussion in regular meetings of neighbors is that men discuss questions there before they come to a political issue, when there is not the heat of the actual fight and the desire to win.

Through regular meetings then, and a genuine discussion, we help to forge the neighborhood bond. But this is not enough. A true community life should be developed. If the multiplicity and complexity of interrelations of interests and wants and hopes are to be brought to the surface to form the substance of politics, people must come more and more to live their lives together. We are ignorant: we should form classes and learn together. The farmer in Virginia goes to the School Centre to learn how to test his seed corn. We need social intercourse: we should meet to exchange experiences and to have a "good time" together. We need opportunity for bringing old and young together, parents and children, for boys and girls to meet in a natural, healthy way. We need true recreation, not the passive looking at the motion pictures, not the deadening watching of other people's acting; we want the real re-creation of active participation. The leisure time of men and women is being increased by legislation, by vocational efficiency, by machinery, and by scientific management. One of the most pressing needs of to-day is the constructive use of leisure. This need can be largely satisfied in the Neighborhood Centre. Festivals, pageants, the celebration of holidays can all be used as recreation, as a means of self-expression, and of building up the neighborhood bond.

Here too the family realizes that its life is embedded in a larger life, and the richer that larger life the more the family gains. The family learns its duty to other families, and it finds that its external relations change all its inner life, as the International League will change fundamentally the internal history of every nation. I knew two sisters who were ashamed of their mother until they could say to their friends, "Mother goes to the lectures every Saturday night at the School Centre." I know men and wives who never went out together until they found an extended home in a School Centre. I know a father, an intelligent policeman, who never had any real friendship with his four daughters until he planned dances for them at the School Centre so that they should not go to the public dance-halls.

Families often need some means of coming to a common understanding; they are not always capable by themselves of making the necessary adjustment of points of view brought from so many sources as the different family outgoings produce. For example, food conservation taught in various ways in the Neighborhood Centre — by cooking classes for women, by lectures for both men and women showing the relation of food to the

whole present world problem, by having regular afternoons for meeting with agents from the Health Department, by comparison between neighbors of the results
of the new feeding — food conservation, that is, taught
as a community problem, is more effective than taught
merely to classes of mothers. For if the mother makes
dishes the father and children refuse to eat, the cooking
classes she has attended will have no community value.
To give community value to all our apparently isolated
activities is one of the primary objects of neighborhood
organization.

The Neighborhood Centre, therefore, instead of separating families, as sometimes feared, is uniting them.
To live their life in the setting of the broader life is continuously to interpret and explain one to the other. And
if we have learned that sacred as our family life must
always be, the significance of that sacredness is its power
of contributing to the life around us, the life of our little
neighborhood, then we are ready to understand that the
nation too is real, that its tasks are mighty and that
those tasks will not be performed unless every one of us
can find self-expression through the nation's needs.

We have seen that the regular meeting of neighbors
gives an external integration of neighborhood life. We
have seen that group discussion begins to forge a real
neighborhood bond. We have seen that a sharing of our
daily life — its cares and burdens, its pleasures and joys,
each with all — furthers this inner, this spiritual union
which is at last to be the core of a new politics. The
fourth way of developing the neighborhood bond is by
citizens taking more and more responsibility for the life
of their community. This will mean a moral integration.
We are not to dig down into our life to find our true
needs and then demand that government satisfy those
needs — the satisfaction also must be found in that

fermenting life from which our demands issue. The methods of neighborhood responsibility will be discussed in chapter XXVI.

The fifth way of developing the neighborhood group is by establishing some regular connection between the neighborhood and city, state and national governments. Then shall we have the political integration of the neighborhood. This will be discussed in chapter XXVII, "From Neighborhood to Nation." Party politics are organized, "interests" are organized, our citizenship is not organized. Our neighborhood life is starving for lack of any real part in the state. Give us that part and as inevitably as the wake follows the ship will neighborhood responsibility follow the integration of neighborhood and state.

XXIV

NEIGHBORHOOD ORGANIZATION VS. PARTY ORGANIZATION

The Will of the People

MANY of us are feeling strongly at the present moment the importance of neighborhood life, the importance of the development of a neighborhood consciousness, the paramount importance of neighborhood organization as the most effective means of solving our city and national problems. What our political life needs to-day is to get at the will of the people and to incorporate it in our government, to substitute a man-governed country for a machine-governed country. If politics are to be no longer mysterious and remote, but the warp and woof of our lives, if they are to be neither a game nor a business, far different methods must be adopted from any we have hitherto known.

Where do we show political vitality at present? In our government? In our party organization? In our local communities? We can see nowhere any clear stream of political life. The vitality of our community life is frittered away or unused. The muddy stream of party politics is choked with personal ambition, the desire for personal gain. Neighborhood organization is, I believe, to be the vital current of our political life. There is a wide-spread idea that we can do away with the evils of the party system by attacking the boss. Many think also that all would be well if we could separate politics and business. But far below the surface are the forces which have allied business and politics;

216

far below the surface we must go, therefore, if we would divorce this badly mated couple.

Neighborhood organization is to accomplish many things. The most important are: to give a knock-out blow to party organization, to make a direct and continuous connection between our daily lives and needs and our government, to diminish race and class prejudices, to create a responsible citizenship, and to train and discipline the new democracy; or, to sum up all these things, to break down party organization and to make a creative citizenship the force of American political life.

An effective neighborhood organization will deal the death blow to party: (1) by substituting a real unity for the pseudo unity of party, by creating a genuine public opinion, a true will of the people,[1] (2) by evolving genuine leaders instead of bosses, (3) by putting a responsible government in the place of the irresponsible party.

First, there is at present no real unity of the people.

It is clear that party organization has succeeded because it was the only way we knew of bringing about concerted action. This must be obtained by the manipulation of other men's minds or by the evolving of the common mind; we must choose between the two. In the past the monarch got his power from the fact that he represented the unity of his people — the tribal or national consciousness. In the so-called democracies of England and America we have now no one man who represents a true collective consciousness. Much of the power of party has come, therefore, from the fact that it gave expression to a certain kind of pseudo collective consciousness: we found that it was impossible to get a common will from a multitude, the only way we could

[1] Public opinion in a true democracy is a potential will. Therefore for practical purposes they are identical and I use them synonymously.

get any unity was through the party. We have accepted party dictatorship rather than anarchy. We have felt that any discussion of party organization was largely doctrinaire because party has given us collective action of a kind, and what has been offered in its place was a scattered and irresponsible, and therefore weak and ineffective, particularism. No "independent" method of voting can ever vie with the organized party machinery: its loose unintegrated nebulosity will be shattered into smithereens by the impact of the closely organized machine.

The problem which many men have wrestled with in their lives — whether they are to adhere to party or to be "independent" — is futile. Personal honesty exhausts no man's duty in life; an effective life is what is demanded of us, and no isolated honesty gives us social effectiveness. When we go up to the gates of another world and say, "I have been honest, I have been pure, I have been diligent" — no guardian of those Heavenly gates will fling them open for us, but we shall be faced with the counter thrust: "How have you used those qualities for making blossom the earth which was your inheritance? We want no sterile virtues here. Have you sold your inheritance for the pottage of personal purity, personal honesty, personal growth?"

To make our "independence" effective, to vie successfully with party organization, we must organize genuine groups and learn in those true collective action. No particularistic theory of politics will ever be strong enough to take the place of party. The political consciousness of men must be transferred from the party to the neighborhood group.

We hear discussed from time to time how far public opinion governs the world, but at present there is no public opinion. Our legislatures are supposed to enact the

will of the people, our courts are supposed to declare
the will of the people, our executive to voice the will of
the people, a will surrounding men like a nimbus apparently from their births on. But there is no will of the
people.[1] We talk glibly about it but the truth is that
it is such a very modern thing that it does not yet exist.
There is, it is true, an overwhelming chaos of ideas on
all the problems which surround us. Is this public
opinion? The urge of the crowd often gets crystallized
into a definite policy ardently advocated. Is this public
opinion? Certain interests find a voice; one party or
another, one group or another, expresses itself. Is this
public opinion? Public opinion is that common understanding which is the driving force of a living whole and
shapes the life of that whole.

We believe that the state should be the incarnation
of the common will, but where is the common will? All
the proposed new devices for getting at the will of the
people (referendum etc.) assume that we have a will to
express; but our great need at present is not to get a
chance to express our wonderful ideas, but to get some
wonderful ideas to express. A more complete representation is the aim of much of our political reform, but our
first requirement is surely to have something to represent. It isn't that we need one kind of government
more than another, as the image-breakers tell us, it isn't
that we need honest intentions, as the preachers tell us,
our essential and vital need is a people creating a will of
its own. In all the sentimental talk of democracy the
will of the people is spoken of tenderly as if it were there
in all its wisdom and all its completeness and we had
only to put it into operation.

[1] Our federal system of checks and balances thwarted the will of the
people. The party system thwarted the will of the people. Our state
governments were never designed to get at the will of the people.

The tragic thing about our situation in America is, not merely that we have no public opinion, but that we think we have. If I have no money in my pocket and know it, I can go to work and earn some; if I do not know it I may starve. But I do not want the American people to starve. The average American citizen says to himself, "It doesn't matter very much what I think because American public opinion is sound at the core." It is our Great Illusion. There has been much apotheosizing of the so-called popular will, but not every circle is a halo, and you can't put a wreath round "the popular will" and call it democracy. The popular will to mean democracy must be a properly evolved popular will — the true will of the people.

Who are the people? Every individual? The majority? A theoretical average? A compromise group? The reason we go astray about public opinion is because we have not as yet a clear and adequate definition of the "people." We are told that we must elevate the "people." There are no "people." We have to create a people. The people are not an imaginary average, shorn of genius and power and leadership. You cannot file off all the points made by talent and efficiency, and call the dead level that is left the people. The people are the integration of every development, of every genius, with everything else that our complex and interacting life brings about. But the method of such integration can never be through crowd association. We may come to think that vox populi is vox Dei, but not until it is the group voice, not until it is found by some more intimate process than listening to the shout of the crowd or counting the votes in the ballot-box.

The error in regard to public opinion can be traced to that same sociological error which is the cause of so many confusions in our political thought: that the social process is the spread of similarities by suggestion and imitation. Any opinion that is shared, simply because it is shared, is called public opinion. But if this opinion is shared because it has spread among large numbers by "unconscious imitation," then it is not a genuine public opinion; to be that, the process by which it has been evolved must be that of intermingling and interpermeating. Public opinion has been defined as the opinions of all the men on the "tops of busses," or the opinion made by "banks, stock-exchanges and all the wire-pullers of the world," or the opinion "imposed on the public by a succession of thinkers." All this is, no doubt, true of much of our so-called public opinion at present, for public opinion to-day is largely crowd opinion. But there is less of this than formerly. And we must adopt those modes of living by which there shall be less and less infection of crowds and more and more an evolving of genuine group thought. When reforms are brought about by crowds being swept into them, they can be undone just as easily; there is no real progress here.

Political parties and business interests will continue to dominate us until we learn new methods of association. Men follow party dictates not because of any worship of party but simply because they have not yet any will of their own. Until they have, they will be used and manipulated and artificially stimulated by those who can command sufficient money to engage leaders for that purpose. Hypnosis will be our normal state until we are roused to claim our own creative power. The promise for the future is the power for working together which lies latent in the great rank and file of men and women to-day, and which must be brought clearly to their view and utilized in the right way. If we see no fruitful future for our political life under the present scheme of party domination, if we can see no bearable future for our industrial life under the present class domination, then some plan must be devised for the will of the people to control the life of the people. Fighting abuses is not our role, but the full understanding that such fighting is a tilting at wind-mills. The abuses in themselves amount to nothing. Our role is to leave them alone and build up our own life with our power of creative citizenship. We need to-day: (1) an *active* citizenship, (2) a *responsible* citizenship, (3) a *creative* citizenship — a citizenship building its own world, creating its own political and social structure, constructing its own life forever.

Our faith in democracy rests ultimately on the belief that men have this creative power. Our vital relation to the Infinite consists in our capacity, as its generating force, to bring forth a group idea, to create the common life. But we have at present no machinery for a constructive life. The organization of neighborhood groups will give us this machinery.

Let us see how neighborhood groups can create a united will, a genuine public opinion.

First, neighborhood groups will naturally discuss their local, intimate, personal concerns. The platitudes and insincerities of the party meeting will give way to the homely realities of the neighborhood meeting. These common interests will become the political issues. Then, and not till then, politics, external at no point to any vital need, will represent the life of our people. Then when we see clearly that the affairs of city and state are our affairs, we shall no longer be apathetic or indifferent in regard to politics. We all *are* interested in our own affairs. When our daily needs become the basis of politics, then party will no longer be left in control because politics bore us, because we feel that they have nothing to do with us.

Already the daily lives of people are passing into the area of government through the increased social legislation of all our states during the last few years. In 1912 a national party was organized with social legislation as part of its platform. The introduction of social programs into party platforms means that a powerful influence is at work to change American politics from a machine to a living thing. When the political questions were chiefly the tariff, the trust, the currency, closely as these questions affected the lives of people, there was so little general knowledge in regard to them that most of us could contribute little to their solution. The social legislation of the last few years has taken up crime, poverty, disease, which we all know a great deal about: laws have been passed regarding child labor, workmen's compensation, occupational disease, prison reform, tuberculosis, mothers' pensions, the liquor question, minimum wage, employment agencies etc.

Tammany is built up on the most intimate local work: no family, no child, is unknown to its organization. And it is founded on the long view: votes are not crudely bought — always; the boy is found a job, the father is helped through his illness, the worn-out mother is sent for a holiday to the country. As politics comes to mean state employment bureaus, sickness and accident insurance, mothers' pensions, Tammany is being shorn of much of its power.

We are sometimes told, however, that while it is conceded that campaign issues should be made up from our intimate, everyday needs, yet it is feared that on each question a different split would come, and thus politics would be too confusing and could not be "handled." Neighborhood organization is going to help us meet this difficulty. In non-partisan neighborhood associations we shall have different alignments on every question. Moreover, we shall have different alignments on the same question in different years. Thus the rigidity of the party organization disappears. The party meeting is to the neighborhood meeting what the victrola is to the human voice: the partisan assembly utters what has been impressed upon it, you hear the machine beating its own rhythm; the neighborhood meeting will give the fresh ever-varied voices from the hearts of men. The party system and the genuine group system is the difference between machine-made and man-made. And this may be true of a good government organization as well as of a Tammany organization — it is true wherever the machine is put above the man. We can get no force without freshness, and you cannot get freshness from a machine, only from living men. Just the very thing which costs the party money — keeping its members together — is its condemnation. Men will make up their minds on question after question in their neighborhood groups. Then they will vote according to these conclusions. Party dictation will never cease until we get group conviction. If our political life is going to show any greater sensitiveness to our real wants and needs than it has shown in the past, there must be some provision made for considering and voting on questions irrespective of party: you can not join a different party every day, but you can separate political issues from partisanship and vote for the thing you want. The reason more of our real wants have not got expressed in our politics is just because people cannot be held together on many issues.

Again, if neighborhood organization takes the place of party organization each question can be decided on its own merit: we shall not have to ask, "How will the management of this affect the power and prestige of our party?"

Also neighborhood groups can study problems, but

the study of problems is fatal to party organization. The party hands out the ephemeral comings-to-the-surface of what will help the party, or the particularistic interests dominating the party. Every question brought forward at all is brought forward as a campaign issue.

Moreover the group discovers and conserves the individual. A party gathering is always a crowd. And party methods are stereotyped, conventional. Under a party system we have no spontaneous political life. The party system gives no exercise to the judgment, it weakens the will, it does away with personal responsibility. The party, as the crowd, blots out the individual. Mass suggestion is dominating our politics to-day. We shall get rid of mass influence exactly as fast as we develop the group consciousness. Men who belong to neighborhood organizations will not be the stuff of which parties are made. The party has prevented us from having genuine group opinion; or if we do by any chance get a group opinion now, it can usually speak only in opposition to party, it cannot get incorporated in our political life.

Every one of us will have an opportunity to learn collective thinking in the small, local, neighborhood group. No one comes to his neighborhood group pledged beforehand to any particular way of thinking. The object of the party system is to stifle all difference of opinion. Moreover, in partisan discussion you take one of two sides; in neighborhood groups an infinitely varied number of points of view can be brought out, and thus the final decision will be richer from what it gains on all sides. The neighborhood group which makes possible different alignments on every question, allows ultimate honesty in the expression of our views. If we get into the habit of suppressing our differences, these differences atrophy and we lose our sensitiveness to their demands. And we have found that the expression and the maintenance of difference is the condition of the full and free development of the race.

But we want not only a genuine public opinion, but a progressive public opinion. We cannot understand once for all, we must be constantly understanding anew. At the same time that we see the necessity of creating the common will and giving voice to it, we must bear in mind that there should be no crystallizing process by which any particular expression of the common will should be taken as eternally right because it is the ex‑pression of the common will. It is right for to-day but not for to-morrow. The flaming fact is our daily life, whatever it is, leaping forever and ever out of the common will. Democracy is the ever-increasing volume of power pouring through men and shaping itself as the moment demands. Constitutional conventions are seeking the machinery by which the reason and justice which have existed among us can be utilized in our life. We must go beyond this and unseal the springs which will reveal the forms for the wisdom and justice of their day. This is life itself, the direct and aboriginal constructor. We meet with our neighbors at our civic club not in order to accumulate facts, but to learn how to release and how to control a constructive force which will build daily for us the habitation of our needs. Then indeed will our government be no longer directed by a "body of law," but by the self-renewing appearing of the will of the people.

The chief need of society to-day is an enlightened, progressive and organized public opinion, and the first step towards an enlightened and organized public opinion is an enlightened and organized group opinion. When public opinion becomes conscious of itself it will have a justified confidence in itself. Then the "people," born of an associated life, will truly govern. Then shall we at last really have an America.

XXV

Leaders or Bosses?

NEIGHBORHOOD organization will prove fatal
to party organization not only through the
creating of a genuine will of the people, but
also through the producing of real leaders to take the
place of the bosses.

American democracy has always been afraid of leadership. Our constitutions of the eighteenth century provided no one department to lead, no one man in the legislature to lead. Therefore, as we must have leadership, there has been much undefined, irresponsible leadership. This has often meant corruption and abuse, bad enough, but worse still it has meant the creation of machinery for the perpetuation of corruption, the encouragement of abuse. Under machine politics we choose for our leaders the men who are most popular for the moment or who have worked out the most thorough system of patronage, or rather of course we do not choose at all. We have two kinds of leaders under our party system, both the wrong kind: we have our actual leaders, the bosses, and our official leaders who have tended to be men who could be managed by the party. Our officials in their campaign speeches say that they are the "servants of the people." But we do not want "servants" any more than we want bosses; we want genuine leaders. Now that more and more direct power is being given to the people it is especially necessary that we should not be led by machine bosses, but that we should evolve the kind of leadership which will serve a true democracy, which will be the expression of a true democracy, and will guide it to democratic ends by democratic methods.

We hope through local group organization to evolve real leaders. There should be in a democracy some sort of regular and ceaseless process by which ability of all sorts should come to the top, and flexibility in our forms so that new ability can always find its greatest point of usefulness, and so that service which is no longer useful can be replaced by that which is. In neighborhood groups where we have different alignments on different questions, there will be a tendency for those to lead at any particular moment who are most competent to lead in the particular matter in hand. Thus a mechanical leadership will give place to a vital leadership. Suppose the subject is sanitation. The man who is most interested, who has the clearest view of the need and who is its most insistent champion, will naturally step forth as the leader in that. The man who knows most about educational matters will lead in those, will be chosen eventually for the school committee or for the educational committee of the state legislature. Thus the different leaders of a democracy appear. Here in the neighborhood group leaders are born. Democracy is the breeding-ground of aristocracy. You have all the chance the world gives. In your neighborhood group show the clearness of your mind, the strength of your grip, your power to elicit and to guide coöperative action, and you emerge as the leader of men.

No adequate statement can be made in regard to leadership until it is studied in relation to group psychology. The leadership of the British Premier, of President Wilson, will become interesting studies when we have a better understanding of this subject. Meanwhile let us look briefly at some of the qualities of leadership.

The leader guides the group and is at the same time himself guided by the group, is always a part of the group. No one can truly lead except from within. One danger of conceiving the leader as outside is that then what ought to be group loyalty will become personal loyalty. When we have a leader within the group these two loyalties can merge.

The leader must have the instinct to trace every evil to its cause, but, equally valuable, he must be able to see the relative value of the cause to each one of his group — in other words, to see the total relativity of the cause to the group. He must draw out all the varying needs of the neighborhood as related to the cause and reconcile them in the remedy. A baby is ill; is the milk perhaps too rich for babies? But probably the rest of the neighborhood demands rich milk. All the neighborhood needs in regard to milk must be elicited and reconciled in the remedy for the sick child. That is, the remedy cannot be thinner milk, but it may be a demand that the milkman have separate milk for babies.

In other words the leader of our neighborhood group must interpret our experience to us, must see all the different points of view which underlie our daily activities and also their connections, must adjust the varying and often conflicting needs, must lead the group to an understanding of its needs and to a unification of its purpose. He must give form to things vague, things latent, to mere tendencies. He must be able to lead us to wise decisions, not to impose his own wise decisions upon us. We need leaders, not masters or drivers.

The power of leadership is the power of integrating. This is the power which creates community. You can see it when two or three strangers or casual acquaintances are calling upon some one. With some hostesses you all talk across at one another as entirely separate individuals, pleasantly and friendlily, to be sure, but still across unbridged chasms; while other hostesses have the power of making you all feel for the moment related, as if you were one little community for the time being. This is a subtle as well as a valuable gift. It is one that leaders of men must possess. It is thus that the collective will is evolved from out the chaos of varied personality and complex circumstance.

The skilful leader then does not rely on personal force; he controls his group not by dominating but by expressing it. He stimulates what is best in us; he unifies and concentrates what we feel only gropingly and scatteringly, but he never gets away from the current of which we and he are both an integral part. He is a leader who gives form to the inchoate energy in every man. The person who influences me most is not he who does great deeds but he who makes me feel I can do great deeds. Many people tell me what I ought to do and just how I ought to do it, but few have made me want to do something. Who ever has struck fire out of me, aroused me to action which I should not otherwise have taken, he has been my leader. The community leader is he who can liberate the greatest amount of energy in his community.

Then the neighborhood leader must be a practical politician. He must be able to interpret a neighborhood not only to itself but to others. He must know not only the need of every charwoman but how politics can answer her call. He must know the great movements of the present and their meaning, and he must know how the smallest needs and the humblest powers of his neighborhood can be fitted into the progressive

movements of our time. His duty is to shape politics
continuously. As the satisfaction of one need, or the expression of one latent power, reveals many more, he must
be always alert and ever ready to gather up the many
threads into one strand of united endeavor. He is the
patient watcher, the active spokesman, the sincere and
ardent exponent of a community consciousness. His
guiding, embracing and dominant thought is to make
that community consciousness articulate in government.

The politician is not a group but a crowd leader. The
leader of a crowd dominates because a crowd wants to
be dominated. Politicians do not try to convince but
to dazzle; they do not deal with facts but with formulæ
and vague generalizations, with the flag and the country. If our politicians and our representatives are not
our most competent men, but those who have the greatest power of suggestion and are most adroit in using it,
the proposal here is that we shall develop methods
which will produce real leaders. We are aiming now in
the reorganization of our state constitutions at responsible official leadership instead of the irresponsible party
boss system which was necessary once because we had
to have leaders of some sort. How far this new movement shall succeed, will depend on how far it has back
of it, or can be made to have back of it, the kind of
organization which will develop group not crowd leaders.

Through neighborhood organization we hope that real
leaders instead of bosses will be evolved. Democracy
does not tend to suppress leadership as is often stated;
it is the only organization of society which will bring out
leadership. As soon as we are given opportunities for
the release of the energy there is in us, heroes and leaders
will arise among us. These will draw their stimulus,
their passion, their life from all, and then in their turn
increase in all passion and power and creating force.

XXVI

A Responsible Neighborhood

WE have said that neighborhood organization must replace party organization by evolving a true will of the people, by giving us leaders instead of bosses, and by making possible a responsible government to take the place of our irresponsible party government. Let us now consider the last point: the possibility of an integrated neighborhood responsibility.

Under our party organization the men who formulate the party platform do not have the official responsibility of carrying it out. Moreover at present representative government rests on the fallacy that when you delegate the job you delegate the responsibility. Most of the abuses which have crept in, business corruption and political bossism alike, are due in large measure to this delegating of responsibility. What we need is a kind of government which will delegate the job but not the responsibility. The case is somewhat like that of the head of a business undertaking, who makes the men under him responsible for their own work and still the final responsibility rests with him. This is not divided responsibility but shared responsibility — a very different thing.

Consider what happens when I want to get a bill through the legislature. I may feel sure that the bill is good and also that "the people" want it, but I can work only through party, and at the state house I have to face all the special interests bound up with party, all the thousand and one "political" considerations, whether

I succeed or fail. But of course I recognize the humor
of this statement: *I* ought never to try to get a bill
through the legislature; special and partial groups have
to do this simply because there is at present no other
way; there must be some other way, some recognized way.
We do not want to circumvent party but to replace party.

Our reform associations, while they have fought party,
have often endeavored to substitute their own organization for the party organization. This has often been the
alternative offered to us — do we want good government
or poor government? We have not been asked if we
would like to govern ourselves. This is why Mitchell
lost last year in New York. One of the New York papers
during the campaign advised Mr. Mitchell "to get
nearer the people." But it is not for government to
"get nearer" the people; it must identify itself with
the people. It isn't enough for the "good" officials to
explain to the people what they are doing; they must
take the people into their counsels. If the Gary system
had ever been properly put up to the fathers it is doubt-
ful if they would have voted against it. Then a good
deal of this advice in regard to city officials "explaining"
their plans in all parts of the city leaves out of account
that the local people have a great deal to give. Some of
the most uneducated, so-called, of the fathers and mothers
might have had valuable points of view to offer in regard to the practical workings of the Gary system.

Tammany won in New York and we heard many people
say, "Well, this is your democracy, the people want bad
government, the majority of people in New York city
have voted for it." Nothing could be more superficial.
What the election in New York meant was that "the
people" are cleverer than was thought; they know that
the question should not be of "good" government or
"bad" government, but only of self-government, and the

only way they have of expressing this is to vote against a government which *seems* to disregard them.

To say, "We are good men, we are honest officials, we are employing experts on education, sanitation etc, you must trust us," will not do; some way must be devised of connecting the experts and the people — that is the first thing to be worked out, then some way of taking the people into the counsels of city administration. All of us criticize things we don't know anything about. As soon as we see the difficulties, *as soon as the responsibility is put upon us*, our whole attitude changes. Take the popular cry "Boston positions for Boston people." This seems a pretty good principle to superficial thinking. But when we know that we have an appropriation of $200,000 a year for a certain department, and are looking for a man to administer it, when we go into the matter and find that there are only two or three experts for this position in the United States, and that not one of these lives in Boston, the question takes the concrete form, "Shall we allow $200,000 of our money to be wasted through inept administration?" It might be said, "But city governments do have the responsibility and yet this is just what they are all the time doing." Certainly, because their position rests on patronage, but I am proposing that the whole system be changed.

Neighborhood organization must be the method of effective popular responsibility: first, by giving reality to the political bond; secondly, by providing the machinery by which a genuine control of the people can be put into operation. At present nearly all our needs are satisfied by external agencies, government or institutional. Health societies offer health to us, recreation associations teach us how to play, civic art leagues give us more beautiful surroundings, associated charities give us poor relief. A kind lady leads my girl to the dentist, a kind young man finds employment for my boy, a stern officer of the city sees that my children are in their places at school. I am constantly being acted upon, no one is encouraging me to act. New York has one hundred municipal welfare divisions and bureaus. Thus am I robbed of my most precious possession — my responsibilities — for only the active process of participation can shape me for the social purpose.

But all this is to end. The community itself must grip its own problems, must fill its needs, must make effective its aspirations. If we want the latest scientific knowledge in regard to food values, let us get an expert to come to us, not wait for some society to send an "agent" to us; if the stores near us are not selling at fair prices, let us make a coöperative effort to set this right. If we want milk and baby hygiene organized, our own local doctors should, in proper coöperation with experts on the one hand and the mothers on the other, organize this branch of public service. The medical experts may be employees of the government, but if the plan of their service be worked out by all three — the experts, the local doctors and the mothers — the results will be: (1) that the needs of the neighborhood will really be met, (2) much valuable time of the expert will be saved, (3) a close follow-up will be possible, (4) the expert can be called in whenever necessary through local initiative, and (5) the machinery will be in existence by which the study of that particular problem can be carried on not as a special investigation but as a regular part of neighborhood life.

Take another example. The Placement Bureau is also a necessary public service: it needs the work of experts and it needs pooled information and centralized machinery; a parent cannot find out all the jobs available in a city for boys of 16 in order to place one boy.

But as long as the secretary of the Placement Bureau appears in the home and takes this whole burden off the parent, and off the community he is serving, his work will not be well done. For the boy will suffer eventually: he cannot be cut off from his community without being hurt; community incentive is the greatest one we know, and somehow there must be worked out some community responsibility for that boy, as well as some responsibility on his part to his community for standing up or falling down on his job. I say that the boy will eventually suffer; his community also will suffer, for it also has need of him; moreover, the community will greatly suffer by the loss of this opportunity of connecting it, through the parents, with the whole industrial problem of the city. The expert service of the Placement Bureau, whether it is administered by city or state, should always be joined to local initiative, effort and responsibility.

And so for every need. If we want well-managed dances for our daughters, we, mothers and fathers, must go and manage them. We do not exist on one side and the government on the other. If you go to a municipal dance-hall and see it managed by officials appointed from City Hall, you say, "This is a government affair." But if you go to a schoolhouse and see a dance managed by men and women chosen by the district, you say, "This is a community affair, government has nothing to do with this." These two conceptions must mingle before we can have any worthy political life. It must be clearly seen that we can operate *as* government as well as *with* government, that the citizen functions through government and the government functions through the citizen. It is not a municipal dance-hall regulated by the city authorities which expresses the right relation between civics and dancing, but dances planned and managed by a neighborhood for itself.

It is not the civic theatre which is the last word in the relation of the drama to the people, it is a community organized theatre. Art and civics do not meet merely by the state presenting art to its members; the civic expression of art is illustrated by locally managed festivals, by community singing, a local orchestra or dramatic club, community dancing etc. Those of us who are working for civic art are working for this: for people to express themselves in artistic forms and to organize themselves for that purpose. The state must give the people every opportunity for building up their own full, varied, healthful life. It seems to be often thought that when the state provides schools, parks, universities etc., there you have the ideal state. But we must go beyond this and find our ideal state in that which shows its members how to build up its own life *in* schools, parks, universities etc.[1]

The question which the state must always be trying to answer is how it can do more for its members at the same time that it is stimulating them to do more for themselves. No, more than this, its doing more for them must take the form of their doing more for themselves. Our modern problem is not, as one would think from some of the writing on social legislation, how much the increased activity of the state can do for the individual, but how the increasing activity of the individual can be state activity, how the widening of the sphere of state activity can be a widening of our own activity. The arguments for or against government action should not take the form of how much or how little government action we shall have, but entirely of how government

[1] The war has shown us that our national agricultural program can best be done on a coöperative neighborhood basis: through the establishment of community agricultural conferences, community labor, seed and implement exchanges, community canning centres, community markets, etc.

action and self-action can coincide. Our one essential political problem is always how to be the state, not, putting the state on one side and the individual on the other, to work out their respective provinces. I have said in the chapter on "Our Political Dualism" that the state and the individual are one, yet this is pure theory until we make them one. But they can never be made one through schemes of representation etc., only by the intimate daily lives of all becoming the constituents of the life of the state.

When a Mothers' Club in one of the Boston School Centres found a united want — that of keeping their children off the streets on Saturday afternoon and giving them some wholesome amusement — and decided to meet this want by asking the city of Boston for permission to use the moving-picture machine of the Dorchester High School for fairy-story films, the mothers to manage the undertaking, two significant facts stand out: (1) they did not ask an outside agency to do something for them, for the men and women of Dorchester, with all the other men and women of Boston, *are* the city of Boston; (2) they were not merely doing something for their children on those Saturday afternoons, they were in a sense officials of the city of Boston working for the youth of Boston. These two conceptions must blend: we do not do for government, government does not do for us, we should be constantly the hands and feet, yes and the head and heart of government.[1]

A most successful effort at neighborhood organization

---

[1] I do not mean to imply that I think it is easy to learn how to identify ourselves with our city, especially for those who live in large cities. The men of a small town know that if they have a new town-hall they will have to pay for it. In a large city men ask for a ward building because they will not have to pay for it, they think. It is all this which neighborhood organization and the integration of neighborhoods, of which I shall speak later, must remedy.

is that of the East Harlem Community Association, which set East Harlem to work on its own problems: first to investigate conditions, and then to find a way of meeting these conditions. The most interesting point about the whole scheme is that the work is not done by "experts" or any one else from outside; there are no paid visitors, but a committee of twelve mothers — one colored woman, two Italian, two Jewish, two Irish, three American, one Polish, and one German — are doing the work well. As a result of the activities of the East Harlem Community Association there are now in a public school building of the neighborhood organized athletic clubs, industrial classes, orchestra, glee, dramatic and art clubs, concerts, good moving pictures, dances, big brother and big sister groups, Mothers' Leagues, Parents' Associations, physical examination of school children etc. Of course these community associations must use expert advice and expert service. Exactly how this relation will be most satisfactorily worked out we do not yet clearly see.[1]

I give this merely as one illustration out of many possible ones. The necessity of neighborhood organization as the basis of future progress is seen by many people to-day. In New York there is a vigorous movement for "Neighborhood Associations"; there are four already in active working order. If the main idea of some of these is services rendered rather than neighborhood organization; if others see too great a separation between needs and the satisfaction of the needs, that is,

---

[1] The plan of Mr. and Mrs. Wilbur Phillips for community organization and for the connection with it of expert service is too comprehensive to describe here, but based as it is on their actual experience, and planning as it does for the training of whole neighborhoods and the arousing of them to responsibility and action, it should be studied by every one, for such plans are, I believe, the best signs we have that democracy is yet possible for America.

if the neighborhoods are always to ask the questions and the experts to find the answers, still these Associations are an interesting and valuable part of the neighborhood movement.[1]

The acute problem of municipal life is how to make us men and women of Boston feel that we *are* the city, directly responsible for everything concerning it. Neighborhood organization, brought into existence largely by the growing feeling of each individual that he is responsible for the life around him, itself then increases and focuses this sense of responsibility. Neighborhood association is vivid and intimate. Whereas the individual seems lost in a big city, through his neighborhood he not only becomes an integral part of the city but becomes keenly conscious of his citizenship.

In a word, what we hope neighborhood organization will do for the development of responsibility is this: that men will learn that they are not to *influence* politics through their local groups, they are to *be* politics. This is the error of some of the reform associations: they want to influence politics. This point of view will never spell progress for us. When we have the organized neighborhood group, when every man sees the problems of political and social reorganization not as abstract matters but as constituting his daily life, when men are so educated in politics as to feel that they themselves are politics functioning, and when our organization is such that this functioning recoils on them, they will so shape their conduct as to change the situation. Then when they are conscious of themselves as masters of the situation they will acknowledge their responsibility.

We see many signs around us to-day of an increased sense of responsibility, of a longing for a self-expression

[1] How much we are all indebted to the settlements as the pioneer neighborhood movement I do not stop to consider here.

that is not to be an individual self-expression but community self-expression. Take the women's clubs: in their first stage their object was personal development; in the second they wished to do something for their town; in the present or third stage women are demanding through some of the more progressive clubs, through women's municipal leagues etc., a more direct share in community life. They are joining together not to benefit themselves, not to benefit others, as others, but because all together they wish to express their community — no, they wish to *be* their community. They are not satisfied with serving, but gathering up the service of all in a common consciousness, each feels herself the whole and seeks to express the whole.

But I do not mean that this greater realization of community is confined to women. How often in the past we have heard a man say complacently, "Well, I suppose I must do my duty and go to the polls and vote to-morrow," or "I must show myself at that rally to-night." But a nobler idea than this is now filling the minds of many men. They go to their civic club not because it is their duty, but because just there working together with their fellows for the furtherance of their common aims, they find their greatest satisfaction. In neighborhood groups men can find that self-realization which becomes by the most wonderful miracle life can offer us community realization. That is, I can learn through my neighborhood group that I am the city, I am the nation, and that fatal transference of responsibility to an invisible and non-existent "they" can be blotted out forever. When neighborhood organization begins to teach that there is no "they," that it is always we, we, we, that mothers are responsible and fathers are responsible, and young men are responsible, and young women are responsible, for their city and their nation, it will begin to teach its chief lesson.

Do I thrill with the passion of service, of joyful, voluntary surrender to a mighty cause as I sail for France to serve the great ends of the Allies? Social and political organization are fatally at fault if they cannot give me the same elation as I go to my Neighborhood Centre and know that there too the world has vital need of me, there too am I not only pouring myself out in world service, but that I am, just in so far, creating, actually building, a new and fairer world.

This is the finest word that can be said for neighborhood organization, for my finding my place through my response to every daily need of my nearest group. For the great word I believe on this subject is not that I *serve* my neighborhood, my city, my nation, but that by this service I *become* my neighborhood, my city, my nation. Surely at this hour in our history we can realize this as never before. The soul of America is being born to-day. The war is binding together class and class, alien and American, men and women. We rejoice that we are alive at this moment, but the keenness of my joy is not because I can serve America but because I am America. I save food in my home not in order that my family income can meet the strain of the higher prices, not because I can thereby help to send more food to the Allies, but because I, saving the food of America for the Allies and the world, am performing America's task, *am* therefore America. This is the deeper thought of neighborhood organization: that through performing my humblest duties I am creating the soul of this great democracy.

Neighborhood organization must then take the place of party organization. The neighborhood group will

answer many of the questions we have put to a party
organization which has remained deaf to our importuni-
ties, dumb to all our entreaties. We have asked for
bread and received the stone times without number.
The rigid formality of the party means stultification,
annihilation. But group politics, made of the very stuff
of life, of the people of the groups, will express the inner,
intimate, ardent desires of spontaneous human beings,
and will contain within its circumference the possibility
of the fullest satisfaction of those desires. Group organization gives a living, pulsing unity made up of the minds
and hearts and seasoned judgments of vital men and
women. Such organization is capable of unbroken
growth. And when this vine of life, which sends its roots
where every two or three are gathered together, has
rooted itself in the neighborhood, faithful care, sedulous
watching, loving ministration will appear with it, will
be the natural way of living. Its impalpable bonds
hold us together, and although we may differ on countless questions, instead of flying asunder we work out the
form in political life which will shelter us and supply our
needs. Faithfulness to the neighborhood bond must
take the place of allegiance to party. Loyalty to a party
is loyalty to a thing — we want a living politics in which
loyalty is always intrinsic. And from the strength of
this living bond shall come the power of our united life.
Always the actor, never the spectator, is the rule of the
new democracy. Always the sharer, never the giver or
the receiver, is the order of our new life.

Do you think the neighborhood group too puny to
cope with this giant towering above us, drunk with the
blood of its many triumphs? The young David went
out to conquer Goliath, strong in the conviction of his
power. Cannot our cause justify an equal faith?

Is our daily life profane and only so far as we rise out

of it do we approach the sacred life? Then no wonder politics are what they have become. But this is not the creed of men to-day: we believe in the sacredness of all our life; we believe that Divinity is forever incarnating in humanity, and so we believe in Humanity and the common daily life of all men.

XXVII

FROM NEIGHBORHOOD TO NATION: THE UNIFYING STATE

HOW can the will of the people be the sovereign power of the state? There must be two changes in our state: first, the state must be the actual integration of living, local groups, thereby finding ways of dealing directly with its individual members. Secondly, other groups than neighborhood groups must be represented in the state: the ever-increasing multiple group life of to-day must be recognized and given a responsible place in politics.[1]

First, every neighborhood must be organized; the neighborhood groups must then be integrated, through larger intermediary groups, into a true state. Neither our cities nor our states can ever be properly administered until representatives from neighborhood groups meet to discuss and thereby to correlate the needs of all parts of the city, of all parts of the state. Social workers and medical experts have a conference on tuberculosis, social workers and educational experts have a conference on industrial education. We must now develop the methods by which the citizens also are represented at these conferences. We must go beyond this (for certain organizations, as the National Settlement Conference at least, do already have neighborhood representation), and develop the methods by which regular meetings of representatives from neighborhood organizations meet to discuss all city and state prob-

[1] This point will be taken up in ch. XXXIII.

lems. Further still, we must give official recognition to such gatherings, we must make them a regular part of government. The neighborhood must be actually, not theoretically, an integral part of city, of state, of nation.

When Massachusetts is thus organized, the neighborhood groups and intermediary, or district, groups should send representatives to city council and state legislature. The Senate might be composed of experts — experts in education, in housing, in sanitation etc.[1] The neighborhood and district centres would receive reports from their representatives to city council and state legislature and take measures on these reports. They should also be required to send regular reports up to their representative bodies. We should have a definitely organized and strongly articulated network of personal interest and representative reporting. Then the state legislature must devise ways of dealing not only with the district group but with the neighborhood groups through the district group, and thus with every individual in the commonwealth. The nation too must have a real connection with every little neighborhood centre through state and district bodies.[2]

America at war has found a way of getting word from Washington to the smallest local units. The Council of National Defense has a "Section of Coöperation with States." This is connected with a State Council of

[1] Or perhaps the Senate might represent the occupational group (see ch. XXXIII). Or perhaps the experts mentioned above might be representatives from occupational groups.

[2] In North Carolina the recently organized State Bureau of Community Service — made up of the administrators of the Department of Agriculture, the Board of Health, the Normal and Industrial College and the Farmers' Union, with the State Superintendent of Public Instruction as its central executive — is making its immediate work the development of local community organization which shall be directly articulated with a unified state organization.

Defense in every state. In most cases the State Council is connected with County Councils, and these often with councils in cities and towns. Beyond this the Council of National Defense has recently (February, 1918) recommended the extension of county organization by the creation of Community Councils in every school district. Its official statement opens with this sentence: "The first nine months of the war have shown the vital importance of developing an official nation-wide organization reaching into the smallest communities to mobilize and make available the efforts of the whole people for the prosecution of the war." And it goes on to say that the government must have such close contact with small units that personal relation with all the citizens is possible.

President Wilson in endorsing this step, said, "[This is an] advance of vital significance. It will, I believe, result when thoroughly carried out in welding the nation together as no nation of great size has ever been welded before. . . . It is only by extending your organization to small communities that every citizen of the state can be reached."

Thus when the government found that it must provide means to its hands for keeping constantly in touch with the whole membership of the nation, it planned to do this by the encouragement and fostering of neighborhood organization. The nation is now seeking the individual through neighborhood groups. It is using the School Centres (it recommends the schoolhouse as the best centre for community organization) for the teaching of Food and Fuel Conservation, for Liberty Loan and Red Cross work, for recruiting for the army, for enlisting workers for war industries, for teaching the necessity and methods of increasing the food supply, for plans to relieve transportation by coöperative shipments and deliveries, for patriotic education etc.[1] This "patriotic education" has an interesting side. In a country which is even nominally a democracy you cannot win a war without explaining your aims and your policy and carrying your people with you step by step. If beyond this the country wishes to be really a democracy, the neighborhood groups must have a share in forming the aims and the policy.

Of course one would always prefer this to be a movement from below up rather than from above down, but it is not impossible for the two movements to go on at the same time, as they are in fact doing now with the rapid development of spontaneous local organization. There were Community Councils in existence in fact if not in name before the recommendation of the Council of National Defense.[2]

Through these non-partisan councils not only national policy can be explained and spread throughout the country, but also what one locality thinks out that is good can be reported to Washington and thus handed on to other sections of the country. It is a plan for sending the news backwards and forwards from individual to nation, from nation to individual, and it is also a plan for correlating the problems of the local community with the problems of the nation and of coöperating nations.

But why should we be more efficiently organized for war than for peace? Is our proverbial carelessness to be pricked into effectiveness only by emergency calls? Is the only motive you can offer us for efficiency — to

---

[1] The Community Council, however, is not to duplicate other organizations but first to coördinate all existing agencies before planning new activities.

[2] And spontaneously many towns and villages turned to the schoolhouse as the natural centre of its war services.

win? Or, if that is an instinctive desire, can we not change the goal and be as eager to win other things as war?

I speak of the new state as resting upon integrated neighborhood groups.[1] While the changes necessary to bring this about would have to be planned and authorized by constitutional conventions, its psychological basis would be: (1) the fact that we are ready for membership in a larger group only by experience first in the smaller group, and (2) the natural tendency for a real group to seek other groups. Let us look at this second point.

We have seen the process of the single group evolving. But contemporaneously a thousand other unities are a-making. Every group once become conscious of itself instinctively seeks other groups with which to unite to form a larger whole. Alone it cannot be effective. As individual progress depends upon the degree of interpenetration, so group progress depends upon the interpenetration of group and group. For convenience I speak of each group as a whole, but from a philosophical point of view there is no whole, only an infinite striving for wholeness, only the *principle* of wholeness forever leading us on.

This is the social law: the law which connects neighborhood with neighborhood. The reason we want neighborhood organization is not to keep people within their neighborhoods but to get them out. The movement for neighborhood organization is a deliberate effort to get people to identify themselves actually, not sentimentally, with a larger and larger collective unit than the neighborhood. We may be able through our neigh-

---

[1] For the moment I ignore the occupational group to be considered later.

borhood group to learn the social process, to learn to evolve the social will, but the question before us is whether we have enough political genius to apply this method to city organization, national organization, and international organization. City must join with city, state with state, actually, not through party. Finally nation must join with nation.

The recommendation of the Council of National Defense which has been mentioned above would repay careful reading for the indications which one finds in it of the double purpose of neighborhood organization. It is definitely stated that the importance of the Community Council is in: (1) initiating work to meet its own war needs; and (2) in making all its local resources available for the nation. And again it is stated that: (1) in a democracy local emergencies can best be met by local action; and (2) that each local district should feel the duty of bearing its full share of the national burden.

Thus our national government clearly sees and specifically states that neighborhood organization is both for the neighborhood and for the nation: that it looks in, it looks out. Thus that which we are coming to understand as the true social process receives practical recognition in government policy.

I have said that neighborhood must join with neighborhood to form the state. This joining of neighborhood and neighborhood can be done neither directly nor imaginatively. It cannot be done directly: representation is necessary not only because the numbers would be too great for all neighborhoods to meet together, but because even if it were physically possible we should have created a crowd not a society. Theoretically when you have large numbers you get a big, composite consciousness made up of infinite kinds of fitting together of infinite kinds of individuals, but practically this varied and multiplied fitting together is not possible beyond a certain number. There must be representatives from the smallest units to the larger and larger, up to the federal state.

Secondly, neighborhoods cannot join with neighborhoods through the imagination alone. Various people have asserted that now we have large cities and solidarity cannot come by actual acquaintance, it must be got by appropriate appeals to the imagination, by having, for instance, courses of lectures to tell one part of a city about another part. But this alone will never be successful. Real solidarity will never be accomplished except by beginning somewhere the joining of one small group with another. We are told too that the uneducated man cannot think beyond his particular section of the universe. We can teach him to think beyond his particular section of the universe by actually making him participate in other sections through connecting his section with others. We are capable of being faithful to large groups as well as small, to complex groups as well as simple, to our city, to our nation, but this can be effected only by a certain process, and that process, while it may begin by a stimulation of the imagination, must, if it is going to bring forth results in real life, be a matter of actual experience. Only by actual union, not by appeals to the imagination, can the various and varied neighborhood groups be made the constituents of a sound, normal, unpartisan city life. Then being a member of a neighborhood group will mean at the same time being a member and a responsible member of the state.

I have spoken of the psychological tendency for group to seek group. Moreover, it is not possible to isolate yourself in your local group because few local needs can be met without joining with other localities, which have these same needs, in order to secure city or state action. We cannot get municipal regulation for the dance-hall in our neighborhood without joining with other neighborhoods which want the same thing and securing municipal regulation for all city dance-halls. If we want better housing laws, grants for industrial education, we join with other groups who want these things and become the state. And even if some need seems purely local, the method of satisfying it ought not to be for the South End to pull as hard as it can for a new ward building, say, while the North End is also pulling as hard as it can for a new ward building, and the winner of such tug-of-war to get the appropriation. If the South End wants a new ward building it should understand how much money is available for ward buildings, and if only enough for one this year, consider where it is most needed. Probably, whatever the evidence, it will be decided that it is most needed in the South End, but a step will be taken towards a different kind of decision in the future.

And we join not only to secure city and state but also federal action. If we want a river or harbor appropriation, we go to Congress. And if such demands are supplied at present on the log-rolling basis, we can only hope that this will not always be so. When group organization has vitalized our whole political life, there may then be some chance that log-rolling will be repudiated.

And we do not stop even at Washington. Immigration is a national and international problem, but the immigrant may live next door to you, and thus the immigration question becomes one of nearest concern. This intricate interweaving of our life allows no man to live to himself or to his neighborhood.

Then when neighborhood joins with neighborhood all the lessons learned in the simple group must be prac-

tised in the complex one. As the group lesson includes
not only my responsibility *to* my group but my responsibility *for* my group, so I learn not only my duty to my
neighborhood but that I am responsible for my neighborhood. Also it is seen that as the individuals of a
group are interdependent, so the various groups are
interdependent, and the problem is to understand just
in what way they are interdependent and how they can
be adjusted to one another. The process of the joining
of several groups into a larger whole is exactly the same
as the joining of individuals to form a group — a reciprocal interaction and correlation.

The usual notion is that our neighborhood association
is to evolve an idea, a plan, and then when we go to
represent it at a meeting of neighborhood associations
from different parts of the city that we are to try to
push through the plan of action decided on by our own
local group. If we do not do this, we are not supposed
to be loyal. But we are certainly to do nothing of
the kind. We are to try to evolve the collective idea
which shall represent the new group, that is, the various
neighborhood associations all acting together. We are
told that we must not sacrifice the interests of the particular group we represent. No, but also we must not
try to make its interests prevail against those of others.
Its real interests are the interests of the whole.

And then when we have learned to be truly citizens
of Boston, we must discover how Boston and other
cities, how cities and the rural communities can join.
And so on and so on. At last the "real" state appears.
We are pragmatists because we do not want to unite
with the state imaginatively, we want to be the state;
we want to actualize and feel our way every moment,
let every group open the way for a larger group, let every
circumference become the centre of a new circumfer-

ence. My neighborhood group opens the path to the State.

But neighborhoods coöperating actively with the city government is not to-day a dream. Marcus M. Marks, President of the Borough of Manhattan, New York City, in 1914 divided Manhattan into sixteen neighborhoods, and appointed for each a neighborhood commission composed of business men, professional men, mechanics, clerks etc. — a thoroughly representative body chosen irrespective of party lines. Mr. Marks' avowed object was to obtain a knowledge of the needs of his constituents, to form connecting links between neighborhoods and the city government. And these bodies need not exist dormant until their advice is asked. Sections 1 and 2 of the Rules and Regulations read:

"1. The Commissions shall recommend, or suggest, to the Borough President, for his consideration and advice, matters which, in their opinion will be of benefit to their districts and to the City.

"2. The Commissions shall receive from the Borough President suggestions or recommendations for their consideration as to matters affecting their districts, and report back their conclusions with respect thereto."

Moreover, beyond the recommendations of the Commission, the coöperation of the whole neighborhood is sought. "Whenever the commissions are in doubt as to the policy they desire to advocate and wish to further sound the sentiment of their localities, meetings similar to town-meetings are held, usually in the local schoolhouse." The "neighborhoods" of Manhattan have coöperated with the city government in such matters as bus franchise, markets, location of tracks, floating baths, pavement construction, sewerage etc. One of the results of this plan, Mr. Marks tells us, is that many types of improvement which were formerly opposed, such as sewerage construction by the owners of abutting property, now receive the support of the citizens because there is opportunity for them to understand fully the needs of the situation and even to employ their own expert if they wish.

The chairmen of the twelve Neighborhood Commissions form a body called the Manhattan Commission. This meets to confer with the President on matters affecting the interests of the entire borough.[1]

This plan, while not yet ideal, particularly in so far as the commissions are appointed from above, is most interesting to all those who are looking towards neighborhood organization as the basis of the new state.

To summarize: neighborhood groups join with other neighborhood groups to form the city — then only shall we understand what it is to be the city; neighborhood groups join with other neighborhood groups to form the state — then only shall we undersand what it is to be the state. We do not begin with a unified state which delegates authority; we begin with the neighborhood group and create the state ourselves. Thus is the state built up through the intimate intertwining of all.

But this is not a crude and external federalism. We have not transferred the unit of democracy from the individual to the group. It is the individual man who must feel himself the unit of city government, of state government: he has not delegated his responsibility to

[1] I have taken this account from the official report. I have been told by New York people that these commissions have shown few signs of life. This does not, however, seem to me to detract from the value of the plan as a suggestion, or as indication of what is seen to be advisable if not yet wholly practicable. The New York charter provides for Local Improvement Boards as connecting links with the central government, but these I am told have shown no life whatever.

his neighborhood group; he has direct relation with larger wholes. I have no medieval idea of mediate articulation, of individuals forming groups and groups forming the nation. Mechanical federalism we have long outgrown. The members of the nation are to be individuals, not groups. The movement for neighborhood organization is from one point of view a movement to give the individual political effectiveness — it is an individualistic not a collectivistic movement, paradoxical as this may seem to superficial thinking. But, as the whole structure of government must rest on the individual, it must have its roots within that place where you can get nearest to him, and where his latent powers can best be freed and actualized — his local group.

What are we ultimately seeking through neighborhood organization? To find the individual. But let no one think that the movement for neighborhood organization is a new movement. Our neighborhood organization, we are often told, had its origin in the New England town-meeting. Yes, and far beyond that in the early institutions of our English ancestors. That our national life must be grounded in the daily, intimate life of all men is the teaching of the whole long stream of English history.

We have seen that the increasing activity of the state, its social policies and social legislation, demands the activity of every man. We have seen in considering direct government that the activity of every man is not enough if we mean merely his activity at the polling booths. With the inclusion of all men and women (practically accomplished) in the suffrage, with the rapidly increasing acceptance of direct government, the *extensive* work of the democratic impulse has ended. Now the *intensive* work of democracy must begin. The great historic task of the Anglo-Saxon people has been to find wise and reasoned forms for the expression of individual responsibility, has been so to bulwark the rights of the individual as to provide at the same time for the unity and stability of the state. They have done this externally by making the machinery of representative government. We want to-day to do it spiritually, to direct the spiritual currents in their flow and interflow so that we have not only the external interpenetration — choosing representatives etc. — but the deeper interpenetration which shows the minds and needs and wants of all men.

We can satisfy our wants only by a genuine union and communion of all, only in the friendly outpouring of heart to heart. We have come to the time when we see that the machinery of government can be useful to us only so far as it is a living thing: the souls of men are the stones of Heaven, the life of every man must contribute fundamentally to the growth of the state. So the world spirit seeks freedom and finds it in a more and more perfect union of true individuals. *The relation of neighbors one to another must be integrated into the substance of the state.* Politics must take democracy from its external expression of representation to the expression of that inner meaning hidden in the intermingling of all men. This is our part to-day — thus shall we take our place in the great task of our race. Our political life began in the small group, but it has taken us long to evolve our relation to a national life, and meanwhile much of the significance and richness of the local life has been lost. Back now to the local unit we must go with all that we have accumulated, to find in and through that our complete realization. Back we must go to this small primary unit if we would understand the meaning of democracy, if we would get the fruits of democracy. As Voltaire said, "The spirit of France is the candle of Europe," so must the spirit of the neighborhood be the candle of the nation.

XXVIII

POLITICAL PLURALISM

ALL that I have written has been based on the assumption of the unifying state. Moreover I have spoken of neighborhood organization as if it were possible to take it for granted that the neighborhood group is to be the basis of the new state. The truth of both these assumptions is denied by some of our most able thinkers.

The unified state is now discredited in many quarters. Syndicalists, guild socialists, some of the Liberals in England, some of the advocates of occupational representation in America, and a growing school of writers who might be called political pluralists are throwing the burden of much proof upon the state, and are proposing group organization as the next step in political method. To some the idea of the state is abhorrent. One writer says, "The last hundred years marked in all countries the beginning of the dissolution of the State and of the resurrection of corporate life [trade unions etc.] . . . In the face of this growth of syndicalism in every direction, . . . it is no longer venturesome to assert that the State is dead."

Others like to keep the word "state" but differ much as to the position it is to occupy in the new order: to some it seems to be merely a kind of mucilage to keep the various groups together; with others the state is to hold the ring while different groups fight out their differences. Still other thinkers, while seeing the open door to scepticism in regard to the state, are nevertheless not ready to pass through, but, preserving the instinct and the reverence for the unity of the state, propose as the most immediate object of our study how the unity can be brought about, what is to be the true and perfect bond of union between the multiple groups of our modern life. All these thinkers, differing widely as they do, yet may be roughly classed together as the upholders of a multiple group organization as the basis for a new state.

This movement is partly a reaction against an atomistic sovereignty, the so-called theory of "subjective" rights, a "senseless" geographical representation, a much berated parliamentary system, and partly the wish to give industrial workers a larger share in the control of industry and in government.

The opposition to "numerical representation" has been growing for some time. We were told thirty years ago by Le Prins that vocational representation is "the way out of the domination of the majority," that the vocational group is the "natural" group "spontaneously generated in the womb of a nation." Twenty-five years ago Benoist said that the state must recognize private associations: universities, chambers of commerce, professional associations, societies of agriculture, syndicates of workmen — "en un mot tout ce qui a corps et vie dans la nation." If the state is to correspond to reality, it must recognize, Benoist insisted, all this group life, all these interests, within it. Moreover, he urged, with our present pulverized suffrage, with sovereignty divided among millions, we are in a state of anarchy; only group representation will save us from "la force stupide de nombre." M. Léon Duguit has given us a so-called "objective" theory of law which means for many people a new conception of the state.

Many say that it is absurd for representation to be based on the mere chance of residence as is the case when the geographical district is the unit. The territorial principle is going, we are told, and that of similar occupational interests will take its place. Again some people are suggesting that both principles should be recognized in our government: that one house in Parliament represent geographical areas, the other occupations.[1] No one has yet, however, made any proposal of this kind definite enough to serve as a basis of discussion.

Syndicalism demands the abolition of the "state" while — through its organization of the syndicate of workers, the union of syndicates of the same town or region and the federation of these unions — it erects a system of its own controlled entirely by the workers. Syndicalism has gained many adherents lately because of the present reaction against socialism. People do not want the Servile State and, therefore, many think they do not want any state.

In England a new school is arising which is equally opposed to syndicalism and to the bureaucracy of state socialism. Or rather it takes half of each. Guild socialism believes in state ownership of the means of production, but that the control of each industry or "guild" — appointment of officers, hours and conditions of work etc. — should be vested in the membership of the industry. The syndicalists throw over the state entirely, the guild socialists believe in the "co-management" of the state. There are to be two sets of machinery side by side but quite distinct: that based on the occupational group will be concerned with economic considerations, the other with "political" considerations, the first culmi-

---

[1] Léon Duguit, Graham Wallis, Arthur Christensen, Norman Angell, etc.

nating in a national Guild Congress, and the second in the State.[1]

"Guild Socialism," edited by A. R. Orage, gives in some detail this systematic plan already familiar to readers of the *New Age*. A later book of the same school "Authority, Liberty and Function," by Ramiro de Maeztu, concerns itself less with detail and more with the philosophical basis of the new order. The value of this book consists in its emphasis on the functional principle.[2]

Mr. Ernest Barker of Oxford, although he formulates no definite system, is a political pluralist.

John Neville Figgis makes an important contribution to pluralism,[3] and although he has a case to plead for the church, he is equally emphatic that all the local groups which really make our life should be fostered and given an increased authority.

In America vocational representation has many distinguished advocates, among them Professor Felix Adler and Professor H. A. Overstreet. Mr. Herbert Croly, who has given profound thought to the trend of democracy, advocates giving increased power and legal recognition to the powerful groups growing up within the state.

[1] The fatal flaw of guild socialism is this separation of economics and politics. First, the interests of citizenship and guild-membership are not distinct; secondly, in any proper system of occupational representation every one should be included — vocational representation should not be trade representation; third, as long as you call the affairs of the guilds "material," and say that the politics of the state should be purified of financial interests, you burn every bridge which might make a unity of financial interests and sound state policy. Guild socialism, however, because it is a carefully worked out plan for the control of industry by those who take part in it, is one of the most well worth considering of the proposals at present before us.

[2] See G. D. H. Cole, "The World of Labor," for the relation of trade unionism to guild socialism.

[3] See especially "Churches in the Modern State" and "Studies in Political Thought from Gerson to Grotius."

Mr. Harold Laski is a pronounced political pluralist, especially in his emphasis on the advantage of multiple, varied and freely developing groups for the enrichment and enhancement of our whole life. Mr. Laski's book, "Studies in the Problem of Sovereignty," is one of the most thought-stimulating bits of modern political writing: it does away with the fetich of the abstract state — it is above all an attempt to look at things as they are rather than as we imagine them to be; it shows that states are not supreme by striking examples of organizations within the state claiming and winning the right to refuse obedience to the state; it sees the strength and the variety of our group life to-day as a significant fact for political method; it is a recognition, to an extent, of the group principle — it sees that sovereignty is not in people as a mass; it pleads for a revivification of local life, and finally it shows us, implicitly, not only that we need to-day a new state, but that the new state must be a great moral force.[1]

Perhaps the most interesting contribution of the pluralists is their clear showing that "a single unitary state with a single sovereignty" is not true to the facts of life to-day. Mr. Barker says, "Every state is something of a federal society and contains different national groups, different churches, different economic organizations, each exercising its measure of control over its members." The following instances are cited to show the present tendency of different groups to claim autonomy:

1. Religious groups are claiming rights as groups. Many churchmen would like to establish the autonomy of the church. It is impossible to have undenomina-

---

[1] See also Mr. Laski's articles: "The Personality of Associations," Harv. Law Rev. 29, 404–426, and "Early History of the Corporation in England," Harv. Law Rev.: 30, 561–588. This is the kind of work which is breaking the way for a new conception of politics.

tional instruction in the schools of England because of the claims of the church.

2. There is a political movement towards the recognition of national groups. The state in England is passing Home Rule Acts and Welsh Disestablishment Acts to meet the claims of national groups. "All Europe is convulsed with a struggle of which one object is a regrouping of men in ways which will fulfil national ideals."

3. "The Trade-Unions claim to be free groups." "Trade-unions have recovered from Parliament more than they have lost in the courts."

Let us consider the arguments of the pluralist school, as they form the most interesting, the most suggestive and the most important theory of politics now before us. It seems to me that there are four weaknesses in the pluralist school [1] which must be corrected before we can take from them the torch to light us on our political way: (1) some of the pluralists ostensibly found their books on pragmatic philosophy and yet in their inability to reconcile the distributive and collective they do not accept the latest teachings of pragmatism, for pragmatism does not end with a distributive pluralism, (2) the movement is in part a reaction to a misunderstood Hegel-

---

[1] It must be understood that all I say does not apply to all the pluralists. For the sake of brevity I consider them as a school although they differ widely. Moreover, for convenience I am using the word pluralist roughly and in a sense inaccurately to include all those who are advocating a multiple group organization as the basis of a new state. Most of these agree in making the group rather than the individual the unit of politics, in their support of group "rights," the "consent" of the group, the "balance" of groups, and in their belief that "rights" should be based on function. But syndicalists and guild socialists are not strictly pluralists since they build up a system based on the occupational group; yet the name is not wholly inapplicable, for, since the guild socialists base their state on balancing groups, that state cannot be called a unified state. It is too early yet to speak of this school with entire accuracy, and in fact there is no "school."

ianism, (3) many of the pluralists are professed followers
of medieval doctrine, (4) their thinking is not based on
a scientific study of the group, which weakens the force
of their theories of "objective" rights and sovereignty,
much as these latter are an advance on our old theories
of "subjective" rights and a sovereignty based on an
atomistic conception of society.

First, the underlying problem of pluralism and pragmatism is, as James proclaims, the relation of "collective" and "distributive." The problem of to-day, we
all agree, is the discovery of the kind of federalism which
will make the parts live fully in the whole, the whole
live fully in the parts. But this is the central problem
of philosophy which has stirred the ages. The heart of
James' difficulty was just this: how can many conscious-
nesses be at the same time one consciousness? How can
the same identical fact experience itself so diversely?
How can you be the absolute and the individual? It is
the old, old struggle which has enmeshed so many, which
some of our philosophers have transcended by the deeper
intuitions, sure that life is a continuous flow and not
spasmodic appearance, disappearance and reappearance.
James struggled long with this problem, but the outcome
was sure. His spirit could not be bound by intellectualistic logic, the logic of identity. He was finally
forced to adopt a higher form of rationality. He gave
up conceptualistic logic "fairly, squarely and irrevocably," and knew by deepest inner testimony that "states
of consciousness can separate and combine themselves
freely and keep their own identity unchanged while
forming parts of simultaneous fields of experience of
wider scope." James always saw the strung-along universe, but he also saw the unifying principle which is
working towards its goal. "That secret," he tells us,
"of a continuous life which the universe knows by heart

and acts on every instant cannot be a contradiction incarnate. . . . Our intelligence must keep on speaking terms with the universe."

When James found that the "all-form" and the "each-forms" are not incompatible, he found the secret of federalism. It is our task to work out in practical politics this speculative truth which the great philosophers have presented to us. The words absolute and individual veil it to us, but substitute state and individual and the problem comes down to the plane of our actual working everyday life. It may be interesting to read philosophy, but the thrilling thing for every man of us to do is to make it come true. We may be heartened by our sojourns on Sinai, but no man may live his life in the clouds. And what does pragmatism mean if not just this? We can only, as James told us again and again, understand the collective and distributive by living. Life is the true revealer: I can never understand the whole by reason, only when the heart-beat of the whole throbs through me as the pulse of my own being.

If we in our neighborhood group live James' philosophy of the compounding of consciousness, if we obey the true doctrine, that each individual is not only himself but the state — for the fulness of life overflows — then will the perfect form of federalism appear and express itself, for then we have the spirit of federalism creating its own form. Political philosophers talk of the state, but there is no state until we make it. It is pure theory. We, every man and woman to-day, must create his small group first, and then, through its compounding with other groups, it ascends from stage to stage until the federal state appears. Thus do we understand by actual living how collective experiences can claim identity with their constituent parts, how "your experience and mine

can be members of a world-experience." In our neighborhood groups we claim identity with the whole collective
will, at that point we are the collective will.

Unless multiple sovereignty can mean ascending rather
than parallel groups it will leave out the deepest truth
which philosophy has brought us. But surely the political pluralists who are open admirers of James will refuse
with him to stay enmeshed in sterile intellectualism, in
the narrow and emasculated logic of identity. Confessedly disciples of James, will they not carry their dis-
cipleship a step further? Have they not with James a
wish for a world that does not fall into "discontinuous
pieces," for "a higher denomination than that distributed, strung-along and flowing sort of reality which
we finite beings [now] swim in"? Their groups must
be the state each at its separate point. When they see
this truth clearly, then the leadership to which their
insight entitles them will be theirs.

I have said that the political pluralists are fighting a
misunderstood Hegelianism. Do they adopt the crudely
popular conception of the Hegelian state as something
"above and beyond" men, as a separate entity virtually
independent of men? Such a conception is fundamentally wrong and wholly against the spirit of Hegel. As
James found collective experience not independent of
distributive experience, as he reconciled the two through
the "compounding of consciousness," so Hegel's related
parts received their meaning only in the conception of
total relativity. The soul of Hegelianism is total relativity, but this is the essence of the compounding of
consciousness. As for James the related parts and their
relations appear simultaneously and with equal reality,
so in Hegel's total relativity: the members of the state
in their right relation to one another appear in all the
different degrees of reality together as one whole total

relativity — never sundered, never warring against the true Self, the Whole.

But there is the real Hegel and the Hegel who misapplied his own doctrine, who preached the absolutism of a Prussian State. Green and Bosanquet in measure more or less full taught the true Hegelian doctrine. But for a number of years the false leadings of Hegel have been uppermost in people's minds, and there has been a reaction to their teaching due to the panic we all feel at the mere thought of an absolute monarch and an irresponsible state. The present behavior of Prussia of course tends to increase the panic, and the fashion of jeering at Hegel and his "misguided" followers is widespread. But while many English writers are raging against Hegelianism, at the same time the English are pouring out in unstinted measure themselves and their substance to establish on earth Hegel's absolute in the actual form of an International League!

The political pluralists whom we are now considering, believing that a collective and distributive sovereignty cannot exist together, throw overboard collective sovereignty. When they accept the compounding of consciousness taught by their own master, James, then they will see that true Hegelianism finds its actualized form in federalism.

Perhaps they would be able to do this sooner if they could rid themselves of the Middle Ages! Many of the political pluralists deliberately announce that they are accepting medieval doctrine.

In the Middle Ages the group was the political unit. The medieval man was always the member of a group — of the guild in the town, of the manor in the country. But this was followed by the theory of the individual not as a member of a group but as a member of a nation, and we have always considered this on the whole an

advance step. When, therefore, the separate groups
are again proposed as the political units, we are going
back to a political theory which we have long outgrown
and which obviously cramps the individual. It is true
that the individual as the basis of government has remained an empty theory. The man with political power
has been the rich and strong man. There has been little
chance for the individual as an individual to become
a force in the state. In reaction against such selfish
autocracy people propose a return to the Middle Ages.
This is not the solution. Now is the critical moment.
If we imitate the Middle Ages and adopt political pluralism we lose our chance to invent our own forms for our
larger ideas.

Again, balancing groups were loosely held together by
what has been called a federal bond. Therefore we are
to look to the medieval empire for inspiration in forming the modern state. But the union of church and guild,
boroughs and shires of the Middle Ages seems to me
neither to bear much resemblance to a modern federal
state nor to approach the ideal federal state. And if
we learn anything from medieval decentralization —
guild and church and commune — it is that political
and economic power cannot be separated.

Much as we owe the Middle Ages, have we not pro-
gressed since then? Are our insights, our ideals, our
purposes at all the same? Medieval theory, it is true,
had the conception of the living group, and this had a
large influence on legal theory.[1] Also medieval theory
struggled from first to last to reconcile its notion of individual freedom,[2] the patent fact of manifold groups,

[1] From this was taken, Gierke tells us, modern German "fellowship."
[2] And the individual was certainly as prominent in medieval theory
as the community of individuals, a fact which the vigorous corporate life
of the Middle Ages may lead us to forget.

and the growing notion of a sovereign state. Our problem it is true is the same to-day, but the Middle Ages hold more warnings than lessons for us. While there was much that was good about the medieval guilds, we certainly do not want to go back to all the weaknesses of medieval cities: the jealousies of the guilds, their selfishness, the unsatisfactory compromises between them, the impossibility of sufficient agreement either to maintain internal order or to pursue successful outside relations.

The Middle Ages had not worked out any form by which the parts could be related to the whole without the result either of despotism of the more powerful parts or anarchy of all the parts. Moreover, in the Middle Ages it was true on the whole that your relation to your class separated you from other classes: you could not belong to many groups at once. Status was the basis of the Middle Ages. This is exactly the tendency we must avoid in any plan for the direct representation of industrial workers in the state.

Is our modern life entirely barren of ideas with which to meet its own problems? Must twentieth century thought with all the richness which our intricately complex life has woven into it try to force itself into the embryonic moulds of the Middle Ages?

The most serious error, however, of the political pluralists is one we are all making: we have not begun a scientific study of group psychology. No one yet knows enough of the laws of associated life to have the proper foundations for political thinking. The pluralists apotheosize the group but do not study the group. They talk of sovereignty without seeking the source of sovereignty.

In the next three chapters I shall consider what the recent recognition of the group, meagre as it is at present, teaches us in regard to pluralism. Pluralism is the dominant thought to-day in philosophy, in politics, in economics, in jurisprudence, in sociology, in many schemes of social reorganization proposed by social workers, therefore we must consider it carefully — what it holds for us, what it must guard against.

XXIX

POLITICAL PLURALISM AND SOVEREIGNTY

WHAT does group psychology teach us, as far as we at present understand it, in regard to sovereignty? How does the group get its power? By each one giving up his sovereignty? Never. By some one from outside presenting it with authority? No, although that is the basis of much of our older legal theory. Real authority inheres in a genuine whole. The individual is sovereign over himself as far as he unifies the heterogeneous elements of his nature. Two people are sovereign over themselves as far as they are capable of creating one out of two. A group is sovereign over itself as far as it is capable of creating one out of several or many. A state is sovereign only as it has the power of creating one in which all are. Sovereignty is the power engendered by a complete interdependence becoming conscious of itself. Sovereignty is the imperative of a true collective will. It is not something academic, it is produced by actual living with others — we learn it only through group life. By the subtle process of interpenetration a collective sovereignty is evolved from a distributed sovereignty. Just so can and must, by the law of their being, groups unite to form larger groups, these larger groups to form a world-group.

I have said that many of the pluralists are opposed to the monistic state because they do not see that a collective and distributive sovereignty can exist together. They talk of the Many and the One without analyzing the process by which the Many and the One are creating each other. We now see that the problem of the compounding of consciousness, of the One and the Many, need not be left either to an intellectualistic or to an intuitive metaphysics. It is to be solved through a laboratory study of group psychology. When we have that, we shall not have to argue any more about the One and the Many: we shall actually see the Many and the One emerging at the same time; we can then work out the laws of the relation of the One (the state) to the Many (the individual), and of the Many (the individual) to the One (the state), not as a metaphysical question but on a scientific basis. And the process of the Many becoming One is the process by which sovereignty is created. Our conceptions of sovereignty can no longer rest on mere abstractions, theory, speculative thought. How absurdly inadequate such processes are to explain the living, interweaving web of humanity. The question of sovereignty concerns the organization of men (which obviously must be fitted to their nature), hence it finds its answer through the psychological analysis of man.

The seeking of the organs of society which are the immediate source of legal sanctions, the seeking of the ultimate source of political control — these are the quests of jurists and political philosophers. To their search must be added a study of the process by which a genuine sovereignty is created. The political pluralists are reacting against the sovereignty which our legal theory postulates, for they see that there is no such thing actually, but if sovereignty is at present a legal fiction, the matter need not rest there — we must seek to find how a genuine social and political control can be produced. The understanding of self-government, of democracy, is bound up with the conception of sovereignty as a psychological process.

The idea of sovereignty held by guild socialists[1] is based largely on the so-called "objective" theory of *le droit* expounded by M. Léon Duguit of Bordeaux. This theory is accepted as the "juridical basis" of a new state, what some call the functionarist state.[2] Man, Duguit tells us, has no rights as man, but only as a member of the social order. His rights are based on the fact of social interdependence — on his relations and consequent obligations. In fact he has no rights, but duties and powers. All power and all obligation is found in "social solidarity," in a constantly evolving social solidarity.[3]

The elaboration of this theory is Duguit's large contribution to political thought. His *droit* is a dynamic law — it can never be captured and fixed. The essential weakness of his doctrine is that he denies the possibility of a collective will, which means that he ignores the psychology of the social process. He and his followers reject the notion of a collective will as "*concept de l'esprit*

[1] See writings of Ramiro de Maeztu in New Age and his book mentioned above.

[2] See "Traité de Droit Constitutionnel" and "Études de Droit Public": I, L'État, Le Droit Objectif et La Loi Positive; II, L'État, Les Gouvernants and Les Agents.

As in French *droit* may be either law or *a* right, Duguit, in order to distinguish between these meanings, follows the German distinction of *objektives Recht* and *subjektives Recht*, and speaks of *le droit objectif* and *le droit subjectif*, thus meaning by *le droit objectif* merely law. But because he at the same time writes of power as resting on function in contradistinction to the classical theory of the abstract "rights" of man, rights apart from law and only declared by law, political writers sometimes speak of Duguit's "objective" theory of law, as opposed to a "subjective" theory of law, when jurists would tell us that law *is* objective, and that subjective right is always merely *a* right, my right. This matter of terminology must be made much clearer than it is at present.

[3] Although how far Duguit had in mind merely the solidarity of French and Roman law has been questioned.

dénué de toute réalité positive." If this is their idea of a
collective will, they are right to reject it. I ask for its
acceptance only so far as it can be proved to have positive reality. There is only one way in the world by
which you can ever know whether there is a collective
will, and that is by actually trying to make one; you
need not discuss a collective will as a theory. If experiment proves to us that we cannot have a collective will,
we must accept the verdict. Duguit thinks that when we
talk of the sovereignty of the people we mean an abstract sovereignty; clearly we ought to mean by the
sovereignty of the people that which they actually
create. It is true that we have none at present. Duguit
is perfectly right in opposing the old theory of the
"sovereign state."

But Duguit says that if there were a collective will
there is no reason why it should impose itself on the
individual wills. "*L'affirmation que la collectivité a le
pouvoir légitime de commander force qu'elle est la collectivité, est une affirmation d'ordre métaphysique ou reli-
gieux. . . .*" This in itself shows a misunderstanding of
the evolution of a collective will. This school does not
seem to understand that every one must contribute to the
collective will; ideally it would have no power unless this
happened, actually we can only be constantly approaching
this ideal.[1] Duguit makes a thing-in-itself of *la volonté
nationale* — it is a most insidious fallacy which we all
fall into again and again. But we can never accept
that kind of a collective will. We believe in a collective
will only so far as it is *really* forming from out our actual
daily life of intermingling men and women. There is

---

[1] I have just read in a work on sociology, "Men surrender their individual wills to the collective will." No, the true social process is not
when they *surrender* but when they *contribute* their wills to the collective
will. See chs. II–VI, "The Group Process."

nothing "metaphysical" or "religious" about this.
Duguit says metaphysics "*doit rester étranger à toute
jurisprudence. . . .*" We agree to that and insist that
jurisprudence must be founded on social psychology.

Five people produce a collective idea, a collective will.
That will becomes at once an imperative upon those
five people. It is not an imperative upon any one else.
On the other hand no one else can make imperatives for
those five people. It has been generated by the social
process which is a self-sufficing, all-inclusive process. The
same process which creates the collective will creates at
the same time the imperative of the collective will. It
is absolutely impossible to give self-government: no
one has the right to give it; no one has the power to
give it. Group A *allows* group B to govern itself? This
is an empty permission unless B has *learned how* to govern itself. Self-government must always be grown.
Sovereignty is always a psychological process.

Many of Duguit's errors come from a misconception
of the social process. Violently opposed to a collective
will, he sees in the individual thought and will the only
genuine "*chose en soi*" (it is interesting to notice that
la chose en soi finds a place in the thought of many pluralists). Not admitting the process of "community" he
asserts that *la règle de droit* is anterior and superior to the
state; he does not see the true relation of *le droit* to
l'état, that they evolve together, that the same process
which creates *le droit* creates *l'état*.[1] The will of the
people, he insists, can not create *le droit*. Here he does
not see the unity of the social process. He separates will
and purpose and the activity of the reciprocal inter-
change instead of seeing them as one. Certainly the will
of the people does not create *le droit*, but the social
process in its entire unity does. "Positive law must

[1] See p. 130.

constantly follow *le droit objeclif.*" Of course. "*Le droit objectif* is constantly evolving." Certainly. But how evolving? Here is where we disagree. The social process creates *le droit objectif*, and will is an essential part of the social process. Purpose is an essential part of the social process. Separate the parts of the social process and you have a different idea of jurisprudence, of democracy, of political institutions. Aim is all-important for Duguit. The rule of *le droit* is the rule of conscious ends: only the aim gives a will its worth; if the aim is juridical (conformed to *la règle de droit*), then the will is juridical. Thus Duguit's pragmatism is one which has not yet rid itself of absolute standards. It might be urged that it has, because he finds his absolute standards in "social solidarity." But any one who believes that the individual will is a *chose en soi*, and who separates the elements of the social process, does not wholly admit the self-sufficing character of that process.

The modern tendency in many quarters, however, in regard to conceptions of social practice, is to substitute ends for will.[1] This is a perfectly comprehensible reaction, but future jurisprudence must certainly unite these two ideas. Professor Jethro Brown says, "The justification for governmental action is found not in consent but in the purpose it serves." Not in that alone.

[1] De Maeztu tells us, "Rights do not arise from personality. This idea is mystic and unnecessary. Rights arise primarily from the relation of the associated with the thing which associates them. . . ." Authority, Liberty, and Function, p. 250.

Mr. Barker substitutes purpose for personality and will as the unifying bond of associations, and says that we thus get rid of "murder in the air" when it is a question of the "competition of ideas, not of real collective personalities." (See "The Discredited State," in *The Political Quarterly*, February, 1915.) This seems a curiously anthropomorphic, so to speak, idea of personality for a twentieth-century writer. The article is, however, an interesting and valuable one.

See also Pollock and Maitland, History of English Law, I, 472.

De Maeztu says, "The profound secret of associations is not that men have need of one another, but that they need the same thing." These two ideas can merge. Professor Brown makes the common good the basis of the new doctrine of natural right.[1] But we must all remember, what I do not doubt this writer does remember, that purpose can never be a *chose en soi*, and that, of the utmost importance, the "new natural law" can be brought into manifestation only by certain modes of association.

It is true, as Duguit says, that the state has the "right" to will because of the thing willed, that it has no "subjective" right to will, that its justification is in its purpose. (This is of course the truth in regard to all our "rights"; they are justified only by the use we make of them.) And yet there is a truth in the old idea of the "right" of a collectivity to will. These two ideas must be synthesized. They *are* synthesized by the new psychology which sees the purpose forming the will at the same time as the will forms the purpose, which finds no separation anywhere in the social process. We can never think of purpose as something in front which leads us on, as the carrot the donkey. Purpose is never in front of us, it appears at every moment with the appearance of will. Thus the new school of jurisprudence founded on social psychology cannot be a teleological school alone, but must be founded on all the elements which constitute the social process. Ideals do not operate in a vacuum. This theorists seem sometimes to forget, but those of us who have had tragic experience of this truth are likely to give more emphasis to the interaction of purpose, will and activity, past and present activity. The recognition that *le droit* is the product of a group process swallows up the question as to whether it is "objective"

[1] See "Underlying Principles of Legislation."

or "subjective"; it is neither, it is both; we look at the matter quite differently.[1]

To sum up this point. We must all, I think, agree with the "objective" conception of law in its essence, but not in its dividing the social process, a true unity, into separate parts. Rights arise from relation, and purpose is bound up in the relation. The relation of men to one another and to the object sought are part of the same process. Duguit has rendered us invaluable service in his insistence that *le droit* must be based on "*la vie actuelle*," but he does not take the one step further and see that *le droit* is born within the *group*, that there is an essential law of the group as different from other modes of association, and that this has many implications.

The *droit* evolved by a group is the *droit* of that group. The *droit* evolved by a state-group (we agree that there is no state-group yet, the state is evolving, the *droit* is evolving, there is only an approximate state, an approximately genuine *droit*) is the *droit* of the state. The contribution of the new psychology is that *le droit* comes from relation and is always in relation. The warning of the new psychology to the advocates of vocational representation is that the *droit* (either as law or right)[2] evolved by men of one occupation only will represent too little intermingling to express the "community" truth. We don't want doctors' ethics and lawyers' ethics, and so on through the varous groups. That is just the trouble

---

[1] The teleological school of sociology is interesting just here. While it marked a long advance on older theories, the true place of selection of ends is to-day more clearly seen. We were told: "Men have wants, therefore they come together to seek means to satisfy those wants." When do men "come together"? When were they ever separated? But it is not necessary to push this further.

[2] I have tried not to jump the track from legal right to ethical right but occasionally one can speak of them together, if it is understood that one is not thereby merging them.

at present. Employers and employees meet in conference. Watch those conferences. The difference of interest is not always the whole difficulty; there is also the
difference of standard. Capitalist ethics and workman
ethics are often opposed. We must accept *le droit* as a
social product, as a group product, but we must have
groups which will unify interests and standards. Law
and politics can be founded on nothing but vital modes
of association.

Mr. Roscoe Pound's exposition of modern law is just
here a great help to political theory. The essential, the
vital part of his teaching, is, not his theory of law based
on interests, not his emphasis upon relation, but his
bringing together of these two ideas. This takes us out
of the vague, nebulous region of much of the older legal
and political theory, and shows us the actual method of
living our daily lives. All that he says of relation implies
that we must seek and bring into use those modes of association which will reveal true interests, actual interests,
yet not particularist interests but the interests discovered through group relations — employer and employed, master and servant, landlord and tenant, etc.
But, and this is of great importance, these groups must
be made into genuine groups. If law is to be a group-
product, we must see that our groups are real groups,
we must find the true principle of association. For this
we need, as I must continually repeat, the study of group
psychology. "Life," "man," "society," are coming
to have little meaning for us: it is your life and my
life with which we are concerned, not "man" but the
men we see around us, not "society" but the many
societies in which we pass our lives. "Social" values?
We want individual values, but individual values discovered through group relations.

To sum up this point: (1) law should be a group-product, (2) we should therefore have genuine groups, (3) political method must be such that the "law" of the group can become embodied in our legislation.

M. Duguit's disregarding of the laws of that inter-mingling which is the basis of his *droit objectif* leads to a partial understanding only of the vote. Voting is for him still in a way a particularist matter. To be sure he calls it a function and that marks a certain advance. Moreover he wishes us to consider the vote an "objective" power, an "objective" duty, not a "subjective" right. This is an alluring theory in a pragmatic age. And if you see it leading to syndicalism which you have already accepted beforehand, it is all the more alluring! But to call the vote a function is only half the story; as long as it is a particularist vote, it does not help us much to have it rest on function, or rather, it goes just half the way. It must rest on the intermingling of all my func-tions, it must rest on the intermingling of all my func-tions with all the functions of all the others; it must rest indeed on social solidarity, but a social solidarity in which every man interpenetrating with every other is thereby approaching a whole of which he is the whole at one point.

Duguit, full of Rousseau, does not think it possible to have a collective sovereignty without every one having an equal share of this collective sovereignty, and he most strenuously opposes *le suffrage universel égalitaire.* But *le suffrage universel égalitaire* staring all the obvious *in*equalities of man in the face, Rousseau's divided sovereignty based on an indivisible sovereignty — all these things no longer trouble you when you see the vote as the expression at one point of some approximate whole produced by the intermingling of men.

True sovereignty and true functionalism are not opposed; the vote resting on "subjective" right and the vote resting on "objective" power are not opposed, but the particularist vote and the genuinely individual vote are opposed. Any doctrine which contains a trace of particularism in any form cannot gain our allegiance.

Again Duguit's ignoring of the psychology of the social process leads him to the separation of governors and governed. This separation is for him the essential fact of the state. Sovereignty is with those individuals who can impose their will upon others. He says no one can give orders to himself, but as a matter of fact no one can really give orders to any one but himself.[1] Here Duguit confuses present facts and future possibilities. Let us *be* the state, let us be sovereign— over ourselves. As the problem in the life of each one of us is to find the way to unify the warring elements within us — as only thus do we gain sovereignty over ourselves — so the problem is the same for the state. Duguit is right in saying that the German theory of auto-limitation is unnecessary, but not in the reasons he gives for it. A psychic entity is subordinate to the *droit* which itself evolves not by auto-limitation, but by the essential and intrinsic law of the group.

But Duguit has done us large service not only in his doctrine of a law, a right, born of our actual life, of our always evolving life, but also in his insistence on the individual which makes him one of the builders of the new individualism.[2] We see in the gradual transformation of the idea of natural law which took place among

[1] The old consent theory assumes that some make the laws and others obey them. In the true democracy we shall obey the laws we have ourselves made. To find the methods by which we can be approaching the true democracy is now our task; we can never rest satisfied with "consent."

[2] Although I do not agree with the form individualism takes in his doctrine.

the French jurists of the end of the nineteenth century, the struggle of the old particularism with the feelings-out for the true individualism. That the French have been slow to give up individual rights, that many of them have not given them up for any collective theory, but, feeling the truth underneath the old doctrine, have sought (and found) a different interpretation, a different basis and a different use, has helped us all immeasurably.

Group psychology shows us the process of man creating social power, evolving his own "rights." We now see that man's only rights are group-rights. These are based on his activity in the group — you can call it function if you like, only unless you are careful that tends to become mechanical, and it tends to an organic functionalism in which lurk many dangers. But the main point for us to grasp is that we can never understand rights by an abstract discussion of " subjective " vs. " objective"—only by the closest study of the process by which these rights are evolved. The true basis of rights is neither a "mystical" idea of related personalities, nor is it to be found entirely in the relation of the associated to the object sought; a truly modern conception of law synthesizes these two ideas. "Function," de Maeztu tells us "[is] a quality independent of the wills of men." This is a meaningless sentence to the new psychology. At present the exposition of the "objective" theory of law is largely a polemic against the "subjective." When we understand more of group psychology, and it can be put forth in a positive manner, it will win many more adherents.

Then as soon as the psychological foundation of law is clearly seen, the sovereignty of the state in its old meaning will be neither acclaimed nor denied. An understanding of the group process teaches us the true nature of sovereignty. We can agree with the pluralist school that the present state has no "right" to sovereignty;[1] we can go further and say that the state will never be more than ideally sovereign, further still and say that the whole idea of sovereignty must be recast and take a different place in political science. And yet, with the meaning given to it by present psychology, it is perhaps the most vital thought of the new politics. The sovereign is not the crowd, it is not millions of unrelated atoms, but men joining to form a real whole. The atomistic idea of sovereignty is dead, we all agree, but we may learn to define sovereignty differently.

Curiously enough, some of the pluralists are acknowledged followers of Gierke and Maitland, and base much of their doctrine on the "real personality" of the group. But the group can create its own personality only by the "compounding of consciousness," by every member being at one and the same time an individual and the "real personality." If it is possible for the members of a group to evolve a unified consciousness, a common idea, a collective will, for the many to become really one, not in a mystical sense but as an actual fact, for the group to have a real not a fictional personality, this process can be carried on through group and group, our task, an infinite one, to evolve a state with a real personality. The imagination of the born pluralist stops with the group.[2]

But even in regard to the group the pluralists seem

[1] Some of the pluralists are concerned, I recognize, with the fact rather than the right of sovereignty.

[2] The trouble with the pluralists is that their emphasis is not on the fact that the group creates its own personality, but on the fact that the state does *not* create it. When they change this emphasis, their thinking will be unchained, I believe, and leap ahead to the constructive work which we eagerly await and expect from them.

sometimes to fall into contradictions. Sovereignty, we
are often told, must be decentralized and divided among
the local units. But according to their own theory by
whom is the sovereignty to be divided? The fact is that
the local units must *grow* sovereignty, that we want
to revivify local life not for the purpose of breaking
up sovereignty, but for the purpose of creating a real
sovereignty.

The pluralists always tell us that the unified state pro-
ceeds from the One to the Many; that is why they discard the unified state. This is not true of the unify*ing*
state which I am trying to indicate. They think that
the only alternative to pluralism is where you begin
with the whole. That is, it is true, the classic monism,
but we know now that authority is to proceed from
the Many to the One, from the smallest neighborhood group up to the city, the state, the nation. This
is the process of life, always a unifying through the
interpenetration of the Many — Oneness an infinite
goal.

This is expressed more accurately by saying, as I have
elsewhere, that the One and the Many are constantly
creating each other. The pluralists object to the One
that comes before the Many. They are right, but we
need not therefore give up oneness. When we say that
there is the One which comes *from* the Many, this
does not mean that the One is *above* the Many. The
deepest truth of life is that the interrelating by which
both are at the same time a-making is constant. This
must be clearly understood in the building of the new
state.

The essential error in the theory of distributed sovereignty is that each group has an isolated sovereignty.
The truth is that each should represent the whole united
sovereignty at one point as each individual is his whole

group at one point. An understanding of this fact seems to me absolutely necessary to further development of political theory.[1] This does not mean that the state must come first, that the group gets its power from the state. This the pluralists rightfully resent. The power within the group is its own genetically and wholly. But the same force which forms a group may form a group of groups.

But the conclusion drawn by some pluralists from the theory of "real personality" is that the state is superfluous because a corporate personality has the right to assert autonomy over itself. They thus acknowledge that pluralism means for them group and group and group side by side. But here they are surely wrong. They ignore the implications of the psychological fact that power developed within the group does not cease with the formation of the group. That very same force which has bound the individuals together in the group (and which the theory of "real personality" recognizes) goes on working, you cannot stop it; it is the fundamental force of life, of all nature, of all humanity, the universal law of being — the out-reaching for the purpose of further unifying. If this force goes on working after the group is formed, what becomes of it? It must reach out to embrace other groups in order to repeat exactly the same process.

When you stop your automobile without stopping your engine, the power which runs your car goes on working exactly the same, but is completely lost. It only makes a noise. Do we want this to happen to our groups? Are they to end only in disagreeable noises? In order that the group-force shall not be lost, we must provide means for it to go on working effectively after

[1] It is also necessary to an understanding of the new international law. See ch. XXXV, "The World State."

it is no longer needed within the group, so to speak. We must provide ways for it to go out to meet the life force of other groups, the new power thus generated again and endlessly to seek new forms of unification. No "whole" can imprison us infinite beings. The centre of to-day is the circumference of to-morrow.

Thus while the state is not necessary to grant authority, it is the natural outcome of the uniting groups. The state must be the collective mind embodying the moral will and purpose of All. From living group to living group to the "real" state — such must be our line of evolution.

Sovereignty, it is true, is a fact, not a theory. Whoever can gain obedience has the sovereign power. But we must go beyond this and seek those political methods by which the command shall be with those who have evolved a genuine authority, that is, an authority evolved by what I have called the true social process. We must go beyond this and seek those methods by which a genuine authority *can* be evolved, by which the true social process shall be everywhere possible. To repeat: first, the true social process must be given full opportunity and scope, then it must be made the basis of political method. Then shall we see emerging a genuine authority which we can all acclaim as sovereign. There is, I agree with the pluralists, a great advantage in that authority being multiple and varied, but a static pluralism, so to speak, would be as bad as a static monism. The groups are always reaching out *towards* unity. Our safeguard against crystallization is that every fresh unity means (as I have tried to show in chapter III) the throwing out of myriad fresh differences — our safeguard is that the universe knows no static unity. Unification means sterilization; unifying means a perpetual generating. We do not want the unified sovereignty of Germany; but when you put the individual and the group first, you get unify*ing* sovereignty.[1]

[1] No one has yet given us a satisfactory account of the history of the notion of sovereignty: just how and in what degree it has been affected by history, by philosophy, by jurisprudence, etc., and how all these have interacted. We have not only to disentangle many strands to trace each to its source, but we have, moreover, just not to disentangle them, but to understand the constant interweaving of all. To watch the interplay of legal theory and political philosophy from the Middle Ages down to the present day is one of the most interesting parts of our reading, but perhaps nowhere is it more fruitful than in the idea of sovereignty. We see the corporation long ignored and the idea of legal partnership influencing the development of the social contract theory, which in its turn reacted on legal theory. We find the juristic conception of group personality, clearly seen as early as Althusius (1557–1638), and revived and expanded by Gierke, influencing the whole German school of "group sociologists." But to-day are not many of us agreed that however interesting such historical tracing, our present notion of sovereignty must rest on what we learn from group psychology?

XXX

The Service State vs. the "Sovereign State"

THE idea at the bottom of occupational representation which has won it many adherents is
that of the interdependence of function. Most
of the people who advocate vocational representation
believe in what they call an organic democracy. This
leads them to believe that the group not the individual
should be the unit of government: a man in an industry
is to vote not as an individual but as a department member because he is thus representing his function. But
man has many functions and then there is something
left over. It is just because our place in the whole can
never be bounded by any one function that we cannot
accept the organism of the Middle Ages, the organic
society of certain sociologists, or the "organic democracy" of the upholders of occupational representation.

Man has many functions or rather he is the interplay
of many functions. The child grows to manhood through
interpenetrating — with his family, at school, at work,
with his play group, with his art group: the carpenter
may join the Arts and Crafts to find there an actualiza-
tion of spirit for which he is fitted, and so on and so on.
All the different sides of our nature develop by the process of compounding. If you shut a man up in his occupation, you refuse him the opportunity of full growth.
The task has been given to humanity to "Know thy-
self," but man cannot know himself without knowing
the many sides of his self. His essential self is the possibility of the multiple expression of spirit.

We see this principle operating every day in our own lives: we cannot do one thing well by doing one thing alone. The interrelations are so manifold that each of us does far more than he wishes, not because our tendency is a senseless ramifying, but because we cannot do our own job well unless we do many other things: we do not take on the extra activities as an *extension* of our life, but simply as an *intensification* of our life at the point of our particular interest. Ideally one should fulfil all the functions of man in order to perform one function. No one ought to teach without being a parent! etc. etc. Man must identify himself with humanity. The great lesson which the pluralist school has to teach is that man cannot do this imaginatively but only actually, through his group relations. What it leaves out is that the task is manifold and infinite because man must identify himself with a manifold and infinite number of groups before he has embraced humanity.

Society, however, does not consist merely of the union of all these various groups. There is a more subtle process going on — the interlocking of groups. And in these interlocking groups we have not only the same people taking up different activities, but actually representing different interests. In some groups I may be an employer, in others an employee. I can be a workman and a stockholder. Men have many loyalties. It is no longer true that I belong to such a class and must always identify myself with its interests. I may belong at the same time to the college club and the business women's club, to the Players' League (representing the actor's point of view) and to the Drama Association (representing the playgoer's point of view). I not only thus get opposite points of view, but I myself can contribute to two opposite points of view. The importance of this has not been fully estimated. I may have to say the collective I or we first of my basket-ball team, next of my trade-union, then of my church club or citizens' league or neighborhood association, and the lines may cross and recross many times. It is just these cross lines that are of inestimable value in the development of society.

Thus while two groups may be competing, certain members of these groups may be working together for the satisfaction of some interest. This is recognized by law. A man can be a member of different corporations. Our possibility of association is not exhausted by contributing to the production of one legal person, we may help to create many different legal persons, each with an entirely different set of liabilities. Then there may be some sort of relation with a definite legal status existing between these bodies: I as member of one corporation may have relation with myself as member of another corporation. We see this clearly in the case of corporations, but it is what is taking place everywhere, this interlocking and overlapping of groups, and is I feel one of the neglected factors in the argument of those who are advocating occupational representation. What we are working for is a plastic social organization: not only in the sense of a flexible interaction between the groups, but in the sense of an elasticity which makes it possible for individuals to change constantly their relations, their groups, without destroying social cohesion. Vocational representation would tend to crystallize us into definite permanent groups.

The present advocacy of organic democracy or "functionalism" is obviously, and in many cases explicitly, a reaction to "individualism": the functional group must be the unit because the individual is so feared. I agree with the denunciation of the individual if you mean the man who seeks only his own advantage. But have we not already seen that that is not the true individual?

And do we not see now that man is a multiple being? Life is a recognition of multitudinous multiplicity. Politics must be shaped for that. Our task is to make straight the paths for the coming of the Lord — the true Individual. Man is struggling for the freedom of his nature. What is his nature? Manifold being. You must have as many different kinds of groups as there are powers in man — this does away with "organic democracy."

The state cannot be composed of groups because no group nor any number of groups can contain the whole of me, and the ideal state demands the whole of me. No one group can seize the whole of me; no one group can seize any part of me in a mechanical way so that having taken one-tenth there are nine-tenths left. My nature is not divisible into so many parts as a house into so many rooms. My group uses me and then the whole of me is still left to give to the whole. This is the constant social process. Thus my citizenship is something bigger than my membership in a vocational group. Vocational representation does not deal with men — it deals with masons and doctors. I may be a photographer but how little of my personality does my photography absorb. We are concerned with what is left over — is that going to be lost? The whole of every man must go into his citizenship.

Some of the guild socialists tell us, however, that a man has as many "rights" as he has functions: a shoe-maker is also a father and a rate-payer. But they do not give us any plan for the political recognition of these various functions. How the father *as* father is to be represented in the state we are not told. The state will never get the whole of a man by his trying to divide him-self into parts. A man is not a father at home, a citizen at the polls, an artisan at work, a business man in his office, a follower of Christ at church. He is at every moment a Christian, a father, a citizen, a worker, if he is at any time these in a true sense. We want the whole man in politics. Clever business men are not engaging workers, they need men, our churches need men, the insistent demand of our political life is for men.

As ideally every function should include every other, as every power of which I am capable should go into my work, occupational representation might do for the millennium, but it is not fitted for the limitations of man in 1918.

I am advocating throughout the group principle, but not the group as the political unit. We do not need to swing forever between the individual and the group. We must devise some method of using both at the same time. Our present method is right so far as it is based on individuals, but we have not yet found the true individual. The groups are the indispensable means for the discovery of self by each man. The individual finds himself in a group; he has no power alone or in a crowd. One group creates me, another group creates me and so on and on. The different groups bring into appearance the multiple sides of me. I go to the polls to express the multiple man which the groups have created. I am to express the whole from my individual point of view, and that is a multiple point of view because of my various groups. But my relation to the state is always as an individual. The group is a method merely. It cannot supplant either the individual on the one hand or the state on the other. The unit of society is the individual coming into being and functioning through groups of a more and more federated nature. Thus the unit of society is neither the group nor the particularist-individual, but the group-individual.

The question is put baldly to us by the advocates of

vocational representation — "Do you want representation of numbers or representation of interests?" They
are opposed to the former, which they call democracy,
because "democracy" means to them the "sovereignty
of the people," which means the reign of the crowd.
Democracy and functionalism are supposed to be opposed.
An industry is to be composed not of individuals but
of departments; likewise the state is to be a union of
industries or occupations.   The present state is conceived as a crowd-state.[1]   If the state is and must necessarily be a crowd, no wonder it is being condemned to-day
in many quarters.   But I do not believe this is the alternative we are facing — the crowd-state or the group-
state.   We want the representation of individuals, but
of true individuals, group-individuals.[2]

The best part of pluralism is that it is a protest against
the domination of numbers; the trouble is that it identi-
fies numbers with individuals.   Some plan must be devised by which we put the individual at the centre of our
political system, without an atomistic sovereignty, and
yet by which we can get the whole of the individual.   I
am proposing for the moment the individual the unit,
the group the method, but this alone does not cover all
that is necessary.   In the French syndicalist organization every syndicate, whatever its size, is represented
by a single individual.   In this way power is prevented
from falling into the hands of a strong federation like
the miners, but of course this often means minority rule.
In England the Trade Union Congress can be dominated
by the five large trades, a state of things which has been
much complained of there.   But we must remember

[1] The French syndicalists avowedly do not want democracy because
it "mixes the classes," because, as they say, interests and aims mingle
in one great mass in which all true significance is lost.

[2] See p. 184.

that while the syndicalists get rid of majority rule, that
is, that the majority of individuals no longer govern,
they merely give the rule to the majority of groups.
They have not given up the *principle* of majority rule,
they simply apply it differently. There is a good deal
of syndicalist thinking that is not a penetrating analysis which presents us with new principles, but a mere
taking of ideas long accepted in regard to the individual
and transferring them to the field of the group. I have
tried to show in chapter XVII, "Democracy Not the Majority," that the pressing matter in politics is not whether
we want majority rule or not, but to decide upon those
methods of association by which we get the greatest
amount of integration. The syndicalists are right, we
do not want a crowd, but I do not think most syndicalists have discovered the true use of the true group.

The task before us now is to think out the way in which
the group method can be a regular part of our political
system — its relation to the individual on the one hand
and to the state on the other. No man should have a
share in government as an isolated individual, but only
as bound up with others: the individual must be the
unit, but an individual capable of entering into genuine
group relations and of using these for an expanding scale
of social, political and international life.

The best part of functionalism is that it presents to
us the Service State in the place of the old Sovereign
State. This has two meanings: (1) that the state is
created by the actual services of every man, that every
man will get his place in the state through the service
rendered: (2) that the state itself is tested by the services it renders, both to its members and to the world-
community.[1] The weakness of functionalism, as so far

[1] This is the basis of Duguit's international law — the place of a state
in an international league is to be determined directly by services rendered.

developed, is that it has provided no method for all the functions of man to be included in the state. The essence of democracy is the expression of every man in his multiple nature.

To sum up: no one group can enfold me, because of my multiple nature. This is the blow to the theory of occupational representation. But also no number of groups can enfold me. This is the reason why the individual must always be the unit of politics, as group organization must be its method. We *find* the individual through the group, we *use* him always as the true individual — the undivided one — who, living link of living group, is yet never embedded in the meshes but is forever free for every new possibility of a forever unfolding life.

XXXI

POLITICAL PLURALISM AND THE TRUE FEDERAL STATE

IN the last two chapters I have taken up the two
fundamental laws of life — the law of interpenetration and the law of multiples. (1) Sovereignty, we
have seen, is the power generated within the group —
dependent on the principle of interpenetration. (2) Man
joins many groups — in order to express his multiple
nature. These two principles give us federalism.

Let us, before considering the conception of federalism
in detail, sum up in a few sentences what has already been
said of these two principles. The fundamental truth of
life we have seen is self-perpetuating activity — activity so regnant, so omnipresent, so all-embracing, that it
banishes even the conception of anything static from
the world of being. Conscious evolution means that we
must discover the essential principle of this activity and
see that it is at work in the humblest of its modes, the
smallest group or meeting of even two or three. The
new psychology has brought to political science the
recognition of interpenetration and the "compounding
of consciousness" as the very condition of all life. Our
political methods must conform to life's methods. We
must understand and follow the laws of association that
the state may appear, that our own little purposes may
be fulfilled. *Little* purposes? Is there any great and
small? The humblest man and the price of his daily
loaf — is this a small matter — it hangs upon the whole
world situation to-day. In order that the needs of the
humblest shall be satisfied, or in order that world pur-

poses shall be fulfilled — it matters not which — this principle of "compounding" must be fully recognized and embodied in our political methods. It is this vital intermingling which creates the real individual and knits men into the myriad relations of life. We win through life our individuality, it is not presented to us at the beginning to be exploited as we will. We win a multiple individuality through our manifold relations. In the workings of this dual law are rooted all of social and political progress, all the hope and the potency of human evolution.

Only the federal state can express this dual principle of existence — the compounding and the multiple compounding. It is an incomplete understanding of this dual law which is responsible for the mistaken interpretation of federalism held by some of the pluralists: a conception which includes the false doctrines of division of power, the idea that the group not the individual should be the unit of the state, the old consent of governed theory, an almost discarded particularism (group rights), and the worn-out balance theory.

The distributive sovereignty school assumes that the essential, the basic part of federalism is the division of power between the central and separate parts: while the parts may be considered as ceding power to the central state, or the central state may be considered as granting power to the parts, yet in one form or another federalism means a divided sovereignty. Esmein says definitely, "*L'État fédératif . . . fractionne la souveraineté. . . .*" [1] No, it should unite sovereignty. There should be no absolute division of power or conferring of power. The activity of whole and parts should be one.

In spite of all our American doctrines of the end of the eighteenth century, in spite of our whole history of states-

[1] Quoted by Duguit.

right theory and sentiment, the division of sovereignty
is not the main fact of the United States government.
From 1789 to 1861 the idea of a divided sovereignty —
that the United States was a voluntary agreement between free, sovereign and independent states, that authority was "divided" between nation and states — dictated
the history of the United States. The war of 1861
was fought (some of the pluralists seem not to know)
to settle this question.[1] The two ideas of federalism
came to a death grapple in our Civil War and the
true doctrine triumphed. That war decided that the
United States was not a delegated affair, that it had a
"real" existence, and that it was sovereign, yet not
sovereign over the states as an external party, for it is
composed of the states, but sovereign over itself, merely
over itself. You have not to be a mystic to understand
this but only an American. Those who see in a federal
union a mere league with rights and powers granted to
a central government, those who see in a federal union
a balancing of sovereign powers, do not understand
true federalism. When we enumerate the powers of
the states as distinct from the powers of our national
government, some people regard this distinction as a
dividing line between nation and states, but the true "fed-
eralist" is always seeing the relation of these powers to
those of the central government. There are no absolute
divisions in a true federal union.

Do we then want a central government which shall
override the parts until they become practically non-

---

[1] It must be remembered, however, that while in the Civil War we
definitely gave up the compact theory held by us since the Mayflower
compact, yet we did not adopt the organism theory. The federal state
we have tried and are trying to work out in America is based on the principles of psychic unity described in chapter X. The giving up of the
"consent" theory does not bring us necessarily to the organic theory of
society.

existent? The moment federalism attempts to transcend the parts it has become vitiated. Our Civil War was not, as some writers assert, the blow to states-rights and the victory of centralization. We shall yet, I believe, show that it was a victory for true federalism.[1] The United States is neither to ignore the states, transcend the states, nor to balance the states, it is to *be* the states in their united capacity.

Of course it is true that many Americans do think of our government as a division of powers between central and local authority, therefore there is as a matter of fact much balancing of interests. But as far as we are doing this at Washington it is exactly what we must get rid of. The first lesson for every member of a federal government to learn is that the interests of the different parts, or the interests of the whole and the interests of the parts, are never to be pitted against each other. As far as the United States represents an interpenetration of thought and feeling and interest and will, it is carrying out the aims of federalism.

We have not indeed a true federalism in the United States to-day; we are now learning the lesson of federalism. Some one must analyze for us the difference between centralization and true federalism, which is neither nationalization, states-rights, nor balance, and then we must work for true federalism. For the federal government to attempt to do that which the states should do, or perhaps even are doing, means loss of force, and loss of education-by-experience for the states. On the other hand, not to see when federal action means at the same time local development and national strength, means a serious retarding of our growth. It is equally true that when the states attempt what the federal gov-

[1] Duguit says that the United States confers the rights of a state on a territory. No, it recognizes that which already exists.

ernment alone should undertake, the consequence is general muddle.

And it is by no means a question only of what the federal government should do and what it should not do. It is a question of the *way* of doing. It is a question of guiding, where necessary, without losing local initiative or local responsibility. It is a question of so framing measures that true federation, not centralization, be obtained. Recently, even before the war, the tendency has been towards increased federal action and federal control, as seen, for instance, in the control of railroad transportation, of vocational education etc. The latter is an excellent example of the possibility of central action being true federal and not nationalized action. The federal government upon application from a state grants to that state an amount for vocational education equal to what the state itself will appropriate. The administration of the fund rests with the state. The federal government thus makes no assumptions. It *recognizes existing facts*. And it does not impose something from without. The state must understand its needs, must know how those needs can best be satisfied; it must take responsibility. The experience of one state joins with the experience of other states to form a collective experience.

As we watch federalism being worked out in actual practice at Washington, we see in that practice the necessity of a distinction which has been emphasized throughout this book as the contribution of contemporary psychology to politics: nationalization is the Hegelian reconciliation, true federalism is the integration of present psychology. This means a genuine integration of the interests of all the parts. If our present tendency is towards nationalization, we must learn the difference between that and federalism and change it into the latter. We need a new order of statesmen in the world to-day — for our nation, for our international league — those who understand federalism.

But I have been talking of federalism as the integration of parts (the states). We should remember also, and this is of the greatest importance, that the United States is not only to be the *states* in their united capacity, but it is to be all the men and women of the United States in *their* united capacity. This it seems difficult for many Europeans to understand; it breaks across their traditional conception of federalism which has been a league, a confederation of "sovereign" parts, not a true federal state. We of Massachusetts feel ourselves not first children of Massachusetts and then through Massachusetts of the United States. We belong directly to the United States not merely through Massachusetts. True federalism means that the individual, not the group, is the unit. A true federal government acts directly on its citizens, not merely through the groups.

America has not led the world in democracy through methods of representation, social legislation, ballot laws or industrial organization. She has been surpassed by other countries in all of these. She leads the world in democracy because through federalism she is working out the secret of the universe actively. Multiple citizenship in its spontaneous unifying is the foundation of the new state. Federalism and democracy go together, you do not decide to have one or the other as your fancy may be. We did not establish federalism in the United States, we are growing federalism. Cohesion imposed upon us externally will lack in significance and duration. Federalism must live through: (1) the reality of the group, (2) the expanding group, (3) the ascending group or unifying process.

The federal state is the unifying state. The political

pluralists, following James, use the "trailing and"[1] argument to prove that we can never have a unified state, that there is always something which never gets included. I should use it to prove that we can and must have a unify*ing* state, that this "and" is the very unifying principle. The "trailing and" is the deepest truth of psychology. It is because of this "and" that our goal must always be the unified state — the unified state to be attained through the federal form. Our spirit it is true is by nature federal, but this means not infinite unrelation but infinite possibility of relation, not infinite strung-alongness but infinite seeking for the unifying of the strung-alongness. I forever discover undeveloped powers. This is the glory of our exhaustless nature. We are the expression of the principle of endless growth, of endless appearing, and democracy must, therefore, so shape its forms as to allow for the manifestation of each new appearing. I grow possibilities; new opportunities should always be arising to meet these new possibilities.

Then through group and group and ascending group I actualize more and more. The "trailing and" is man's task for ever and ever — to drag in more spirit, more knowledge, more harmony. Federalism is the only possible form for the state because it leaves room for the new forces which are coming through these spiritual "ands," for the myriad centres of life which must be forever springing up, group after group, within a vital state. Our impulse is at one and the same time to develop self and to transcend self. It is this ever transcending self which needs the federal state. The federal

---

[1] "The word 'and' trails along after every sentence. Something always escapes. . . . The pluralistic world is thus more like a federal republic than like an empire or a kingdom." "A Pluralistic Universe," 321–322.

state is not a unified state, I agree, but it is a unifying state, not a "strung-along" state.

Thus it is the federal state which expresses the two fundamental principles of life — the compounding of consciousness and the endless appearings of new forces.

I have said that the pluralists' mistaken interpretation of federalism includes the particularist notions of "consent" and "rights" and "balance," and that all these come from a false conception of sovereignty. What does the new psychology teach us of "consent"? Power is generated within the true group not by one or several assuming authority and the others "consenting," but solely by the process of intermingling. Only by the same method can the true state be grown.

If divorce is to be allowed between the state and this group or that, what are the grounds on which it is to be granted? Will incompatibility be sufficient? Are the manufacturing north and agricultural south of Ireland incompatible? Does a certain trade association want, like Nora, a "larger life"? The pluralists open the gates to too much. They wish to throw open the doors of the state to labor: yes, they are right, but let them beware what veiled shapes may slip between those open portals. Labor must indeed be included in the state, it is our most immediate task, but let us ponder well the method.

The pluralists assume that the unified state must always claim authority over "other groups." [1] But as he who expresses the unity of my group has no authority over me but is simply the symbol and the organ of the group, so that group which expresses the unity of all groups — that is, the state — should have no authority *as a separate group*, but only so far as it gathers up into

[1] When they say that the passion for unity is the urge for a dominant One, they think of the dominant One as outside.

itself the whole meaning of these constituent groups. Just here is the crux of the disagreement between the upholders of the pluralistic and of the true monistic state: the former think of the other groups as "coextensive" or "complementary" to the state — the state is one of the groups to which we owe obedience; to the latter they and all individuals are the constituents of the state.[1]

I have said that our progress is from Contract to Community.[2] This those pluralists cannot accept who take the consent of the group as part of their theory of the state. They thereby keep themselves in the contract stage of thinking, they thereby and in so far range themselves with all particularists.[3]

Secondly, in the divided sovereignty theory the old particularist doctrine of individual rights gives way merely to a new doctrine of group rights, the "inherent rights" of trade-unions or ecclesiastical bodies. "Natural rights" and "social compact" went together; the "inherent rights" of groups again tend to make the

---

[1] One of the pluralists says, "I cannot see that . . . sovereignty is the unique property of any one association." No, not sovereignty over "others," but sovereignty always belongs to any genuine group; as groups join to form another real group, the sovereignty of the more inclusive group is evolved — that is the only kind of state sovereignty which we can recognize as legitimate. (See ch. XXIX on " Political Pluralism and Sovereignty.")

[2] See ch. XV.

[3] Mr. Laski is an exception to many writers on "consent." When he speaks of consent he is referring only to the actual facts of to-day. Denying the sovereignty postulated by the lawyers (he says you can never find in a community any one will which is certain of obedience), he shows that as a matter of fact the state sovereignty we have now rests on consent. I do not wish to confuse the issue between facts of the present and hopes for the future, but I wish to make a distinction between the "sovereignty" of the present and the sovereignty which I hope we can grow. This distinction is implicit in Mr. Laski's book, but it is lacking in much of the writing on the "consent of the governed."

federal bond a compact.[1] The state resting on a numerical basis, composed of an aggregate of individuals, gives
way only to a state still resting on a numerical basis
although composed now of groups instead of individuals.
As in the old days the individuals were to be "free,"
now the groups are to be "independent." These new
particularists are as zealous and as jealous for the group
as any nineteenth-century "individualist" was for the individual. Mr. Barker, who warns us, it is true, against
inherent rights which are not adjusted to other inherent
rights, nevertheless says, "If we are individualists now,
we are corporate individualists. Our individuals are becoming groups. We no longer write Man *vs.* the State
but The Group *vs.* the State." But does Mr. Barker
really think it progress to write Group *vs.* the State?
If the principle of individual *vs.* the state is wrong, what
difference does it make whether that individual is one
man or a group of men? In so far as these rights are based
on function, we have an advance in political theory; in
so far as we can talk of group *vs.* the state, we are held
in the thralls of another form of social atomism. It is
the pluralists themselves who are always saying, when
they oppose crowd-sovereignty, that atomism means
anarchy. Agreed, but atomism in any form, of groups
as well as individuals, means anarchy, and this they do
not always seem to realize.

Mr. Barker speaks of the present tendency "to restrict
the activity of the state in order to safeguard the rights
of the groups." Many pluralists and syndicalists are
afraid of the state because for them the old dualism is

[1] Wherever you have the social contract theory in any form, and
assent as the foundation of power, there is no social process going on;
the state is an arbitrary creation of men. Group organization to-day
must give up any taint whatever of the social contract and rest squarely
and fully on its legitimate psychological basis.

unsolvable. But as I have tried to show in the chapter on "Our Political Dualism" that the rights of the state and the citizen are never, ideally, incompatible, so now we should understand that our present task is to develop those political forms within which rights of group and state can be approaching coincidence.

As long as we settle down within any one group, we are in danger of the old particularism. Many a trade-unionist succumbs to this danger. Love of a group will not get us out of particularism. We can have egoism of the group as well as egoism of the individual. Indeed the group may have all the evils of the individual — aggrandizement of self, exploitation of others etc. Nothing will get us out of particularism but the constant recognition that any whole is always the element of a larger whole. Group life has two meanings, one as important as the other: (1) it looks in to its own integrated, coördinated activity, (2) it sees that activity in relation to other activities, in relation to a larger whole of which it is a part. The group which does not look out deteriorates into caste. The group which thinks only of itself is a menace to society; the group which looks to its manifold relations is part of social progress. President Wilson as head of a national group has just as clear a duty to other national groups as to his own country.

Particularism of the individual is dead, in theory if not in practice. Let us not now fall into the specious error of clinging to our particularism while changing its name from individual to group.

The outcome of group particularism is the balance of power theory, perhaps the most pernicious part of the pluralists' doctrine. The pluralist state is to be composed of sovereign groups. What is their life to be? They are to be left alone to fight, to compete, or, word most favored by this school, to balance. With de Maeztu the balance of power is confessedly the corner-stone of the new state. "The dilemma which would make us choose between the State and anarchy is false. There is another alternative, that of plurality and the balance of powers, not merely within the nation but in the family of nations."[1]

But whenever you have balance in your premise, you have anarchy in your conclusion.

The weakness of the reasoning involved in the balance of power argument has been exposed in so much of the war literature of the last three years, which has exploded the balance of power theory between nations, that little further criticism is needed here. Unity must be our aim to-day. When you have not unity, you have balance or struggle or domination — of one over others. The nations of Europe refuse domination, aim at balance, and war is the result.

It seems curious that these two movements should be going on side by side: that we are giving up the idea of the balance of nations, that we are refusing to think any longer in terms of "sovereign" nations, and yet at the same time an increasing number of men should be advocating balancing, "sovereign" groups within nations. The pluralists object to unity, but unity and plurality are surely not incompatible. The true monistic state is merely the multiple state working out its own unity from infinite diversity. But the unifying state shows us what to do with that diversity. What advantage is that diversity if it is to be always "competing," "fighting," "balancing?" Only in the unifying state do we get the full advantage of diversity where it is gathered up into significance and pointed action.

The practical outcome of the balance theory will be

[1] This is perhaps a remnant of the nineteenth-century myth that competition is the mode of progress.

first antagonistic interests, then jealous interests, then competing interests, then dominating interests — a fatal climax.

The trouble with the balance theory is that by the time the representatives of the balancing groups meet, it is too late to expect agreement. The chief objection to pluralism is, perhaps, that it is usually merely a scheme of representation, that its advocates are usually talking of the kind of roof they want before they have laid the foundation stones. No theory of the state can have vitality which is merely a plan of representation. The new state must rest on a new conception of living, on a true understanding of the vital modes of association. The reason why occupational representation must bring balance and competition is because the integrating of differences, the essential social process, does not take place far enough back in our life. If Parliaments are composed of various groups or interests, the unification of those interests has to take place in Parliament. But then it is too late. The ideas of the different groups must mingle earlier than Parliament. We must go further back than our legislatures for the necessary unifying. We do not want legislatures full of opposing interests. The ideas of the groups become too crystallized by the time their representatives get to the Parliament, in fact they have often hardened into prejudices. Moreover, the representatives could not go against their constituencies, they would be pledged to specific measures. The different groups would come together each to try to prevail, not to go through the only genuine democratic process, that of trying to integrate their ideas and interests.

When the desire to prevail is once keenly upon us, we behave very differently than when our object is the seeking of truth. Suppose I am the representative in Congress of a group or a party. A bill is under consideration.

I see a weakness in that bill; if I point it out some one
else may see a remedy for it and the bill may be im-
mensely improved. But do I do this? Certainly not.
I am so afraid of the bill being lost if I show any
weakness in it that I keep this insight to myself and my
country loses just so much. I cannot believe that occupational representation will foster truth seeking or truth
speaking. It seems to me quite a case of the frying pan
into the fire. Compromise and swapping will be the
order in Parliaments based solely on the vocational
principle. The different interests must fight it out in
Parliament. This is fundamentally against democracy
because it is against the psychological foundation of
democracy, the fundamental law of association. Democracy depends on the blending, not the balancing, of
interests and thoughts and wills. Occupational representation assumes that you secure the interests of the
whole by securing the interests of every class, the old
particularist fallacy transferred to the group.

Moreover, it is often assumed that because the occupational group is composed of men of similar interests
we shall have agreement in the occupational group; it
is taken for granted that in these economic groups the
agreement of opinion necessary for voting will be automatic. But do poets or carpenters or photographers
think alike on more than a very few questions? What
we must do is to get behind these electoral methods to
some fundamental method which shall *produce* agreement.

Moreover, if the Cabinet were made up of these warring elements, administration would be almost impossible. Lloyd-George's Cabinet at present is hampered by
too much "difference." I have throughout, to be sure,
been advocating the compounding of difference as the
secret of politics, but the compounding must begin further back in our life than Parliaments or Cabinets.

And if you had group representation in England would not the Cabinet be made up of the most powerful of the groups, and would not a fear of defeat at any particular time mean overtures to enough of the other groups to make success in the Cabinet? And would not an entirely improper amount of power drift to the Premier under these circumstances? Have we any leaders who would, could any one trust himself to, guide the British Cabinet for the best interests of Great Britain under such conditions as these?

To sum up: a true federalism cannot rest on balance or group-rights or consent. Authority, obedience, liberty, can never be understood without an understanding of the group process. Some of the advocates of guild socialism oppose function to authority and liberty, but we can have function *and* liberty *and* authority: authority of the whole through the liberty of all by means of the functions of each. These three are inescapably united. A genuine group, a small or large group, association or state, has the right to the obedience of its members. No group should be sovereign over another group. The only right the state has to authority over "other" groups is as far as those groups are constituent parts of the state. All groups are not constituent parts of the state to-day, as the pluralists clearly see. Possibly or probably all groups never will be, but such perpetually self-actualizing unity should be the process. Groups are sovereign over themselves, but in their relation to the state they are interdependent groups, each recognizing the claims of every other. Our multiple group life is the fact we have to reckon with; unity is the aim of all our seeking. And with this unity will appear a sovereignty spontaneously and joyfully acknowledged. In true federalism, voided of division and balance, lies such sovereignty.

XXXII

POLITICAL PLURALISM (CONCLUDED)

I HAVE spoken of the endeavor of the pluralist school to look at things as they are as one of its excellencies. But a progressive political science must also decide what it is aiming at. It is no logical argument against a sovereign state to say that we have not one at present, or that our present particularistic states are not successful. Proof of actual plural sovereignty does not constitute an argument against the ideal of unified or rather a unifying sovereignty. The question is do we want a unifying state? And if so, how can we set about getting it?

The old theory of the monistic state indeed tended to make the state absolute. The pluralists are justified in their fear of a unified state when they conceive it as a monster which has swallowed up everything within sight. It reminds one of the nursery rhyme of one's childhood:

> Algy met a bear
> The bear was bulgy
> The bulge was Algy.

The pluralists say that the monistic state *absorbs* its members. (This is a word used by many writers).[1] But the ideal unified state is not all-absorptive; it is all-inclusive — a very different matter: we are not, individual or group, to be absorbed into a whole, we are to be constitutent members of the whole. I am speaking throughout of the ideal unified state, which I call a uni-*fying* state.

[1] See p. 39, note.

311

The failure to understand a unifying state is responsible for the dread on the one hand of a state which will "demand" our allegiance, and on the other of our being left to the clash of "divided" allegiances. Both these bugbears will disappear only through an understanding of how each allegiance can minister to every other, and also through a realization that no single group can embrace my life. It is true that the state as state no more than family or trade-union or church can "capture my soul." But this does not mean that I must divide my allegiance; I must find how I can by being loyal to each be loyal to all, to the whole. I am an American with all my heart and soul and at the same time I can work daily for Boston and Massachusetts. I can work for my nation through local machinery of city or neighborhood. My work at office or factory enriches my family life; my duty to my family is my most pressing incentive to do my best work. There is no competing here, but an infinite number of filaments cross and recross and connect all my various allegiances. We should not be obliged to choose between our different groups. Competition is not the soul of true federalism but the interlocking of all interests and all activities.

The true state must gather up every interest within itself. It must take our many loyalties and find how it can make them one. I have all these different allegiances, I should indeed lead a divided and therefore uninteresting life if I could not unify them, Life *would* be "just one damned thing after another." The true state has my devotion because it gathers up into itself the various sides of me, is the symbol of my multiple self, is my multiple self brought to significance, to self-realization. If you leave me with my plural selves, you leave me in desolate places, my soul craving its meaning, its home. The home of my soul is in the state.

But the true state does not "demand" my allegiance. It is the spontaneously uniting, the instinctive self-unifying of our multiple interests. And as it does not "demand" allegiance, so also it does not "compete" with trade-unions etc., as the present state often does, for my allegiance. We have been recently told that the tendency of the state is to be intolerant of "any competing interest or faith or hope," but if it is, the cure is not to make it tolerant, but to make it recognize that the very substance of its life is all these interests and faiths and hopes. Every group which we join must increase our loyalty to the state because the state must recognize fully every legitimate interest. Our political machinery must not be such that I get what I need by pitting the group which most clearly embodies my need against the state; it must be such that my loyalty to my trade-union is truly part of my loyalty to the state.

When I find that my loyalty to my group and my loyalty to the state conflict (if I am a Quaker and my country is at war, or if I am a trade-unionist and the commands of nation and trade-union clash at the time of a strike), I must usually, as a matter of immediate action, decide between these loyalties. But my duty to either group or state is not thereby exhausted: I must, if my disapproval of war is to be neither abandoned nor remain a mere particularist conviction, seek to change the policy of my state in regard to its foreign relations; I must, knowing that there can be no sound national life where trade-unions are pitted against the state, seek to bring about those changes in our industrial and political organization by which the interests of my trade-union can become a constituent part of the interests of the state.

I feel capable of more than a multiple allegiance, I feel capable of a unified allegiance. A unified allegiance the new state will claim, but that is something very different from an "undivided" allegiance. It is, to use James' phrase again, a compounding of allegiances. "Multiple allegiance" leaves us with the abnormal idea of competing groups. "Supplementary allegiance" gives us too fragmentary an existence. "Coöperative allegiance" comes nearer the truth. Can we not perhaps imagine a coöperative or unified allegiance, all these various and varying allegiances actually living in and through the other?

We need not fear the state if we could understand it as the unifying power: it is the state-principle when two or three are gathered together, when any differences are harmonized. Our problem is how all the separate community sense and community loyalty and community responsibility can be gathered up into larger community sense and loyalty and control.

One thing more it is necessary to bear in mind in considering the unified state, and that is that a unifying state is not a static state. We, organized as the state, may issue certain commands to ourselves to-day, but organized as a plastic state, those commands may change to-morrow with our changing needs and changing ideals, and they will change through *our* initiative. The true state is neither an external force nor an unchanging force. Rooted in our most intimate daily lives, in those bonds which are at the same time the strongest and the most pliant, the "absolutism" of the true state depends always upon *our* activity. The objectors to the unified state seem to imply that it is necessarily a ready-made state, with hard and fast articulations, existing apart from us, imposing its commands upon us which we must obey; but the truth is that the state must be in perfect flux and that it is utterly dependent upon us for its appearance. In so far as we actualize it, it appears to us; we recognize that it is wrong, then we see it in a higher form and actualize that. The true state is not an arbitrary creation. It is a process: a continual self-modification to express its different stages of growth which each and all must be so flexible that continual change of form is twin-fellow of continual growth.

But the objections that can be raised against the pluralists do not destroy the great value of their contribution to political thought.

First, they prick the bubble of the present state's right to supremacy. They see that the state which has been slowly forming since the Middle Ages with its pretences and unfulfilled claims has not won either our regard or respect. Why then, they ask, should we render this state obedience? "[The state must] prove itself by what it achieves." With the latter we are all beginning to agree.

Genuine power, in the sense not of power actually possessed, but in the sense of a properly evolved power, is, we have seen, an actual psychological process. Invaluable, therefore, is the implicit warning of the pluralists that to attain this power is an infinite task. Sovereignty is always a-growing; our political forms must keep closely in touch with the specific stage of that growth. In rendering the state obedience, we assume that the state has genuine power (because the consequences of an opposite assumption would be too disastrous) while we are trying to approximate it. The great lesson of Mr. Laski's book is in its implication that we do not have a sovereign state until we make one. Political theory will not *create* sovereignty, acts of Parliament cannot *confer* sovereignty, only living the life will turn us, subjects indeed at present, into kings of our own destiny.

Moreover, recently some of the pluralists are beginning

to use the phrase coöperative sovereignty [1] which seems happily to be taking them away from their earlier "strung-along" sovereignty. If they press along this path, we shall all be eager to follow.

Secondly, they recognize the value of the group and they see that the variety of our group life to-day has a significance which must be immediately reckoned with in political method. Moreover they repudiate the idea that the groups are given authority by the state. An able political writer recently said, "All other societies rest on the authority given by the state. The state itself stands self-sufficient, self-directing. . . ." It is this school of thought which the pluralists are combating and thereby rendering invaluable service to political theory.

Third, and directly connected with the last point, they plead for a revivification of local life. It is interesting to note that the necessity of this is recognized both by those who think the state has failed and by those who wish to increase the power of the state. To the former, the group is to be the substitute for the repudiated state. As for the latter, the Fabians have long felt that local units should be vitalized and educated and interested, for they thought that socialism would begin with the city and other local units. Neighborhood education and neighborhood organization is then the pressing problem of 1918. All those who are looking towards a real democracy, not the pretence of one which we have now, feel that the most imminent of our needs is the awakening and invigorating, the educating and organizing of the local unit. All those who in the humblest way, in settlement or community centre, are working for this, are working at the greatest political problem of the twentieth century.

[1] Mr. Laski, I think.

In the fourth place the pluralists see that the interest of the state is not now always identical with the interests of its parts. It is to the interest of England to win this war, they say, but England has yet to prove that it is also for the interest of her working people.

In the fifth place, we may hail the group school as the beginning of the disappearance of the crowd. Many people advocate vocational representation because they see in it a method of getting away from our present crowd rule, what they call numerical representation. They see our present voters hypnotized by their leaders and manipulated by "interests," and propose the occupational group as a substitute for the crowd. New political experiments must indeed be along this line. We must guard only (1) that the "group" itself shall not be a crowd, (2) that the union of groups shall not be a numerical union.

Finally, this new school contains the prophecy of the future because it has with keenest insight seized upon the problem of identity, of association, of federalism,[1] as the central problem of politics as it is the central problem of life. The force of the pluralist school is that it is not academic; it is considering a question which every thoughtful person is asking himself. We are faced to-day with a variety of group interests, with many objects demanding our enthusiasm and devotion; our duty itself shines, not a single light showing a single path, but shedding a larger radiance on a life which is most gloriously not a path at all. Shall Boston or Washington hold me, my family, my church, my union? With the complexity of interests increasing every day on the outside, inside with the power of the soul to "belong"

[1] It does not matter in the terms of which branch of study you express it — philosophy, sociology, or political science — it is always the same problem.

expanding every day (the English and the French flags
stir us hardly less than the American now), with the
psychologists talking of pluralism and the political sci-
entists of multiple sovereignty, with all this yet the soul
of man seeks unity in obedience to his essential nature.
How is this to be obtained? Social evolution is in the
hands of those who can solve this problem.

What is the law of politics that corresponds in importance to the law of gravitation in the physical world?
It is the law of interpenetration and of multiples. I am
the multiple man and the multiple man is the germ of
the unified state. If I live fully I become so enriched
by the manifold sides of life that I cannot be narrowed
down to mere corporation or church or trade-union or
any other special group. The miracle of spirit is that
it can give itself utterly to all these things and yet remain
unimpaired, unexhausted, undivided. I am not a serial
story to be read only in the different instalments of my
different groups. We do not give a part to one group
and a part to another, but we give our whole to each
and the whole remains for every other relation. Life
escapes its classifications and this is what some of the
writers on group organization do not seem to understand. This secret of the spirit is the power of the federal principle. True federation multiplies each individual.
We have thought that federal government consisted of
mechanical, artificial, external forms, but really it is the
spirit which liveth and giveth life.

Let the pluralists accept this principle and they will
no longer tell us that they are torn by a divided allegiance. Let them carry their pragmatism a step further
and they will see that it is only by actual living that we
can understand an undivided allegiance. James tells
us that "Reality falls in passing into conceptual analysis;
it mounts in living its own undivided life — it buds and

bourgeons, changes and creates." This is the way we must understand an undivided allegiance. I live forever the undivided life. As an individual I am the undivided one, as the group-I, I am again the undivided one, as the state-I, I am the undivided one — I am always and forever the undivided one, mounting from height to height, always mounting, always the whole of me mounting.

XXXIII

INCREASING RECOGNITION OF THE OCCUPATIONAL GROUP

FROM the confessedly embryonic stage of thinking in which the movement for group organization still is, two principal questions have emerged:
(1) shall the groups form a pluralistic or a unifying state,
(2) shall the economic group be the sole basis of representation? The first question I have tried to answer,
the second offers greater difficulties with our present
amount of experience. Men often discuss the occupational vs. the neighborhood group on the pivotal question — which of these is nearest a man? Benoist's plea
for the occupational group was that politics must represent *la vie*. But, agreed as to that, we still question
whether the occupational group is the most complete
embodiment of *la vie*.

It is not, however, necessary to balance the advantages of neighborhood and occupational group, for I am
not proposing that the neighborhood group take the
place of the occupational. We may perhaps come to
wish for an integration of neighborhood and industrial
groups — and other groups too as their importance and
usefulness demand — as their "objective" value appears.
In our neighborhood group we shall find that we can
correct many partial points of view which we get from
our more specialized groups. A director of a corporation
will be more valuable to his state and even to his corporation if he is at the same time the member of a neighborhood group. It may be that we shall work out some

machinery by which the neighborhood group can include the occupational group. All our functions must be expressed, but somewhere must come that coördination which will give them their real effectiveness. We are not yet ready to say what the machinery will be, only to recognize some of the principles which should guide us in constructing that machinery. The power of an individual is his power to live a vital group life. The more your society is diversified in group life, the higher the stage of civilization. Perhaps the destiny of the neighborhood group is to interpret and correlate, to give full significance and value to, all the spontaneous association which our increasingly fuller and more varied life is constantly creating. It may be that the neighborhood group is not so much to *include* the others as to make each see its relation through every other to every other.[1] The possible solution, mentioned above, of the two houses of our legislatures and parliaments dividing neighborhood and occupational representation, seems a little crude now to our further analysis unless some practical integration is being worked out at the same time in the local unit. But all this must be a matter of experiment and experience, of patient trial and open-minded observation.[2]

The salient fact, however, is that neighborhood and occupational groups, either independently or one through the other, must both find representation in the state. But we must remember that it is industry which must be included in the state, not labor, but labor and capital. This war certainly shows us the importance of the great

[1] See pp. 199–201.

[2] Some writers talk of trade representation vs. party organization as if in the trade group you are rid of party. Have they studied the politics of trade unionism? In neither the trade group nor the neighborhood group do you automatically get rid of the party spirit. That will be a slow growth indeed.

organizations of industry. Let them be integrated openly
with the state on the side of their public service, rather
than allow a back-stairs connection on the side of their
"interests." And let them be integrated in such manner
that labor itself is at last included in our political organization. This will not be easy; as a matter of fact we
have no more difficult, as we have no more important,
problem before us than the relation within the state of
one powerful organized body to another and of these
bodies to the state. The average American is against the
growth of corporate bodies. But this prejudice must
go: we need strong corporate bodies not to compete
with the state but to minister to the state. Individualism and concentrated authority have been struggling for supremacy with us since the beginning of our
government. From the beginning of our government we
have been seeking the synthesis of the two. That synthesis is to be found in the recognition of organized
groups, but not, I believe, by taking away power from
the state and giving to the group. Some of the pluralists,
in their reaction to the present fear of powerful groups,
advocate that groups should be given more and more
power. I agree with them so far, but their implication
is that we shall thereby have shorn the Samson locks of
the state. This I do not believe we want to do.

Every one sees the necessity to-day of the increase of
state control as a war measure, but some tell us that we
should guard against its dangers by giving to certain
organizations within the state enough power to "balance" the state. I insist that balance can never be the
aim of sound political method. We must first change
our conception of the state — substitute the Service
State for the Sovereign State — then methods must be
devised within which such new conception can operate.
We should, indeed, give more and more power to the

groups, or rather, because we can never "give" power, we should recognize all the power which springs up spontaneously within the state, and seek merely those methods by which that self-generating power shall tend immediately to become part of the strength of the state.

How absurd our logic has been. We knew that it took strong men to make a strong state; we did not realize that those groups which represent the whole industry and business of the country need not be rivals of the state, but must be made to contribute to the state, must be the means by which the state becomes great and powerful at the same time that it uses that power for the well-being and growth of all. Our timidity has been but the reflection of our ignorance. A larger understanding is what we need to-day. There is no need to condemn the state, as do the pluralists; there is no need to condemn our great corporate bodies, as do their opponents. But full of distrust we shall surely be, on one side or the other, until we come truly to understand a state and to create a state which ministers continuously to its parts, while its parts from hour to hour serve only the enhancement of its life, and through it, the enhancement of the life of its humblest member.

The tendency to which we have long been subject, to do away with everything which stood between man and the state, must go, but that does not mean that we must fly to the other extreme and do away with either the individual or the state. One of the chief weaknesses of political pluralism is that it has so many of the earmarks of a reaction — the truth is that we have groups *and* man *and* the state, all to deal with.

Neighborhood groups, economic groups, unifying groups, these have been my themes, and yet the point which I wish to emphasize is not the kind of group, but that the group whatever its nature shall be a genuine group, that we can have no genuine state at all which does not rest on genuine groups. Few trade-unionists in demanding that their organization shall be the basis of the new state examine that organization to see what right it has to make this demand. Most trade-unionists are satisfied in their own organizations with a centralized government or an outworn representative system. Labor can never have its full share in the control of industry until it has learnt the secrets of the group process. Collective bargaining must first be the result of a genuine collective will before it can successfully pass on to directorate representation, to complete joint control.[1]

It is significant that the guild socialists, in considering how acrimonious disputes between guilds are to be avoided, say that "the labor and brains of each Guild naturally [will evolve] a hierarchy to which large issues of industrial policy might with confidence be referred," and "at the back of this hierarchy and finally dominating it, is the Guild democracy. . . ." But then guild socialism is to have no different psychological basis from our present system. This is exactly what we rely on now so patiently, so unsuccessfully — the lead of the few, the following of the crowd, with the fiction that, as our government is based on numbers, the crowd can always have what it wants; therefore, at any moment what we have is what we have chosen — Tammany

---

[1] Yet perhaps the trade-union has been one of the truest groups, one of the most effective teachers of genuine group lessons which we have yet seen. Increased wages, improved conditions, are always for the group. The trade-unionist feels group-wants; he seeks to satisfy these through group action. Moreover the terms of a collective bargain cannot be enforced without a certain amount of group solidarity. In strikes workmen often sacrifice their own interests for what will benefit the union: the individual-I may prefer his present wages to the privations of a strike; the group-I wants to raise the wages of the whole union.

rule for instance. We need a new method: the group process must be applied to industrial groups as well as to neighborhood groups, to business groups, to professional societies — to every form of human association. If the labor question is to be solved by a system of economic control based on economic representation instead of upon vital modes of association, "industrial democracy" will fail exactly as so-called political democracy has failed.

Perhaps this warning is particularly necessary at the present moment because "group" control of industry seems imminent. Through the pressure of the war guild socialism has made practical as well as theoretical headway in England. There are two movements going on side by side, both due it is true to the emergency of war, but neither of which will be wholly lost when the war is over; it is the opinion of many, on the contrary, that these movements are destined to shape a new state for England. First, the government has assumed a certain amount of control over munition plants, railroads, mines, breweries, flour mills and factories of various kinds, and it has undertaken the regulation of wages and prices, control of markets and food consumption, taxation of profits etc.[1]

Secondly, at the same time that the state is assuming a larger control of industry, it is inviting the workmen themselves to take part in the control of industry. "The Whitley Report, adopted by the Reconstruction Committee of the Cabinet, proposes not only a Joint Standing Industrial Council for each great national industry, for the regular consideration of matters affecting the progress and well-being of the trade, but District Councils

[1] I have not in this brief statement distinguished between government "ownership," "control," "regulation," etc. See "War-Time Control of Industry" by Howard L. Gray.

and Works Committees within each business upon which capital and labor shall be equally represented." These bodies will take up "questions of standard wages, hours, overtime, apprenticeship, shop discipline, . . . technical training, industrial research and invention, the adoption of improved machinery and processes, and all those matters which are included under ' scientific management.' "[1]

This is a step which goes far beyond arbitration and conciliation boards. It gives to labor a positive share in the control of industry. "Although it is not at present proposed to give any legal recognition to this new machinery of economic government or any legal enforcement of its decision, . . . it may reasonably be expected that [these national industrial councils] will soon become the effective legislature of the industry."

Most noteworthy is the general acceptance of this plan. "All classes appear to be willing and even anxious to apply the principle of representative self-government not only to the conduct of the great trades but to their constituent businesses." Undoubtedly the English laborer has an increasing fear of bureaucracy and this is turning him from state socialism: his practical experience during the war of "tyrannical" bureaucracy in the government controlled industries has lost state socialism many supporters.

The establishment of the Standing Industrial Councils is a step towards guild socialism although (1) the determination of lines of production, the buying and selling processes, questions of finance, everything in fact outside shop-management, is at present left to the employers, and (2) the capitalist is left in possession of his capital. But this movement taken together with the one mentioned above, that is, the trend towards state-ownership or joint ownership or partial control, has large signifi-

[1] " Representative Government in British Industry" by J. A. Hobson, in *New Republic*, September 1, 1917.

cance: the state to own the means of production, the producers to control the conditions of production, seems like the next step in industrial development, in government form, — the fact that these two go together, that government form is to follow industrial development, gives us large hope for the future.

The British Labor Party in 1917 formulated a careful plan for reorganization with a declared object of common ownership of means of production and "a steadily increasing participation of the organized workers in the management."[1] This wording is significant.

In America also the pressure of war has led to the recognition of labor in the control of industry. Adjustment boards containing labor representatives have been required of almost all private employers signing contracts with the War and Navy Departments.[2] The policy of the administration is to recognize collective bargaining. And the President's Mediation Commission, which imposed collective agreements on the copper industry of Arizona, stated in its official report, "The leaders of industry must . . . [enable] labor to take its place as a coöperator in the industrial enterprise." Moreover, the workman is gaining recognition not only in the management of the industry in which he is engaged, but also at Washington. On most of the important government boards which deal with matters affecting labor, labor is represented. The work of the War Labor Board and the War Labor Policies Board mark our advance in the treatment of labor questions.

The "National Party," inaugurated in Chicago in

[1] See p. 120.

[2] Following the precedent of England which provided, under the Munitions of War act and other legislation, machinery (joint boards representing employers and employed) for the prevention and adjustment of labor disputes.

October, 1917, composed largely of socialists, had for one
plank in its platform, "The chief industries should be
controlled by administrative boards upon which the
workers, the managers and the government should all
be represented." Thus the old state socialism is passing.

In France long before the war we see the beginnings
of syndicalism in the steps taken to give to the actual
teaching force of universities a share in the administration of the department of education.   In 1896–1897 university councils were established, composed of deans and
two delegates elected by each university faculty.   While
these councils are under ministerial control, this is hailed
as the beginning of functionarist decentralization in
France.   In 1910 was organized the representation of all
the personnel of the service of post, telephone and tele-
graph in regional and central councils of discipline, and
also advisory representation to the heads of the service.

The best part of syndicalism is its recognition that
every department of our life must be controlled by those
who know most about that department, by those who
have most to do with that department.   Teachers should
share both in the legislation and the administration
affecting education.   Factory laws should not be made
by a Parliament in which factory managers and employees are not, or are only partially, represented.

One movement toward syndicalism we see everywhere:
the forming of professional groups — commercial, literary, scientific, artistic — is as marked as the forming of
industrial groups.   Any analysis of society to-day must
study its groupings faithfully.   We are told too that in
France these professional groups are beginning to have
political power, as was seen in several large towns in
the municipal elections before the war.   Similar instances are not wanting in England and America.

In Germany there are three strong "interest" organizations which have a large influence on politics: the "Landlords' League" which represents the conservatives, the "Social Democrats" who represent labor, and the "Hanseatic League for Manufactures, Trade and Industry" founded in 1909 with the express object of bringing forward its members as candidates for the Reichstag and Landtags.[1]

We have an interesting instance in the United States of political organization on occupational lines from which we may learn much—I refer to the Nonpartisan league of North Dakota composed of farmers which, inaugurated in 1915, in 1916-7 carried the state elections of North Dakota, electing a farmer-governor, and putting their candidates in three of the supreme court judgeships, and gaining 105 out of the 138 seats in the state legislature. The first object of the league was the redress of economic injustice suffered by the farmer. They saw that this must be done through concerted control of the political machinery. Of the legislation they wished, they secured: (1) a new office of State Inspector of Grains, Weights and Measures, (2) partial exemption of farm improvements from taxation, (3) a new coöperative corporation law, and (4) a law to prevent railroads from discriminating, in supplying freight-cars, against elevators owned by farmers' coöperative societies.

In 1917 a Farmers' Nonpartisan League of the state of New York was organized. In September, 1917, the North Dakota League became the "National Nonpartisan League," the organization spreading to several of the neighboring states: Minnesota, South Dakota, Idaho, Montana, etc. At the North Dakota state primaries held in the summer of 1918, nearly all the League's candidates were nominated, thus insuring the continuance of its control of the state government.

[1] Christensen, "Politics and Crowd Morality," p. 238.

In Denmark we are told the battle rages between the agrarian party and the labor party. More and more the struggle in Parliamentary countries is becoming a struggle between interests rather than between parties based on abstract principles. This must be fully taken into account in the new state.

The hoped-for relation of industry to the state might be summed up thus: we want a state which shall include industry without on the one hand abdicating to industry, or on the other controlling industry bureaucratically. The present plans for guild socialism or syndicate control, while they point to a possible future development, and while they may be a step on the way, as a scheme of political organization have many weak points. Such experiments as the Industrial Councils of England are interesting, but until further technique is worked out we shall find that individual selfishness merely gives way to group selfishness. From such experiments we shall learn much, but the new ship of state cannot ride on such turbulent waters.

The part labor will take in the new state depends now largely upon labor itself. Labor must see that it cannot reiterate its old cries, that it need no longer demand "rights." It is a question of a new conception of the state and labor seeing its place within it. For a new state is coming — we cannot be blind to the signs on every side, we cannot be deaf to the voices within. Labor needs leaders to-day who are alive not to the needs of labor, but to the needs of the whole state: then it will be seen as a corollary how labor fits in, what the state needs from labor, what labor needs from the state, what part labor is to have *in* the state.

PART IV

THE DUAL ASPECT OF THE GROUP:

A UNION OF INDIVIDUALS, AN INDIVIDUAL IN A LARGER UNION

XXXIV

THE MORAL STATE AND CREATIVE CITIZENSHIP

WE see now that the state as the appearance of the federal principle must be more than a coördinating agency. It must appear as the great moral leader. Its supreme function is moral ordering. What is morality? The fulfilment of relation by man to man, since it is impossible to conceive an isolated man: the father and mother appear in our mind and with the three the whole infinite series. The state is the ordering of this infinite series into their right relations that the greatest possible welfare of the total may be worked out. This ordering of relations is morality in its essence and completeness. The state must gather up into itself all the moral power of its day, and more than this, as our relations are widening constantly it must be the explorer which discovers the kind of ordering, the kind of grouping, which best expresses its intent.

But "things are rotten in Denmark." The world is at present a moral bankrupt, for nations are immoral and men worship their nations. We have for centuries been thinking out the morals of individuals. The morality of the state must now have equal consideration. We spring to that duty to-day. We have the ten commandments for the individual; we want the ten commandments for the state.

How is the state to gain moral and spiritual authority?

Only through its citizens in their growing understanding of the widening promise of relation. The neighborhood group feeds the imagination because we have daily to consider the wants of all in order to make a synthesis of those wants; we have to recognize the rights of others and adapt ourselves to them. Men must recognize and unify difference and then the moral law appears in all its majesty in concrete form. This is the universal striving. This is the trend of all nature — the harmonious unifying of all. The call of the moral law is constantly to recognize this. Our neighborhood group gives us preeminently the opportunity for moral training, the associated groups continue it, the goal, the infinite goal, the emergence of the all-inclusive state which is the visible appearance of the total relativity of man in all right connections and articulations.

The state accumulates moral power only through the spiritual activity of its citizens. There is no state except through me. James' deep-seated antagonism to the idealists is because of their assertion that the absolute is, always has been and always will be. The contribution of pragmatism is that we must work out the absolute. You are drugging yourselves, cries James, the absolute is real as far as you make it real, as far as you bring forth in tangible, concrete form all its potentialities. In the same way we have no state until we make one. This is the teaching of the new psychology. We have not to "postulate" all sorts of things as the philosophers do ("organic actuality of the moral order" etc.), we have to *live* it; if we can make a moral whole then we shall know whether or not there is one. We cannot become the state imaginatively, but only actually through our group relations. Stamped with the image of All-State-potentiality we must be forever making the state. We are pragmatists in politics as the new school of philosophy is in religion: just as they say that we are one with God not by prayer and communion alone, but by doing the God-deed every moment, so we are one with the state

by actualizing the latent state at every instant of our
lives. As God appears only through us, so is the state
made visible through the political man. We must gird
up our loins, we must light our lamp and set forth, we
must *do* it.

The federal state can be the moral state only through
its being built anew from hour to hour by the activity
of all its members. We have had within our memory
three ideas of the individual's relation to society: the
individual as deserving "rights" *from* society, next with
a duty *to* society, and now the idea of the individual
as an activity *of* society. Our relation to society is so
close that there is no room for either rights or duties.
This means a new ethics and a new politics. Citizenship is not a right nor a privilege nor a duty, but an
activity to be exercised every moment of the time.
Democracy does not exist unless each man is doing his
part fully every minute, unless every one is taking his
share in building the state-to-be. This is the trumpet
call to men to-day. A creative citizenship must be made
the force of American political life, a trained, responsible citizenship always in control creating always its own
life. In most of the writing on American politics we find
the demand for a "creative statesmanship" as the most
pressing need of America to-day. It is indeed true that
with so much crystallized conservatism and chaotic
radicalism we need leadership and a constructive leadership, but the doctrine of true democracy is that every
man is and must be a creative citizen.

We are now awaking to this need. In the past the
American conception of government has been a machine-
made not a man-made thing. We have wanted a perfect
machine which could be set going like an international
exhibition by pressing the button, but who is going to
press the button? We have talked about the public

without thinking that we were the public, of public
opinion as something quite distinct from any opinion of
our own. It is partly because men have not wanted the
trouble of governing themselves that they have put all
their faith in "good" officials and "good" charters.
"I hate this school, I wish it would burn up," wrote a
boy home, "there's too much old self-government about
it, you can't have any fun." Many of us have not
wanted that kind of government.

The idea of the state as a collection of units has fatally
misled us in regard to our duty as citizens. A man often
thinks of his share in the collective responsibility for
Boston as a 1/500,000 part of the whole responsibility.
This is too small a part to interest him, and therefore
he often disregards such an infinitesimal duty altogether.
Of course we tell him about little drops of water, little
grains of sand etc., but hitherto such eloquence has produced little effect. This is because it is untrue. We must
somehow make it clear that the part of every man in a
great city is not analagous to the grain of sand in the
desert, it is not a 1/500,000 part of the whole duty. It
is a part so bound up with every other part that no
fraction of a whole can represent it. It is like the key
of a piano, the value of which is not in its being 1/56 of
all the notes, but in its infinite relations to all the other
notes. If that note is lacking every other note loses its
value.

Another twist in our ideas which has tended to reduce
our sense of personal responsibility has been that we
have often thought of democracy as a happy method by
which all our particular limitations are lost sight of in
the general strength. Matthew Arnold said, "Democracy is a force in which the concert of a great number
of men makes up for the weakness of each man taken
by himself." But there is no mysterious value in people

conceived of all together. A lot of ignorant or a lot of bad people do not acquire wisdom and virtue the moment we conceive them collectively. There is no alchemy by which the poornesses and weaknesses of the individual get transmuted in the group; there is no trick by which we can lose them in the whole. The truth is that all that the individual has or is enhances society, all that the individual lacks, detracts from society. The state will become a splendid thing when each one of us becomes a splendid individual. Democracy does not mean being lost in the mass, it means the contribution of every power I possess to social uses. The individual is not lost in the whole, he makes the whole.

A striking exception to the attitude of the average American in the matter of his personal responsibility was Mr. John Jay Chapman's visit to Coatesville, Pennsylvania, to do penance for "that blot on American history" — the burning a negro to death in the public square of Coatesville — because he felt that "it was not the wickedness of Coatesville but the wickedness of all America."

But there are signs to-day of a new spirit among us. We have begun to be restless under our present political forms: we are demanding that the machine give way to the man, we want a world of men governed by the will of men. What signs have we that we are now ready for a creative citizenship?

Every one is claiming to-day a share in the larger life of society. Each of us wants to pour forth in community use the life that we feel welling up within us. Citizens' associations, civic clubs and forums are springing up every day in every part of the country. Men are seeking through direct government a closer share in lawmaking. The woman suffrage movement, the labor movement, are parts of this vital and irresistible current. They have not come from surface springs, their sources are deep in the life forces of our age. There is a more fundamental cause of our present unrest than the superficial ones given for the woman movement, or the selfish ones given for our labor troubles: it is not the "demand for justice" from women nor the "economic greed" of labor, but the desire for one's place, for each to give his share, for each to control his own life — this is the underlying thought which is so profoundly moving both men and women to-day.

But a greater awakening has come since April, 1917. It has taken the ploughshare of fire to reveal our true selves: this war is running the furrows deep in the hearts of men and turning up desires of which they were unconscious themselves in their days of ease. Men are flocking to Washington at the sacrifice of business and personal interests willing to pour out their all for the great stake of democracy; the moment came when the possession of self-government was imperilled and all leapt forward ready to lay down their lives to preserve it. This war has revealed the deeper self with its deeper wishes to every man and he sees that he prizes beyond life the power to govern himself. Now is the moment to use all this rush of patriotism and devotion and love of liberty and willingness to serve, and not let it sink back again into its hidden and subterranean depths. Let us develop the kind of institutions which will call forth and utilize these powers and energies for peace as for war, for the works of peace are glorious if men can but see the goal. Let us make a fitting abiding place for men's innate grandeur. Let us build high the walls of democracy and enlarge its courts for our daily dwelling.

Then must men understand that in peace as in war ours is to be a life of endeavor, of work, of conscious

effort towards conscious ends. The ordinary man is
not to do his work and then play a little in order to re-
fresh himself, with the understanding that the world of
industry and the government of his country are to be
run by experts. They are to be run by him and he is to
prepare himself to tackle his job. The leisure-time
problem is not how the workman can have more time
for play, it is how he can have more time for association,
to take his share in the integrated thought and will and
responsibility which is to make the new world. The
"good citizen" is not he who obeys the laws, but he who
has an active sense of being an integral part of the state.
This is the essence and the basis of effective good citizenship. We are not part of a nation because we are living
within its boundaries, because we feel in sympathy with
it and have accepted its ideas, because we have become
naturalized. We are part of a nation only in so far as
we are helping to make that nation.

For this we must provide methods by which every
man is enabled to take his part. We are no longer to
put business and political affairs in the hands of one
set of men and then appoint another set as watch-dogs
over them, with the people at best a sort of chorus in
the background, at the worst practically non-existent.
But we are so to democratize our industrial and our
political methods that all will have a share in policy
and in responsibility. Exhortation to good citizenship
is useless. We get good citizenship by creating those
forms within which good citizenship can operate, by
making it possible to acquire the habit of good citizenship by the practice of good citizenship.

The neighborhood group gives the best opportunity
for the training and for the practice of citizenship. The
leader of a neighborhood group should be able to help
every one discover his greatest ability, he should see

the stimulus to apply, the path of approach, that the constituents of his neighborhood should not merely serve, but should serve in exactly that way which will best fit themselves into the community's needs. The system of war registration where men and women record what they are best able to do, might, through the medium of the neighborhood group, be applied to the whole country. The chief object of neighborhood organization is not to right wrongs, as is often supposed, but to found more firmly and build more widely the right.

Moreover, neighborhood organization gives us a definite objective for individual responsibility. We cannot understand our duty or perform our duty unless it is a duty to *something*. It is because of the erroneous notion that the individual is related to "society" rather than to a group or groups that we can trace much of our lack of responsibility. A man trusts vaguely that he is doing his duty to "society," but such vagueness gets him nowhere. There is no "society," and therefore he often does no duty. But let him once understand that his duty is to his group — to his neighborhood group, to his industrial group — and he will begin to see his duty as a specific, concrete thing taking definite shape for him.

But my gospel is not for a moment of citizenship as a mere duty. We must bring to politics passion and joy. It is not through the cramping and stultification of desire that life is nobly lived, it is through seeing life in its fulness. We want to use the whole of man. You cannot put some of his energies on one side and some on the other and say some are good and some bad — all are good and should be put to good use. Men follow their passions and should do so, but they must purify their passions, educate them, discipline and direct them. We turn our impulses to wrong uses, but our impulses are not wrong. The forces of life should be used, not stifled.

It is not corruption, dishonesty, we have to fight; it is ignorance, lack of insight, desires not transmuted. We want a state which will transmute the instincts of men into the energies of the nation. You cannot dam the stream entirely, you can only see that it flows so as to irrigate and fructify. It all comes down to our fear of men. If we could believe in men, if we could see that circle which unites human passion and divine achievement as a halo round the head of each human being, then social and political reorganization would no longer be a hope but a fact. The old individualism feared men; the corner-stone of the new individualism is faith in men. We need a constructive faith and a robust faith, faith in men, in this world, in this day, in the Here and the Now.

From the belief of savages in the spirits who ruled their fate to the "power outside ourselves that makes for righteousness," through the weak man's reliance on luck and the strong man's reliance on his isolated individuality, we have had innumerable forms of the misunderstanding of responsibility. But all this is now changing. The distinguishing mark of our age is that we are coming to a keen sense of personal responsibility, that we are taking upon ourselves the blame for all our evils, the charge for all our progress. We are beginning to realize that the redemptive power is within the social bond, that we have creative evolution only through individual responsibility.

The old ways of thinking are breaking up. The New Life is before us. Are we ready? Are we making ourselves ready? A new man is needed for the New Life — a man who understands self-discipline, who understands training, who is willing to purge himself of his particularist desires, who is conscious of relations as the stuff of his existence.

To sum up this chapter: the moral state is the task of man. This must be achieved through the creative power of man as brought into visibility and actuality through his group life. The great cosmic force in the womb of humanity is latent in the group as its creative energy; that it may appear the individual must do his duty every moment. We do not get the whole power of the group unless every individual is given full value, is giving full value. It is the creative spontaneity of each which makes life march on irresistibly to the purposes of the whole. Our social and political organization must be such that this group life is possible. We hear much of "the wasted forces of our nation." The neighborhood organization movement is a movement to use some of the wasted forces of this nation — it is the biggest movement yet conceived for conservation. Have we more "value" in forests and water-power in America than in human beings? The new generation cries, "No, this release of the spiritual energy of human beings is to be the salvation of the nation, for the life of all these human beings is the nation." The success of democracy depends (1) upon the degree of responsibility it is possible to arouse in every man and woman, (2) on the opportunity they are given to exercise that responsibility. The new democracy depends upon you and me. It depends upon you and me because there is no one else in the world but you and me. If I pledge myself to the new democracy and you pledge yourself to the new democracy, a new motor force will be born in the world.

We need to-day new principles. We can reform and reform but all this is on the surface. What we have got to do is to change some of the fundamental ideas of our American life. This is not being disloyal to our past, it is exactly the opposite. Let us be loyal to our inheritance and tradition, but let us understand what that inheritance and tradition truly is. It is not *our* tradition to stick to an outworn past, a conventional ideal, a rigid religion. We are children of men who have not been afraid of new continents or new ideas. In our blood is the impulse to leap to the highest we can see, as the wills of our fathers fixed themselves on the convictions of their hearts. To spring forward and then to follow the path steadfastly is forever the duty of Americans. We must *live* democracy.

XXXV

THE WORLD STATE

WE have seen the true state emerging through the working of the federal principle, dual in its nature: (1) created by the law of interpenetration, the unifying of difference, and (2) representing the multiple man in his essential nature. Through the further working of this principle the world-state appears.

The lesson of the group is imperative for our international relations. No "alliances," no balance of power, no agreements, no Hague tribunals will now satisfy us; we know that it is only by creating a genuine community of nations that we can have stability and growth — world peace, world progress. What are the contributions of group psychology to the League of Nations?

There is no way out of the hell of our present European situation until we find a method of compounding difference. Superficial moralists try to get us to like some other nationality by emphasizing all the things we have in common, but war can never cease until we see the value of differences, that they are to be maintained not blotted out. The white-man's burden is not to make others like himself. As we see the value of the individual, of every individual, so we must see the value of each nation, that all are needed. The pacifists have wanted us to tolerate our enemies and the more extreme ones to turn the other cheek when smitten. But tolerance is intolerable. And we cannot dwell among enemies. The ideal of this planet inhabited by Christian enemies all turning the cheek does not seem to me a happy one.

We must indeed, as the extreme militarists tell us, "wipe out" our enemies, but we do not wipe out our enemies by crushing them. The old-fashioned hero went out to conquer his enemy; the modern hero goes out to disarm his enemy through creating a mutual understanding.

The failure of international society in the past is a fact fraught with deep significance: the differences between nations are not to be overcome by one class of people in a country uniting with the same class in another country. The upper classes of Petrograd, Berlin, Paris and London have very much the same manners and habits. This has not brought peace. Artists the world over have a common language. Workingmen have tried to break down international barriers by assuming that their interests were so identical that they could unite across these barriers. But this has failed to bring peace as. the other *rapprochements* have failed. Why? Because they are all on the wrong track. International peace is never coming by an increase of similarities (this is the old-fashioned crowd-philosophy); international peace is coming by the frankest and fullest kind of recognition of our differences. Internationalism and cosmopolitanism must not be confused. The aim of cosmopolitanism *is* for all to be alike; the aim of internationalism is a rich content of widely varying characteristic and experience.

If it were true that we ought to increase the likenesses between nations, then it would be legitimate for each nation to try to impose its ideals upon others. In that case England would try to spread her particular brand of civilization, and Germany hers, for if some one kind of civilization has to prevail, each will want it to be his own. There is not room on this planet for a lot of similar nations, but only for a lot of different nations. A group of nations must create a group culture which shall be broader than the culture of one nation alone. There must be a world-ideal, a whole-civilization, in which the ideals and the civilization of every nation can find a place. The ideal of one nation is not antagonistic to the ideal of another, nor do these ideals exist in a row side by side, but these different kinds of civilization are bound up in one another. I am told that this is mysticism. It is the most practical idea I have found in the world.

It is said that a mighty struggle is before us by-and-by when East meets West, and in that shock will be decided which of these civilizations shall rule the world — that this is to be the great world-decision. No, the great world-decision is that each nation needs equally every other, therefore each will not only protect, but foster and increase the other that thereby it may increase its own stature.

Perhaps one of the most useful lessons to be learned from the group process is a new definition of patriotism. Patriotism must not be herd-instinct. Patriotism must be the individual's rational, self-conscious building of his country every moment. Loyalty means always to create your group, not to wave a flag over it.[1] We need a patriotism which is not "following the lead" but involved in a process in which all take part. In the place of sentimental patriotism we want a common purpose, a purpose evolved by the common life, to be used for the common life. Some of our biologists mislead us when they talk of the homogeneity of the herd as the aim of nations. The nation may be a herd at present. What we have to do is to make it a true group. Internationalism must be based upon group units, not upon herd or crowd units, that is, upon people united not by herd instinct but by group conviction. If a nation is a crowd,

[1] See pp. 58–59.

partiotism is mere hypnotism; if a nation is a true
federal state built up of interlocking and ascending
groups, then patriotism is self-evolved. When you are
building up an association or a nation you have to preach
loyalty; later it is part of the very substance which has
been built.

Then genuine loyalty, a self-evolved loyalty, will
always lead the way to higher units. Nationalism looks
out as well as in. It means, in addition to its other
meanings, every nation being responsible to a larger
whole. It is this new definition of patriotism which
America is now learning. It is this new patriotism
which must be taught our children, which we must
repeat to one another on our special patriotic day, July
4th, and on every occasion when we meet. This new
patriotism looks in, it looks out: we have to learn that
we are not wholly patriotic when we are working with
all our heart for America merely; we are truly patriotic
only when we are working also that America may take
her place worthily and helpfully in the world of nations.
Nationalism is not my nation for itself or my nation
against others or my nation dominating others, but
simply my nation taking its part as "an equal among
equals."

Shall this hideous war go on simply because people
will not understand nationalism? Nationalism and
internationalism are not opposed. We do not lop off
just enough patriotism to our country to make enough
for a world-state: he who is capable of the greatest
loyalty to his own country is most ready for a wider
loyalty. There is possible no world-citizenship the ranks
of which are to be filled by those who do not care very
much for their own country. We have passed through
a period when patriotism among cultivated people
seemed often to be at a discount — the ideal was to be

"citizens of the world." But we see now that we can never be "citizens of the world" until we learn how to be citizens of America or England or France. Internationalism is not going to swallow up nationalism. Internationalism will accentuate, give point, significance, meaning, value, reality, to nationalism.

Whether we can have a lasting peace or not depends upon whether we have advanced far enough to be capable of loyalty to a higher unit, not as a substitute for our old patriotism to our country, but in addition to it. Peace will come by the group consciousness rising from the national to the international unit. This cannot be done through the imagination alone but needs actual experiments in world union, or rather experiments first in the union of two or more nations. Men go round lecturing to kind-hearted audiences and say, "Can you not be loyal to something bigger than a nation?" And the kind-hearted audiences reply, " Certainly, we will now, at your very interesting suggestion, be loyal to a league of nations." But this is only a wish on their part, its realization can never come by *wishing* but only by *willing*, and willing is a process, you have to put yourself in a certain place from which to will. We must, in other words, try experiments with a league of nations, and out of the actual life of that league will come loyalty to it. We are not ready for the life of the larger group because some teacher of ethics has taught us "to respect other men's loyalties." We are ready for it when our experience has incorporated into every tissue of our thought-life the knowledge that we need other men's loyalties. Loyalty, therefore, is not the chickens running back to the coop, also it is not a sentiment which we decide arbitrarily to adopt, it is the outcome of a process, the process of belonging.

Of course there must be some motive for the larger

union: we shall probably first get nations into an international league through their economic interests; then when we have a genuine union the sense of belonging begins. When men have felt the need of larger units than nations and have formed "alliances," they have not felt that they belonged to these alliances. The sense of belonging ended at the British Empire or the German Empire. But the reason Germany became one empire and Italy one nation was because an economic union brought it home to the people daily that they were Italians, not Venetians, Germans, not Bavarians. We must feel the international bond exactly as we feel the national bond. Some one in speaking of the difficulties of internationalism has said, "It is easier to make sacrifices for those whom you know well, your own countrymen, than for strangers." But internationalism has not come when we decide that we are willing to make sacrifices for strangers. This fallacy has been the stumbling block of some of the pacifists. To make sacrifices for "strangers" will never succeed. We make sacrifices for our own nation because of group feeling. We shall make sacrifices for a league of nations when we get the same feeling of a bond.

We may, perhaps, look forward to Europe going through something of the same process which we have gone through in the United States. The colonies joined in a federal government. The union was something entirely apart from themselves. The men of Massachusetts were first and last men of Massachusetts. We belonged for good reasons to a larger unit, but it was only very slowly that we gained any actual feeling of belonging to the United States, of loving it because we were a constituent part of it, because we were helping to make it, not just as an external authority to which we had promised loyalty. The American colonies did not undertake to look pleasant and be kind to one another, they went to work and learned how to live together. And state jealousy has been diminished every year, not by any one preaching to us, but by the process of living together. This is what may happen in a league of nations.

The great lesson of the group process, in which all others are involved, is that particularism, however magnified, is no longer possible. There is no magic by which selfishness becomes patriotism the moment we can invoke the nation. The change must be this: as we see now that a nation cannot be healthy and virile if it is merely protecting the rights of its members, so we must see that we can have no sound condition of world affairs merely by the protection of each individual nation — that is the old theory of individual rights. Each nation must play its part in some larger whole. Nations have fought for national rights. These are as obsolete as the individual rights of the last century. What raises this war to a place never reached by any war before is that the Allies are not fighting for national rights. As long as history is read the contribution of America to the Great War will be told as America's taking her stand squarely and responsibly on the position that national particularism was in 1917 dead.

And as we are no longer to talk of the "rights" of nations, so no longer must "independent" nations be the basis of union. In our present international law a sovereign nation is one that is independent of other nations — surely a complete legal fiction. And when stress is laid on independence in external relations as the nature of sovereignty, it is but a step to the German idea that independence of others can develop into authority over others. This tendency is avoided when we think of sovereignty: (1) as *looking in*, as authority over

its own members, as the independence which is the result
of the complete interdependence of those members;
and when we at the same time (2) think of this independence as *looking out* to other independences to form
through a larger interdependence the larger sovereignty
of a larger whole. Interdependence is the keynote of
the relations of nations as it is the keynote of the relations of individuals within a nation. As no man can be
entirely free except through his perfected relation to his
group, so no nation can be truly independent until a
genuine union has brought about interdependence. As
we no longer think that every individual has a final purpose of his own independent of any community, so we
no longer think that each nation has a "destiny" independent of the "destiny" of other nations.

The error of our old political philosophy was that the
state always looks in: it has obligations to its members,
it has none to other states; it merely enters into agreements with them for mutual benefit thereby obtained.
International law of the future must be based not on
nations as "sovereigns" dealing with one another, but
on nations as members of a society dealing with one
another. The difference in these conceptions is enormous. We are told that cessions of sovereignty must
be the basis of an international government. We cannot
have a lasting international union until we entirely reform such notions of sovereignty: that the power of the
larger unit is produced mechanically by taking away
bits of power from all the separate units. Sovereignty
is got by giving to every unit its fullest value and thereby
giving birth to a new power — the power of a larger
whole. We must give up "sovereign" nations in the
old sense, but with our present definition of sovereignty
we may keep all the real sovereignty we have and then
unite to evolve together a larger sovereignty.

This idea must be carefully worked out: we can take each so-called "sovereign power" which we are thinking of "delegating" to a League of Nations and we can see that that delegating does not make us individual nations less "sovereign" and less "free" but more so — it is the Great Paradox of our time. The object of every proper "cession" of sovereignty is to make us freer than ever before. Is it to be "sovereign" and "free" for nations suspiciously and fearfully to keep sleepless watch on one another while they build ship for ship, plane for plane? Have England and Germany been proudly conscious of their "freedom" when thinking of Central Africa? When the individual nations give up their separate sovereignty — as regards their armaments, as regards the control of the regions which possess the raw materials, as regards the great waterways of the world, as regards, in fact, all which affects their joint lives — the falling chains of a real slavery will reverberate through the world. For unrelated sovereignty, with world conditions as they are to-day, is slavery.

The idea of "sovereign" nations must go as completely as is disappearing the idea of sovereign individuals. The isolation of sovereign nations is so utterly complete that they cannot really (and I mean this literally) even see each other. The International League is the one solution for the relation of nations. Whenever we say we can have a "moral" international law on any other basis, we write ourselves down pure sentimentalists.

There are many corollaries to this project. We do not need, for instance, a more vigorous protection of neutrals, but the abolition of neutrals. The invasion of the rights of neutrals in this war by both sides shows that we can no longer have neutrals in our scheme of union; all must come within the bond.

Further, diplomatic relations will be entirely changed.

"Honor among thieves" means loyalty to your group: while to lie or to try to get the better of your own particular group is an unpardonable offence, you may deceive an outsider. We see now the psychological reason for this. Diplomatic lying will not go until diplomatists instead of treating with one another as members of alien groups consider themeslves all as members of one larger group — the League of Nations.

Moreover, one nation cannot injure another merely; the injury will be against the community, and the community of nations will look upon it as such. Under our present international system the attack of one nation on another is the same as the attack of one outlaw on another. But under a civilized international system, the attack of one individual on another is an attack on society and the whole society must punish it. The punishment, however, will not consist in keeping the offender out of the alliance. If the Allies win, Germany should not be punished by keeping her out of a European league; she must be shown how to take her place within it. And it must be remembered that we do not join a league of nations solely to work out our relations to one another, but to learn to work for the larger whole, for international values. Until this lesson is learned no league of nations can be successful.

Finally, the League of Nations is against the theory of the balance of power, but this has been already considered in the chapter on The Federal State.

To sum up all these particularist fallacies: live and let live can never be our international motto. *Laissez-faire* fails as ignominiously in international relations as within a single nation. Our new motto must be, Live in such manner that the fulness of life may come to all. This is "the ledge and the leap" for twentieth-century thought.

Organized coöperation is in the future to be the basis of international relations. We are international in our interests. We do not want an American education, an English education, a French education. "Movements" seek always an international society. We have international finance. Our standards of living are becoming internationalized. Socially, economically, in the world of thought, national barriers are being broken down. It is only in politics that we are national. This must soon change: with all these *rapprochements* we cannot be told much longer of fundamental differences between us which can be settled only by murdering each other.

People thought that Italy could not be united, that the duchies of Germany would never join. Cavour and Bismark had indeed no easy part. But if one hundred millions of people in Central Europe can be made to see the evils of separation, cannot others? With our greater facilities of communication, with our increased commercial intercourse and our increased realization of the interdependence of nations (a manufacturing nation cannot get along without the food-producing nations, etc.), this ought not now to be impossible. Or has the single state exhausted our political ability? Are we willing to acknowledge this? We have had very little idea yet of a community of nations. The great fault of Germany is not that she overestimates her own power of achievement, which is indeed marvellous, but that she has never yet had any conception of a community of nations. Let her apply all her own theory of the subordination of the individual to the whole to the subordination of Germany to an allied Europe, and she would be a most valuable member of a European league.

The group process thus shows us that a genuine community of nations means the correlation of interests, the development of an international ethics, the creation

of an international will, the self-evolving of a higher
loyalty, and above all and including all, the full responsibility of every nation for the welfare of every other.

With such an aim before us courts of arbitration seem
a sorry makeshift. We are told that as individuals no
longer fight duels but take their disputes into the courts,
so nations must now arbitrate, that is, take their dispute
to some court. But what has really ousted duels has not
been the courts but a different conception of the relation
between men; so what will do away with war will not be
courts of arbitration, but a different conception of the
relations between nations. We need machinery not
merely for settling disputes but for preventing disputes
from arising; not merely for interpreting past relations,
but for giving expression to new relations; not merely
to administer international law, but to make international law — not a Hague court but an international
legislature.

A community of nations needs a constitution, not
treaties. Treaties are of the same nature as contract.
Just as in internal law contract is giving way to the truer
theory of community, so the same change must take
place in international law. It is true that the first step
must be more progressive treaties before we can hope
for a closer union, but let us keep clearly before us the
goal in order that in making these treaties they shall be
such that they will open the way in time to a real federation, to an international law based not on "sovereign"
nations.

We have already seen that it is the *creation* of a collective will which we need most in our social and political
life, not the enforcing of it; it is the same with a league
of nations — we must create an international will. We
want neither concession nor compromise. And a vague
"brotherhood" is certainly not enough. As we have

seen the group as the workshop for the making of the collective will, so we see that we cannot have an international will without creating a community of nations. Group psychology will revolutionize international law. The group gets its authority through the power it has *in itself* of integrating ideas and interests. No so-called collective will which is not a genuine collective will, that is, which is not evolved by this process, will have real authority; therefore no stable international relations are possible except those founded on the creation of an actual community of nations.

What interests us most in all the war literature is any proposed *method* of union. The importance of an international league as a peace plan is that you can never aim directly at peace, peace is what you get through other things. Much of the peace propaganda urges us to choose peace rather than war. But the decision between "war" or "peace" never lies within our power. These are mere words to gather up in convenient form of expression an enormous amount that is underneath. All sorts of interests compete, all sorts of ideas compete or join: if they can join, we have peace; if they must compete, we have war. But war or peace is merely an outcome of the process; peace or war has come, by other decisions, long before the question of peace or war ever arises.

All our hope therefore of future international relations lies, not in the ethical exhortations of the pacifists, nor in plans for an economic war, but in the recognition of the possibility of a community of nations.

In making a plea for some experiment in international coöperation, I remember, with humiliation, that we have fought because it is the easy way. Fighting solves no problems. The problems which brought on this war will all be there to be settled when the war ends. But we have war as the line of least resistance. We have war when the mind gives up its job of agreeing as too difficult.[1] It is often stated that conflict is a necessity of the human soul, and that if conflict should ever disappear from among us, individuals would deteriorate and society collapse. But the effort of agreeing is so much more strenuous than the comparatively easy stunt of fighting that we can harden our spiritual muscles much more effectively on the former than the latter. Suppose I disagree with you in a discussion and we make no effort to join our ideas, but "fight it out." I hammer away with my idea, I try to find all the weakest parts of yours, I refuse to see anything good in what you think. That is not nearly so difficult as trying to recognize all the possible subtle interweavings of thought, how one part of your thought, or even one aspect of one part, may unite with one part or one aspect of one part of mine etc. Likewise with coöperation and competition in business: coöperation is going to prove so much more difficult than competition that there is not the slightest danger of any one getting soft under it.

The choice of war or peace is not the choice between effort and stagnation. We have thought of peace as the lambs lying down together after browsing on the consciousness of their happy agreements. We have thought of peace as a letting go and war as a girding up. We have thought of peace as the passive and war as the active way of living. The opposite is true. War is not the most strenuous life. It is a kind of rest-cure compared to the

[1] It has usually been supposed that wars have been the all-important element in consolidating nations; I do not want to disregard this element, I want only to warn against its over emphasis. Moreover, the way in which wars have had a real and permanent influence in the consolidation of nations is by the pressure which they have exerted upon them in showing them that efficiency is obtained by the closest coöperation and coördination of all our activities, by a high degree of internal organization.

task of reconciling our differences. I knew a young business man who went to the Spanish war who said when he came back that it had been as good as going to a sanitarium; he had simply obeyed commands and had not made a decision or thought a thought since he left home. From war to peace is not from the strenuous to the easy existence; it is from the futile to the effective, from the stagnant to the active, from the destructive to the creative way of life.

If, however, peace means for you simply the abstinence from bloodshed, if it means instead of the fight of the battlefield, the fight of employer and employed, the fight of different interests in the legislature, the fight of competing business firms, that is a different matter. But if you are going to try to *solve* the problems of capital and labor, of competing business interests, of differing nations, it is a tougher job than standing up on the battlefield.

We are told that when the North Sea fishermen found that they were bringing flabby codfish home to market, they devised the scheme of introducing one catfish into every large tank of codfish. The consequent struggle hardened the flesh of the fish and they came firm to market. The conclusion usually drawn from all such stories is that men need fighting to keep them in moral condition. But what I maintain is that if we want to train our moral muscles we are devising a much harder job for them if we try to agree with our catfish than to fight him.

Civilization calls upon us to "Agree with thine adversary." It means a supreme effort on our part, and the future of the world depends upon whether we can make this effort, whether we are equal to the cry of civilization to the individual man, to the individual nation. It is a supreme effort because it is not, as sometimes thought, a matter of feeling. To feel kindly, to desire peace — no, we must summon every force of our natures, trained minds and disciplined characters, to find the *methods* of agreement. We may be angry and fight, we may feel kindly and want peace — it is all about the same. The world will be regenerated by the people who rise above both these passive ways and heroically seek, by whatever hardship, by whatever toil, the methods by which people *can* agree.

What has this young twentieth century gone out to fight? Autocracy? The doctrine of the right of might? Yes, and wherever found, in Germany or among ourselves. And wherever found these rest on the consciousness of separateness. It is the conviction of separateness which has to be conquered before civilization can proceed. Community must be the foundation stone of the New State.

. . . .

The history of modern times from the point of view of political science is the history of the growth of democracy; from the point of view of social psychology it is the history of the growth of the social consciousness. These two are one. But the mere consciousness of the social bond is not enough. Frenssen said of Jörn Uhl, "He became conscious of his soul, but it was empty and he had now to furnish it." We have become conscious of a social soul, we have now to give it content. It is a long way from the maxim, "Religion is an affair between man and his Maker," to the cry of Mazzini, "Italy is itself a religion," but we surely to-day have come to see in the social bond and the Creative Will, a compelling power, a depth and force, as great as that of any religion we have ever known. We are ready for a new revelation of God. It is not coming through any

single man, but through the men and men who are band-
ing together with one purpose, in one consecrated service,
for a great fulfilment. Many of us have felt bewildered
in a confused and chaotic world. We need to focus both
our aspirations and our energy; we need to make these
effective and at the same time to multiply them by their
continuous use. This book is a plea for the more abund-
ant life: for the fulness of life and the growing life. It is
a plea against everything static, against the idea that
there need be any passive material within the social bond.
It is a plea for a splendid progress dependent upon every
splendid one of us. We need a new faith in humanity,
not a sentimental faith or a theological tenet or a philosophical conception, but an active faith in that creative
power of men which shall shape government and industry,
which shall give form equally to our daily life with our
neighbor and to a world league.

APPENDIX

APPENDIX

THE TRAINING FOR THE NEW DEMOCRACY

THE training for the new democracy must be from the cradle — through nursery, school and play, and on and on through every activity of our life. Citizenship is not to be learned in good government classes or current events courses or lessons in civics. It is to be acquired only through those modes of living and acting which shall teach us how to grow the social consciousness. This should be the object of all day school education, of all night school education, of all our supervised recreation, of all our family life, of our club life, of our civic life.

When we change our ideas of the relation of the individual to society, our whole system of education changes. What we want to teach is interdependence, that efficiency waits on discipline, that discipline is obedience to the whole of which I am a part. Discipline has been a word long connected with school life — when we know how to teach *social* discipline, then we shall know how to "teach school."

The object of education is to fit children into the life of the community.[1] Every coöperative method conceivable, therefore, must be used in our schools for this end. It is at school that children should begin to learn group initiative, group responsibility — in other words social functioning. The group process must be learnt by practice. We should therefore teach subjects which require a working together, we should have group recitations, group investigations, and a gradual plan of self-government. Every child must be shown his place in the life that builds and his relation to all others who are building. All the little daily and hourly experiences of

[1] The western states feel that they are training members of society and not individuals and that is why it seems proper to them to take public money to found state universities.

his interrelations must be constantly interpreted to him. Individual competition must, of course, disappear. All must see that the test of success is ability to work with others, not to surpass others.

Group work is, indeed, being introduced into our more progressive schools. Manual training, especially when the object made is large enough to require the work of two or more, cooking classes, school papers, printing classes etc., give opportunity for organization into groups with the essential advantage of the group: coördinated effort.

Moreover, we should have, and are beginning to have, group recitations. A recitation should not be to test the pupil but to create something. Every pupil should be made to feel that his point of view is slightly different from any one's else, and that, therefore, he has something to contribute. He is not to "recite" something which the teacher knows already; he is to contribute not only to the ideas of his fellow-pupils but also to those of his teacher. And this is not impossible even for the youngest. Once when I was in Paris I made the acquaintance of little Michael, a charming English boy of five, who upon being taken to the Louvre by his mother and asked what he thought of the Mona Lisa, replied, with a most pathetic expression, "I don't think she looks as if she liked little boys." That was certainly a contribution to Mona Lisa criticism.

But after the child has been taught in his group recitation to contribute his own point of view, he must immediately be shown that he cannot over-insist upon it; he must be taught that it is only a part of the truth, that he should be eager for all the other points of view, that all together they can find a point of view which no one could work out alone. In other words we can teach collective thinking through group recitations.

A group recitation may give each pupil the feeling that a whole is being created: (1) by different points of view being brought out and discussed, and (2) by every one contributing something different: one will do some extra reading, one will bring clippings from newspapers and periodicals, one will take

his camera to the Art Museum and take pictures of the casts.
Thus we get life, and the lesson of life, into that hour.   Thus
may we learn the obligation and the joy of "belonging," not
only when our school goes to play some other school, but in
every recitation hour of the day.   The old idea was that no
one should help another in a recitation; the new idea is that
every one is to help every one else.   The kind of competition
you have in a group recitation is whether you have added as
much as any one else.   You now feel responsible not only for
your contribution but that the recitation as a whole should be
a worthy thing.   Such an aim will overcome much of the present class-room indifference.

Many more of the regular school activities could be arranged on a group basis than is now thought possible — investigation for instance.   This is a big word, but the youngest
children sent out to the woods in spring are being taught
"original research."

Again, every good teacher teaches her pupils to "assemble"
his different thoughts, shows them that a single thought is not
useful, but only as it is connected with others.   The modern
teacher is like the modern curator who thinks the group significance of a particular classification more important than the
significance of each isolated piece.   The modern teacher does
not wish his pupils' minds to be like an old-fashioned museum —
a hodge-podge of isolated facts — but a useful workshop.

Again, to learn genuine discussion should be considered an
essential part of our education.   Every child must be trained
to meet the clash of difference — difference of opinion, difference of interest — which life brings.   In some universities
professors are putting aside one hour a week for a discussion
hour.   This should be done in all colleges and schools, and
then it should be seen to that it is genuine discussion that
takes place in that hour.

Moreover, in many schools supervised playground and
gymnasium activities are being established, athletic clubs
encouraged, choruses and dramatic leagues developed, not
only because of their value from the health or art point of
view, but because they teach the social lesson.

The question of self-government in the schools is too complicated a subject and has met with too many difficulties, notwithstanding its brilliant successes, to take up here, but undoubtedly some amount of self-control can be given to certain groups, and in the upper grades to whole schools, and when this can be done no training for democracy is equal to the practice of democracy.

The aim is to create such a mental atmosphere for children that it is natural for them to wish to take their part, to make them understand that citizenship is not obeying the laws nor voting, nor even being President,[1] but that all the visions of their highest moments, all the aspirations of their spiritual nature can be satisfied through their common life, that only thus do we get "practical politics."

In our industrial schools it is obviously easier to carry further the teaching of coördinated effort than in the regular day schools.

Our evening schools must adopt the methods of the more progressive day schools, and must, as they are doing in many cases, add to the usual activities of evening schools.

The most conscious and deliberate preparation for citizenship is given by the "School Centres" now being established all over the United States. The School Centre movement is a movement to mould the future, to direct evolution instead of trusting to evolution. The subject of this book has been the necessity for community organization, but the ability to meet this necessity implies that we know how to do that most difficult thing in the world — work with other people: that we are ready to sacrifice individual interests to the general good, that we have a fully developed sense of responsibility, that we are trained in initiative and action. But this is not true. If the School Centres are to fill an important place in neighborhood life, they must not only give an opportunity for the development of neighborhood consciousness and neighborhood organization, but they must train up young people to be ready for neighborhood organization. We who believe

[1] A little girl I know said, "Mother, if women get the vote, shall I *have* to be President?"

in the School Centre as one of the most effective means we have for reconstructing city life believe that the School Centre can furnish this training. We hear everywhere of the corruption of American municipal politics, but why should the next generation do any better than the present unless we are training our young men and women to a proper understanding of the meaning of good citizenship and the sense of their own! responsibility? The need of democracy to-day is a trained citizenship. We must deliberately train for citizenship as for music, art or trade. The School Centres are, in fact, both the prophecy of the new democracy and a method of its fulfilment. They provide an opportunity for its expression, and at the same time give to men and women the opportunity for the training needed to bring it to its highest expression.

The training in the School Centres consists of: group-activities, various forms of civic clubs and classes, and practice in self-government.

First, we have in the Centres those activities which require working together, such as dramatic and choral clubs, orchestras and bands, civic and debating clubs, folk-dancing and team-games. We want choral unions and orchestras, to be sure, because they will enrich the community life at the same time that they emphasize the neighborhood bond, we want civic and debating clubs because we all need enlightenment on the subjects taken up in these clubs, but the primary reason for choosing such activities is that they are group activities where each learns to identify himself with a social whole. This is the first lesson for all practical life. Take two young men in business. One says of his firm, "*They* are doing so and so": his attitude is that the business is a complete whole, without him, to which he may indeed be ministering in some degree. Another young man who has been a few weeks with an old-established firm says "*We* have done so and so for years," "*Our* policy is so and so." You perhaps smile but you know that he possesses one of the chief requirements for rising.

In our group the centre of consciousness is transferred from our private to our associate life. Thus through our group activities does neighborhood life become a preparation for neighborhood life; thus does it prepare us for the pouring out of strength and strain and effort in the common cause.

Then the consciousness of the solidarity of the group leads directly to a sense of responsibility, responsibility in a group and for a group. Sooner or later every one in a democracy must ask himself, what am I worth to society? Our effort in the Centres is to help the birth of that moment. This is the social lesson: for people to understand that their every act, their work, their home-life, the kind of recreation they demand, the kind of newspapers they read, the bearing of their children, the bringing up of their children — that all these so-called private acts create the city in which they live. It is not just when we vote, or meet together in political groups, or when we take part in some charitable or philanthropic or social scheme, that we are performing our duty to society. Every single act of our life should be looked at as a social act.

Moreover, we learn responsibility for our group as well as to our group. We used to think, "I must do right no matter what anyone else does." Now we know how little that exhausts our duty; we must feel an equally keen responsibility for our whole group.

These then are the lessons which we hope group activities will teach — solidarity, responsibility and initiative, — how to take one's place worthily in a self-directed, self-governing community.

In the first year of one of our Boston Centres, the people of a certain nationality asked if they might meet regularly at the Centre. At their first meeting, however, they broke up without accomplishing anything, without even deciding to meet again, simply because those present had never learned how to do things with other people. Each man seemed a little island by himself. They explained to me the fact that they made no plans for further meeting by saying that they found they did not know parliamentary law, and some of them must learn parliamentary law before they could organize. I did not feel, however, that that was the real reason. I was sure it was because they had never been accustomed to do

things in groups — they had probably never belonged to a
basket-ball team or a dramatic club — and we have to learn
the trick of association as we have to learn anything else.

But the Centres prepare for citizenship not only by group
activities but also by direct civic teaching. This takes the
form not only of lectures, classes in citizenship, but also of
societies like the "junior city councils" or the "legislatures"
where municipal and state questions are discussed, and young
men's and young women's civic clubs. And it must be remembered that the chief value of these clubs is not the information
acquired, not even the interest aroused, but the lesson learned
of genuine discussion with all the advantages therefrom.[1]

But I have written as if it were our young people who were
to be educated by the group activities of the Centres, as if the
young people were to have the training for democracy and the
older people the exercise of democracy. Nothing could be
further from my thoughts. The training for democracy can
never cease while we exercise democracy. We older ones need
it exactly as much as the younger ones. That education is a
continuous process is a truism. It does not end with gradua-
tion day; it does not end when "life" begins. Life and education must never be separated. We must have more life in our
universities, more education in our life. Chesterton says of
H. G. Wells, "One can lie awake nights and hear him grow."
That it might be said of all of us! We need education all
the time and we all need education. The "ignorant vote"
does not (or should not) mean the vote of the ignorant, we
get an ignorant vote very often from educated people; an
ignorant vote means ignorance of some particular subject.

A successful business man said to me the other day, "I
graduated from college with honors, but all I learned there
has done me little good directly. What I got out of college
was an attitude towards life: that life was a matter of constantly learning, that my education had begun and was going
on as long as I lived." Then he went on to say, "This is the
attitude I want somehow to get into my factory. Boys and

[1] See pp. 208–212.

girls come to me with the idea, 'School is over, learning is behind me, now work begins.' This is all wrong. I am now planning a school in connection with my factory, not primarily on account of what they will learn in the school, but in order to make them see that their life of steady learning is just beginning and that their whole career depends on their getting this attitude." Now this is what we want the Centres to do for people: to help them acquire the attitude of learning, to make them see that education is for life, that it is as valuable for adults as for young people.

We have many forms of adult education: extension courses, continuation and night schools, correspondence schools, courses in settlements, Young Men's Christian Associations etc. And yet all these take a very small per cent of our adult population. Where are people to get this necessary education? Our present form of industry does not give enough. Tending a machine all day is not conducive to thought;[1] a man thus employed gets to rely entirely on his foreman. The man who lets his foreman do his thinking for him all day tends to need a political boss at night. We must somehow counteract the paralyzing effect of the methods of modern industry. In the School Centre we have an opportunity for adult education in the only forms in which many people, tired out with the day's work, can take it: discussion, recreation, group activities and self-governing clubs. The enormous value of that rapidly spreading movement, the forum movement, and its connection with the School Centres, there is space here only to mention.

Many people, however, even if not the majority, are eager and hungry for what one man spoke to me of as "real education." University extension work is spreading rapidly and in many cases adapting itself marvellously to local needs; a much closer connection could be made between the opportunities of the university and the training of the citizen for his proposed increased activity in the state by having university extension work a recognized part of the School Centre, so that every one, the farmer or the humblest workman, might

[1] Also men have less opportunity for discussion at work than formerly.

know that even although he cannot give all his time to college life, he may have the advantage of its training. In the School Centre should be opportunity for the study of social and economic conditions, the work of constitutional conventions, the European situation and our relation to it, the South American situation and our relation to it, etc. etc.

Moreover, we must remember when we say we all need more education, that even if we could be "entirely" educated, so to speak, at any one minute, the next minute life would have set new lessons for us. The world is learning all the time about health, food values, care of children etc. All that science discovers must be spread. Adult education means largely the assimilation of new ideas; from this point of view no one can deny its necessity.

I have said that the Centres prepare for citizenship through group activities, through civic clubs and classes and through actual practice in self-government. The Centres may be a real training in self-government, a real opportunity for the development of those qualities upon which genuine self-direction depends, by every club or group being self-governed, and the whole Centre self-directed and self-controlled by means of delegates elected from each club meeting regularly in a Central Council. If we want a nation which shall be really self-governed not just nominally self-governed, we must train up our young people in the ways of self-direction.

Moreover, the development of responsibility and self-direction will be the most effective means of raising standards. We are hearing a great deal just now of regulated recreation, regulated dance halls etc. We must give regulation a secondary place. There is something better than this which ought to be the aim of all recreation leaders, that is, to educate our young people to want higher standards by interpreting their own experience to them and by getting them to think in terms of cause and effect. You can force a moral code on people from above yet this will change them very little, but by a system of self-governing clubs with leaders who know how to lead, we can make real progress in educating people to higher standards. This is true of athletic games as well as of dances.

APPENDIX

We find, indeed, that it is true of all parts of our Centre work.
Through the stormy paths of club election of officers, I have
seen leaders often guide their young men to an understanding
of honest politics. It is usually easier, it is true, to do *for*
people, it is easier to "regulate" their lives, but it is not the
way to bring the results we wish. We need education, not
regulation.

Self-government in the Centres then means not only the
election of officers and the making of a constitution, but a real
management of club and Centre affairs, the opportunity to
take initiative, to make choices and decisions, to take responsibility. The test of our success in the Centres will always be
how far we are developing the self-shaping instinct. But we
must remember that we have not given self-government by
allowing the members of a club to record their votes. Many
people think a neighborhood association or club is self-governing if a question is put to them and every one votes upon it.
But if a club is to be really self-governed it must first learn
collective thinking. This is not a process which can be hurried,
it will take time and that time must not be grudged. Collective thinking must be reverenced as an act of creation. The
time spent in evolving the group spirit is time spent in creating the dynamic force of our civilization.

Moreover each Centre should be begun, directed and supported (as far as possible) by the adult people of a community
acting together for that end. A Centre should not be an
undertaking begun by the School Committee and run by the
School Committee, but each Centre should be organized by
local initiative, to serve local needs, through methods chosen
by the people of a district to suit that particular district.
The ideal School Centre is a Community Centre. A group of
citizens asks for the use of a schoolhouse after school hours,
with heat, light, janitor, and a director to make the necessary
connection between the local undertaking and the city department. Then that group of citizens is responsible for the Centre: for things worth while being done in the schoolhouse, and
for the support of the activities undertaken. By the time
such a School Centre is organized by such an association of

citizens, neighbors will have become acquainted with one another in a more vital way than before, and they will have begun to learn how to think and to act together as a neighborhood unit.

We are coming to a more general realization of this. In the municipal buildings in the parks of Chicago, the people are not given free lectures, free moving pictures, free music, free dances etc.; they are invited to develop their own activities. To the Recreation Centres of New York, operated by the Board of Education, are being added the Community Centres controlled by local boards of neighbors. In Boston we have under the School Committee a department of "The Extended Use of School Buildings," and the aim is to get the people of each district to plan, carry out and supervise what civic, educational and recreational activities they wish in the schoolhouses.

A Chicago minister said the other day that the south side of Chicago was the only part of the city where interest in civic problems and community welfare could be aroused, and this he said was because of the South Park's work in field houses, clubrooms and gymnasiums for the last ten or twelve years.

When the chairman of the Agricultural Council of Defense of Virginia asked a citizen of a certain county what he thought the prospects were of being able to rouse the people in his county in regard to an increased food production, the prompt reply was, "On the north side of the county we shall have no trouble because we have several Community Leagues there, but on the south side it will be a hard job."

The School or Community Centre is the real continuation school of America, the true university of true democracy.